THE ASSOCIATION FOR SCOTTISH LITERARY STUDIES
NUMBER FORTY-TWO

A SONG OF GLASGOW TOWN

THE COLLECTED POEMS OF MARION BERNSTEIN

*

THE ASSOCIATION FOR SCOTTISH LITERARY STUDIES

The Association for Scottish Literary Studies aims to promote the study, teaching and writing of Scottish literature, and to further the study of the languages of Scotland.

To these ends, the ASLS publishes works of Scottish literature (of which this volume is an example); literary criticism and in-depth reviews of Scottish books in *Scottish Literary Review*; short articles, features and news in *ScotLit*; and scholarly studies of language in *Scottish Language*. It also publishes *New Writing Scotland*, an annual anthology of new poetry, drama and short fiction, in Scots, English and Gaelic. ASLS has also prepared a range of teaching materials covering Scottish language and literature for use in schools.

All the above publications are available as a single 'package', in return for an annual subscription. Enquiries should be sent to:

> ASLS, Scottish Literature, 7 University Gardens, University of Glasgow, Glasgow G12 8QH. Telephone/fax +44 (0)141 330 5309 or visit our website at **www.asls.org.uk**

A list of Annual Volumes published by ASLS can be found at the end of this book.

THE ASSOCIATION FOR SCOTTISH LITERARY STUDIES

A SONG OF GLASGOW TOWN

THE COLLECTED POEMS OF MARION BERNSTEIN

In loving memory of Donna K. Cohen
1943–2010

Edited by Edward H. Cohen,
Anne R. Fertig and Linda Fleming

GLASGOW

2013

Published in Great Britain, 2013
by The Association for Scottish Literary Studies
Scottish Literature
University of Glasgow
7 University Gardens
Glasgow G12 8QH

ASLS is a registered charity no. SC006535

www.asls.org.uk

ISBN: 978-1-906841-13-3

A catalogue record for this book
is available from the British Library.

The Association for Scottish Literary Studies acknowledges
support from Creative Scotland towards
the publication of this book.

Typeset by AFS Image Setters Ltd, Glasgow
Printed and bound by Bell & Bain Ltd, Glasgow

Marion Bernstein
Frontispiece, *Mirren's Musings*, 1876

Contents

Poems published 25 April 1874 to 6 May 1876 but not collected in *Mirren's Musings*

Poems collected in *Mirren's Musings*, June 1876, but not previously published

Poems published 8 July 1876 to 6 January 1906, subsequent
to the printing of *Mirren's Musings*

Acknowledgements

We are especially grateful to Margery Palmer McCulloch, who has served with sound judgment as the editorial adviser to this volume. We are indebted, as well, to Duncan Jones, Director, and the Publications Board of the Association for Scottish Literary Studies for their generous support of our project.

During the years in which this edition was in progress, we have relied on the expertise and encouragement of many friends and scholars. Foremost among these are Florence Boos, David Finkelstein, Tom Leonard, Emily Russell, and Nerys Tunnicliffe. Also generous with their assistance have been the staffs of the British Library Newspaper Library, the Mitchell Library, the National Library of Scotland, and the University of Glasgow Library.

Rollins College has supported the work of Edward Cohen and Anne Fertig with grants from its Ashforth Fund and stipends from its Student-Faculty Collaborative Research Program. The British Academy and Rollins College have awarded, respectively, Linda Fleming and Edward Cohen with travel grants to support their participation in the 2009 meeting of the Australasian Victorian Studies Association.

For permission to quote from Marion Bernstein's applications for financial relief, we appreciate the kindness of the Royal Literary Fund, London, and the Royal Society for the Relief of Indigent Gentlewomen of Scotland, Edinburgh. For permission to reprint portions of articles previously published, we thank the editors of the *Journal of the Edinburgh Bibliographical Society*, the *Scottish Literary Review*, and the *Victorians Institute Journal*.

For our cover illustration, we are pleased to acknowledge permission of the Aberdeen Art Gallery & Museums Collections to reprint 'Autumn' (1898) by the Glasgow painter Bessie MacNicol, 1869–1904.

A Note on the Text

Marion Bernstein once predicted that her verses would 'crumble to dust' and that her memory would 'pass away.'[1] Almost a century after her death, however, she was resurrected when Tom Leonard included a small selection of her early poems in *Radical Renfrew*.[2] A few of her works have since appeared in *Mungo's Tongues*, *Glasgow Poets Past and Present*, *A History of Scottish Women's Writing*, *The New Penguin Book of Scottish Verse*, and *Working-Class Women Poets in Victorian Britain*.[3] The poems most frequently reprinted or cited are those published in her only collection, *Mirren's Musings*, 1876:

> Title: MIRREN'S MUSINGS. | A COLLECTION OF | SONGS AND POEMS. | BY | MARION BERN-STEIN. | PRICE 2/6. | GLASGOW: | McGEACHY, 93 UNION STREET, AND M. BERNSTEIN, | 5 DUN-ROBIN PLACE, PAISLEY ROAD. | 1876.

> Π, [A]–E^8, G–I^8, K^8. 73 leaves, comprising: one leaf with portrait tipped to front free endpaper; p. [i] title; p. [ii] printer's notice; pp. [iii]–[iv] PREFACE; pp. v–vi TO MISS MARION BERNSTEIN; p. vii TO MISS MARION BERNSTEIN; p. [viii] blank; pp. [ix]–xii CONTENTS; p. [xiii] ADVERTISEMENT; p. [xiv] blank; pp. [1]–129 MIRREN'S MUSINGS.

> Octavo. Leaf measures 18.1 × 11.9 cm. White wove paper; leaves trimmed and with gilt edges. Bound in dark blue, pebble grain publishers' cloth; front cover stamped in gold: 'Mirren's Musings | Bernstein | 2.6.'

> Known extant copies: British Library (YA.1986.a.5670); Mitchell Library (ACS/P244); National Library of Scotland (ABS.2.206.012); Paisley Central Library (P/Bern PC 1926); University College London Library (MOCATTA TE 42 BER); University of Aberdeen Library (82189 Ber).

In 1990, in conjunction with the publication of *Radical Renfrew*, Leonard recorded a series of 'Forgotten Voices' for Radio Scotland, and in one of these programmes he expressed the wish that someone would cull Bernstein's uncollected verses from the pages of the *Glasgow Weekly Herald*, the *Glasgow Weekly Mail*, and other local newspapers in which they had appeared.[4] In undertaking this task, we have discovered that establishing a definitive chronological text presents several challenges.

In all, Marion Bernstein published 198 poems. Of these, 171 were first printed in newspapers, and many may be dated by their temporal proximity to events or topics reported in the press, such as: lines (122) on a riveters' strike in Govan in 1878; an account (141) of a 'fearsome gale' in which 160 east-coast fishermen were drowned in October 1881; an attack (151) on a Highland laird inspired by testimony taken by the Napier Commission in August 1883; a rallying cry (157) to the women of Glasgow who had failed to participate in the great franchise demonstration on 6 September 1884; even an acrostic sonnet (166) on Elizabeth Mouat, who was rescued in February 1886 after drifting helplessly in a fishing smack—for seven days and nights—from the Shetland Islands to the coast of Norway. Only a handful of Bernstein's published poems, however, bear actual dates of composition. The earliest—'To Annie on Her Birthday' (98)—is dated 2 November 1873, the day her sister turned twenty-nine. The latest—'To King Edward on His Coronation' (193)—is dated 9 August 1902. We do not know, moreover, whether she dated her manuscripts. Of the two surviving specimens of her handwriting, one is her application for a grant from the Royal Literary Fund, in which she explains: 'Many of my papers were mislaid during a removal, when I was not well enough to look after them properly.'[5] For these reasons, we have elected to present Marion Bernstein's poems—as far as possible—in the order of their publication.

To our knowledge, no scholar has previously compared the newspaper versions of the early poems and the versions in *Mirren's Musings*. The editors of the papers did take liberties in altering Bernstein's texts to conform to their house styles and in excising lines and stanzas from her submissions. In every instance, we have assumed that the poet restored her intentions when she published her collection and we have presented these poems as they appear in that work.

In an 'Advertisement' in *Mirren's Musings*, Bernstein announced her ambition 'to publish another volume, containing an equal number of entirely different poems, in about a year.'[6] No such volume appeared, however, and she may have been discouraged by the disruptions she encountered with the printing of her collection.[7] She continued, nevertheless, to compose poems on diverse subjects and to publish them over the next three decades in the pages of the *Advent Review and Herald of the Sabbath*, the *Christian Leader*, the *Glasgow Weekly Herald*, the *Glasgow Weekly Mail*, the *Helensburgh and Gareloch Times*, and the *People's Journal for Glasgow and Edinburgh*. We have now unearthed eighty-eight Bernstein poems printed chiefly in these papers between 8 July 1876 and 6 January 1906. In representing these texts, we have silently corrected the misspellings, inconsistent uses of quotation marks and other punctuation, and obvious inadvertencies characteristic of nineteenth-century newspaper verse.

Finally, four anomalies must be noted. First, at least two Bernstein poems never saw print. On 9 May 1874, the poetry editor of the *Glasgow Weekly Mail* wrote: 'M.B.— The writing of Lowland Scotch is a lost art, and you need not feel discouraged when we say you have not discovered it. "A Gey Guid Riddance" and "The Starling" are not up to the mark—your mark' (p. 3). Neither text has been recovered. Second, under a poem published in the *Glasgow Weekly Herald* on 3 January 1885, Bernstein's name is clearly visible, but the text has been torn from the only known extant copy of this issue. Third, of the 101 Bernstein poems collected in *Mirren's Musings*, twenty-six had not been previously published in newspapers. When we have external evidence to assign approximate dates of composition, we do so in our notes on the individual texts. But for most of them, especially the religious verses in which she expresses her Christian faith and her commitment to the Saturday Sabbath, we know only that they were composed before June 1876, when the publication of the book was first reported in the *Glasgow Weekly Mail*.[8] We have arranged these twenty-six (85–110) in the order of their placement in *Mirren's Musings*. Fourth, in the *Women's Suffrage Journal*, 2 November 1871, p. 119, the following poem was printed above Bernstein's initials:

A Manly Sentiment
Dedicated to the Brave (Wife Beating) Briton.

Suggested by a leading article on a man at Sheffield, who kicked his wife
to death, saying as he dragged her along, 'You know I can do as I like
to you, you are mine! I shall only get a twelvemonth for you.'

Only my wife! My chattels and goods,
To do with whatever I will.
Who can stop me from claiming the right of my sex,
To abuse her, or batter, or kill?

To steal or embezzle are serious crimes;
Shop-lifting is not in my line;
For poaching, or picking some sticks from a hedge
Penal servitude might be the fine!!

But to outdo a fiend in a raid on my wife
Is the sport that to me is most dear,
I can kick her, or beat her, or maim her for life,
And 'a twelvemonth' is all I need fear.

Perchance if the Judge is to mercy inclined
I'll be let off this time, with a fine,
And as soon as I'm back to my house and my wife,
I'll serve her far worse, for 'she's mine'!

Even when I'm in prison, she's punished, not I.
For she has the burden to bear,
If she starve half the time, she must keep up my house,
While I have warmth, clothes, and good fare.

Then hurrah! for the laws of this glorious land,
Where liberty's all for the strong.
Long, long, may the men make the laws to shield them!
Long flourish oppression and wrong!

While these quatrains lack the syntactic sophistication of
verses known to be Bernstein's, several elements—including
the scornful tone, the fictive speaker, and the epigraph in
which the source for the poem is attributed to an episode
reported in a newspaper[9]—are consistent with tropes she
frequently employed. We cannot assert with full confidence,

however, that 'A Manly Sentiment' is Marion Bernstein's poem.

Endnotes

[1] *One Hundred Modern Scottish Poets*, ed. by D. H. Edwards (Brechin: Edwards, 1880), pp. 52–53.

[2] *Radical Renfrew: Poetry from the French Revolution to the First World War by Poets Born, or Sometime Resident in, the County of Renfrewshire*, ed. by Tom Leonard (Edinburgh: Polygon, 1990), pp. 296–303.

[3] *Mungo's Tongues: Glasgow Poems 1630–1990*, ed. by Hamish Whyte (Edinburgh: Mainstream, 1993), pp. 141–43; Edwin Morgan, *Glasgow Poets Past and Present: The Story of a City* (Hamilton, NZ: University of Waikato, 1993), p. 8; Valentina Bold, 'Beyond "The Empire of the Gentle Heart": Scottish Women Poets of the Nineteenth Century', in *A History of Scottish Women's Writing*, ed. by Douglas Gifford and Dorothy McMillan (Edinburgh: Edinburgh University Press, 1997), pp. 246–61; *The New Penguin Book of Scottish Verse*, ed. by Robert Crawford and Mick Imlah (London: Penguin, 2000), p. 367; *Working-Class Women Poets in Victorian Britain: An Anthology*, ed. by Florence S. Boos (Peterborough, ON: Broadview Press, 2008), pp. 337–47.

[4] Tom Leonard, 'The Forgotten Voices: Some Scottish Poetry from 1789 to 1918', 1991 (Edinburgh: National Library of Scotland, Acc. 11807).

[5] Royal Literary Fund, Form of Application for an Author, 4 October 1904 (London: British Library, RLF File 2686.) The other specimen of Bernstein's handwriting appears in a privately owned presentation copy of *Mirren's Musings*.

[6] Marion Bernstein, *Mirren's Musings* (Glasgow: McGeachy [and] Bernstein, 1876), p. [xiii].

[7] Bernstein's commitment to the arrangement of the prefatory material, to the inclusion of her portrait, and to the expense of the gilt-edged leaves and cloth binding suggests that she regarded the book as an artistic product and insisted on its perfection. But on 12 February 1876, the editor of the *Glasgow Weekly Mail* reported: 'Mirren writes that she has been greatly tried by the printers in getting out her book. One firm she gave up altogether; and now another' (p. 7).

[8] On 24 June 1876, the editor of the *Glasgow Weekly Mail* announced: 'It affords us much satisfaction to be able to inform our readers that our versatile poetical correspondent, Marion Bernstein, has got out her book at last, after many vexatious delays. Speaking our praise of it in a sentence, we may say that it is a highly creditable production to both authoress and printer, and well worth its space on any household library shelf. Mirren has the knack of saying smart things in a clever manner occasionally, and is not without a suspicion of sarcastic acidity, which gives an enjoyable flavour to her rhymes' (p. 7).

[9] A reference to this incident had appeared as a letter to the editor—headed 'Sarcasm' and signed 'Only a Woman'—in the *Sheffield Daily Telegraph*, 2 September 1871, p. 7.

Introduction

When Marion Bernstein died in 1906, at the age of fifty-nine, she had resided in Glasgow more than half her life.[1] She had published nearly two hundred poems in local weekly newspapers in which she had interacted with readers, editors, and fellow poets who were citizens of the city and its environs. One of her major poems, moreover, had appeared in the first volume of D. H. Edwards's celebrated series of *Modern Scottish Poets*. She had eked out a living as a music teacher, and many of her students had been pupils at the prestigious Park School for Girls in Lynedoch Street. When her health was failing and she could no longer support herself, she had survived on grants from Colquhoun's Bequest for Incurables, Glasgow, and the Indigent Gentlewomen's Fund, Edinburgh. She had come to regard herself and to be regarded as a Glaswegian and as a Scot.[2]

In 'A Note on the Text' the present editors have established the significance of the first collection of Bernstein's poems—*Mirren's Musings*—published at the mid-point of her life in 1876. She laboured long on the production of the volume and endeavoured, within her limited financial resources, to fashion the book itself as a work of art.[3] In gathering her poems from the pages of newspapers and arranging them for publication between hard covers, she set her sights on literary status and lasting fame. As we have noted, she announced in an advertisement in her collection that she intended to publish another volume of entirely different poems 'in about a year'. That book never appeared, but she continued to write and to submit her verses for another thirty years. It has fallen to us, therefore, to retrieve almost a hundred poems not included in *Mirren's Musings*. Most of these have remained unknown to scholarship, and we expect readers to be pleased by the variety of subjects and the evenness of quality that Bernstein sustained throughout her poetic career.[4]

In the following pages we examine a constellation of events and themes by which Bernstein established her agency and identity as a person and as a poet: the two tragedies of her early life; her evolving interests in Glasgow and in Scotland; her preoccupations with time and with her disability; her commitment to her religious faith; and her advocacy for social justice and gender equality. We conclude with a brief discussion of her poetic practice.

Early Life

Bernstein was born in London on 16 September 1846 and baptised at the Church of St John on Bethnal Green.[5] Her father, Theodore Bernstein, had emigrated to England from Prussia, and he was identified in the 1841 census as a 'tutor' residing in Liverpool.[6] Her mother, Lydia Pulsford, was the daughter of a 'gentleman' from Surrey.[7] Her parents had married in 1843 at All Souls, Langham Place, St Marylebone.[8] Their first child, Lydia Annie, was born the following year in Clapham.[9] Their third child, Theodore, was born in 1852.[10]

In her earliest years, Bernstein lived with her parents and her sister in Victoria Terrace, adjacent to Victoria Park, in London's East End. The park, which had opened to the public in 1845, provided a rare space of greenery for working- and middle-class families, and the pleasant childhood memories related in her poems were probably drawn from her gambols there. Two tragic events in her childhood, however, cast a pall over her life. The first of these, to which she refers regularly in her verse, was the disability that resulted from a crippling illness. The second, to which she never alludes, was the premature death of her father.

Bernstein's recollections of her life in Victoria Park—presented in 'Mirren's Autobiography' (132)—touch on early joy displaced by sorrow. She recalls the days when her 'strength and activity' won her the name 'Little Sturdyboots'. She remembers, on the other hand, how suddenly her 'first trouble came', how her weakness 'increased day by day', and how 'the cold breath of sickness prevented [her] prime'. It is difficult from these symptoms to diagnose the cause of her disability; nevertheless, the evidence of the sudden onset of her illness in childhood and of the steadily increasing weakness in her constitution suggests that she was stricken with infantile paralysis.[11] She represents herself here as having grown up 'to womanhood feeble and lame' and elsewhere as an aging invalid suffering from 'chronic infirmity'.

It is impossible to know whether Theodore Bernstein, on leaving Prussia, had intended to remain in England or, like many transmigrants from Europe, to travel on to the Americas. In the public records, he was identified variously as a tutor, a teacher, a linguist, a translator, even as a professor of romance languages. If he had hoped—with his 'knowledge of eight languages'—to secure a position at a public school or even at a university, then he must have been sorely disappointed. For by 1851, when he was thirty-seven years old, he and his family had removed from Victoria Terrace to 3 Upper Baker Street, in Marylebone, and in the census taken that year he was described as a 'tobacconist'.[12] He tried desperately to make a decent living, but in July 1855, two months before Marion's ninth birthday, Theodore Bernstein, 'Tobacconist and Cigar Dealer, and Teacher and Translator of Languages', was brought up before the court as an insolvent debtor.[13] Regrettably, his downward spiral continued. He must have suffered greatly from the trials of providing for his family and from the shameful consequences of his accumulated debts. In 1856 he was admitted as a pauper patient to the Camberwell House Lunatic Asylum, and early in 1859, diagnosed with dementia, he was transferred 'in depressed circumstances' to the Surrey County Asylum.[14] There his condition deteriorated, and he was removed after six months to the Middlesex County Lunatic Asylum, Colney Hatch, where he suffered a series of 'epileptic fits' and 'died generally exhausted' on 26 November.[15]

How and where the rest of the Bernstein family was living in these years is not known. In the 1861 census they are shown to be residing in a seafront boarding house in Hastings, at 5 Coburg Place, where the widow Lydia was the 'proprietress' and her three children were 'scholars'.[16] After this date, unfortunately, the trail grows cold, and for at least ten years no record of their whereabouts exists. We do know that both daughters, Lydia Annie and Marion, acquired the training during this decade that prepared them for careers as music teachers,[17] and we know that Marion was introduced to the wide range of literary works she would cite in her poetry.[18] In the 1871 census, sister Lydia is enumerated as a 'lodger' and 'vocalist' living in London near Cavendish Square,[19] and in the register of marriages in

Sunderland in the first quarter of 1873 she is cross-listed with Benjamin Malyon, a lithographic printer.[20] One of Bernstein's few dated poems, 'To Annie on Her Birthday' (98), was composed on 2 November 1873, and we speculate that the entire family—mother, daughters, son, and son-in-law—had by then begun their migration north of the Tweed.

Glasgow and Scotland

Glasgow in the last quarter of the nineteenth century presented a picture of striking contrasts. Between 1871 and 1901, when its area and population doubled, the city experienced unprecedented prosperity and widespread poverty; rapid expansion and stifling congestion; immigration from Ireland and the Highlands, but equivalent emigration to North America, New Zealand, and Australia; advances in the shipbuilding and engineering industries, but declines in the production of textiles and chemicals; and increasing confidence in commerce and investment until the stunning collapse of the City of Glasgow Bank in 1878. Eleanor Gordon and Gwyneth Nair, in their study of Glasgow in the Victorian years, remark that 'its economy, occupational structure, architecture, housing, and class formation and class relations have all been invoked to conjure up images of a city which reaped the benefits and suffered the ravages of its emergence as a leading industrial city.'[21]

The first notice of the Bernstein family in Glasgow appeared in the *Post-Office Directory for 1874–1875*, where Marion's mother is listed as a resident—presumably with Marion and her brother Theodore—at 5 Dunrobin Place, Paisley Road.[22] We cannot say how easily or how frequently Bernstein ranged beyond her flat and explored the city. She refers in her poems to overcrowding on the city's trams (2), to the antics of street performers (54), and to the dangers of negotiating dimly lit staircases (56), but she more often describes herself as an invalid confined to her bed or to her room. Living on the south bank of the Clyde, in the police burgh of Kinning Park, she was near enough to the river to hear the sounds of heavy industry and to see and smell the smoke rising from the chimneys of local factories producing soap and paint.[23] One of her first

published poems, 'Wanted in Glasgow' (2), captures the
same sensory experiences of urban life—the 'noise and
smoky breath'—related in Alexander Smith's 'Glasgow' in
1857.

Critical tradition has it that the Glasgow poets of the later
nineteenth century, nostalgic for the Scottish countryside,
showed little interest in the town as a source of inspiration.[24] On 5 September 1874 the editor of the *Glasgow
Weekly Mail* complained that contributors to his poetry column had a tendency 'to run in a rut' and to submit verses
'on conventional country life' (p. 7). His challenge—'Has
city life no phases worthy of poetic mention?'—led to a
number of responses, including accounts of public drunken-
ness and complaints about increasing crime. In 'A Song of
Glasgow Town' (23), Bernstein describes the Clyde as a
sewer and the factories as sources of pollution. She con-
ceives the competing landscapes as conspiring against the
quality of human life:

On every side I see
A crowd of giant chimney stalks
As grim as grim can be.
There's always smoke from some of them—
Some black, some brown, some grey.

She constructs her song, like the city itself, upon a foundation of antitheses: wealth and want, learning and ignorance,
beauty and ugliness. New to Glasgow, Bernstein observes
her surroundings critically. Still, she salutes 'the Glasgow
people' and celebrates the city's past and potential.

From the time she arrived in Glasgow, Bernstein found
a cordial audience for her poetry in the pages of the local
weekly newspapers. Of her extant poems, a quarter were
published in the *Glasgow Weekly Herald* and half in the
Glasgow Weekly Mail. The *Weekly Herald*, with a balanced
coverage of local, national, and global news, was the more
conservative of the two papers. On the second page of
every issue there appeared a column of 'Original Poetry'
with two or three pieces, contributed mostly by men, on
topics of general human interest. In the 1870s the few
poems Bernstein published in these columns were chiefly
expressions of her faith. But it was in the *Weekly Mail* that

she first made her mark by contributing poems on current events and contemporary concerns reported in the paper. Published every Saturday, each eight-page issue cost one penny. The first page was devoted to local or regional news of a social or sensational bent. In the issue dated 28 February 1874, in which Bernstein's first poem appeared, the leading story was an account of a 'terrific gale' in the west of Scotland. There were also excerpts from other papers on events of singular interest: 'Painful Suicide in Dublin', 'Horrible Murder in Paris', and 'Shocking Atrocities in the South Seas'. Other pages reported incidents in Glasgow and its environs: a drowning in the Kelvin, a miners' strike in Falkirk, and an outbreak of smallpox in Wigtown. The paper also responded to questions from readers, chiefly on legal matters, and announced recent local births, marriages, and deaths. The lion's share of the *Weekly Mail* and the *Weekly Herald* alike was given over to advertisements, which frequently occupied a quarter of page 3, half of page 5, and all of page 8. Wanted were clerks, couriers, confectioners, paper makers, wagon makers, servants, and stereotypers. Among the products for sale were books and bibles, cocoa and chocolate, mangles, sewing machines, cartes de visites, and 'fine old whisky for toddy'; patent medicines included Cockle's Antibilious Pills and Dr Paris's Nervous Restorative Lozenges. Services offered were hat cleaning, 'blood purifying', and voice and piano lessons. Several columns were regularly devoted to shipping and to opportunities for emigration. News, features, and advertisements of this sort, both in the *Weekly Herald* and the *Weekly Mail*, suggest that the Saturday papers were aimed at readers with wide-ranging interests and expanding expectations. The content also reflects the growth of economic opportunity in an increasingly urbanised Scotland.

Up until the end of 1873, the poetry column in the *Weekly Mail* had appeared irregularly. In January 1874, however, the liberal editor Charles Cameron[25] was elected to Parliament and was succeeded by his assistant, James Ramsay Manners.[26] Not as politically engaged as his predecessor, Manners was nevertheless an astute editor whose attention to social change served him well during a period when he led the paper to unprecedented prosperity. Between 1874 and 1880 its circulation increased fifty-four percent to 200,000; and, according to the *Newspaper Press Directory* for 1877, its readership was 'about four times that of any other newspaper in Edinburgh and Glasgow.'[27] The paper remained liberal in 'colour', but Manners took pains to cultivate a broad readership. In addition to the commercial success he achieved, Manners was responsible for two important changes concerning the publication of poetry in the paper. One was the establishment of a regular poetry column that appeared in almost every issue from 14 February 1874 until well into the twentieth century. Situated either on page 3 or page 7, the column included 'original' poems by men and women alike. Another feature introduced early in Manners's tenure, from 21 February 1874, was a weekly inventory of poems submitted but not published in the poetry column: poems declined; poems recommended for revision and resubmission; even fragments or stanzas of poems cited as examples of good or poor poetic practice. Adjoining the poetry column, this list of 'responses' created a competition between the poems selected and the poems rejected. These two innovations had several consequences. First, the regular appearance of the poetry column created a new venue for poets and furthered competition with the *Weekly Herald*; secondly, comments directed to authors of declined submissions recorded the evolving editorial policies of the poetry column; thirdly, although Bernstein often disagreed, these policies enhanced the quality of poetic production in the paper; and, fourthly, the interplay amongst the poetry editor, the poets, and the readers fostered a community sustained in the *Glasgow Weekly Mail* throughout the decade.

Most likely, the overseeing of the poetry column and the 'response' column was delegated to an anonymous subeditor who was identified as 'T. E.' in statements of editorial policy and was known to poets and readers simply as 'The Editor'. Some contributors—including Bernstein—speculated on his identity (6). He offered consolation or criticism to authors whose verses he rejected, and his comments could be gentle or biting. To one poet he wrote: 'You are fortunate in having more time to write than we have to read' (9 January 1875, p. 7). From the first, however, he admired Marion Bernstein's wit and quickly admitted her to the *Weekly Mail*'s fold of 'regular correspondents'.

Indeed, it was he who playfully gave her the sobriquet 'Mirren'—which he defined as 'an affectionate Scottish synonym for Marion' and which she embraced and eventually adopted for her collection of *Musings*. The poetry published in the *Weekly Mail* and the *Weekly Herald* between 1875 and 1900 offers a unique snapshot of the public culture of Glasgow, for the poets and readers alike were chiefly Victorian working-class and middle-class men and women, and their verses shaped—in Natalie Houston's words—a 'shared public discourse of current events'.[28]

After she published 'Wanted in Glasgow' (2) and 'A Song of Glasgow Town' (23), Bernstein began to find inspiration in a variety of stories reported in the *Weekly Mail*. From these sources she composed poems on the practice of cremation (4, 35, 91), on a formula for calculating 'the square contents of a circle' (8), and on the cruelty of fox hunting (16). She wrote on accounts of the natural and the occult—on a rare May Day snowstorm (118) and on a prediction of the world's end (127). Becoming bolder, she sparred with the poetry editor and challenged his many proscriptions, such as amatory poems, epistolary poems, obituary poems, poems about Robert Burns, and poems that exceeded thirty-two lines. Occasionally, if he responded snappishly, one or more of the paper's readers would spring in verse to Bernstein's defence. She enjoyed the repartee, and these exchanges also encouraged her to write and publish poems on more serious topics, especially on social justice and gender equality.

News of local interest, too, captured Bernstein's attention. In 'The Hero of the Clyde' (30), she narrates the story of Jamie Lambert, who had lived many years on the banks of the river and claimed to have saved the lives of more than a hundred people swept away by the currents; blind and elderly, he was living in 1875 in the Asylum for Indigent Old Men, in Rotten Row, and Bernstein encourages charitable contributions to acknowledge his humane services to the city. In 'Gas on the Stair' (56) she writes no longer as a newcomer but as one fully engaged in Glaswegian affairs. She complains to officials in the city proper about the practice of curtailing the distribution of gas to the contiguous suburbs during the summer months. Her tone is playful, but there is also a hint that she—especially

as a disabled person—fears falling and having to 'be carried
upstairs an unfortunate wreck'.

One of Bernstein's most daring ventures was her poem
on 'The Govan Riveters' Strike' (122). Although the shipbuilding industry on the Clyde expanded spectacularly
during the last three decades of the nineteenth century,
there were also years of economic stagnation and decline.
Between 1877 and 1879 the local newspapers reported news
of financial collapse: threats of strikes, rising unemployment, and the disastrous failure of the City of Glasgow
Bank. In October 1878 the Clyde Shipbuilders' and Engineers' Association averted a general strike by agreeing to
reductions in the workers' wages and hours. On 9 November, however, the *Weekly Mail* reported that 'a few squads
of boilermakers and riveters came out on strike' (p. 5)
rather than accept these conditions. As winter approached
and living conditions deteriorated, Bernstein's poem caught
some of her readers by surprise:

> Ye riveters of Govan,
>   Who stay at home at ease,
> And live upon the 'strike fund'
>   As idle as you please,
> While wiser men and better,
>   Who lazy ways don't like,
> Must starve through keeping idle,
>   Because you're out on strike.

Whilst Bernstein's position on the strike may seem anti-
thetical to the sympathy she often expresses for the working classes, it is consistent with the political perspective
shared by many Glaswegians of differing social back-
grounds, who regarded strikes as threats to the wealth and
progress of Clydeside. Her poem also caused some discomfort for the *Weekly Mail*, whose editor responded: 'While
we permit the opinions of our correspondent, we do not of
course endorse them; it is an easy thing to say but exceedingly difficult to prove that either strikes or trades-unions
have influenced the Clyde trade in any degree.'

The poetry column of the *Weekly Mail* also provided a
place where Bernstein could interact, in print, with fellow
Glasgow poets. She composed a sonnet in response to a

threnody by Mary Cross (160). She exchanged poems on women's rights and women's suffrage with Jessie Russell (40) and on the migratory habits of swallows with Mary Inglis (62, 110). She wrote a parody of James Nicholson's popular comic poem 'Im-ph-m' (116). She also submitted a poem 'On the Death of "Rhyming Willie"' (117), who had laboured as a blacksmith and composed verses in Scots, in which she celebrates William Penman's wit and extends her sympathy to his 'widow' and the 'little ones'. Bernstein's was among the first of fifty-four poetic tributes submitted to honour Penman, and the publication of her lines signals her participation in the society of Glasgow's newspaper poets. She had capitalised on the conventions of the *Weekly Mail* and its poetry column, to paraphrase Alexis Easley, 'as a way of constructing and complicating' her authorial identity.[29]

Whilst the city centre was suffering from the consequences of overcrowding, the worst in all of Britain, Glasgow's suburbs and outlying districts were experiencing an explosion in the construction of housing. Many of the new terraced houses, however, remained unoccupied or were subdivided into flats. Middle-class citizens often preferred these tenement arrangements because their jobs were never wholly secure or because they preferred to negotiate the cost of the short-term leases that owners were willing to grant. Bernstein lived longer at 5 Dunrobin Place than at any other Glasgow address. There she enjoyed a suburban respectability, although the adjoining Paisley Road was a busy commercial thoroughfare and her neighbourhood was becoming anxious about loitering and other threatening behaviours. She captured the comedy of her removal to 244 St George's Road, on 6 September 1879, in 'A Rainy Day Flitting' (128). We speculate that she relocated to the West End, together with her mother and brother, in order to be nearer to her sister Lydia, who was living with her husband at 187 Dumbarton Road, and to be more accessible to potential clients seeking her services as a music teacher. She would be just a short walk there from the Park School for girls, established in 1880, whose headmistress frequently sent her students to Bernstein for lessons in voice and piano.[30] Thereafter, Bernstein lived in a succession of tenement flats at various addresses in Rupert Street, Sandyford Place, John Street, Buchanan Street, Rosevale Place, Great

George Street, West Princes Street, Elderslie Street, Craignethan Gardens, West Regent Street, St Vincent Crescent, Thornwood Drive, and Kildonan Terrace. 'St Vincent Loch' (194), one of Bernstein's later poems, takes its title and setting from one of her last addresses in Glasgow, 30 St Vincent Crescent. The site had been developed as a middle-class residential property, and fronting the dwellings were gardens, a bowling green, and a large pond where children sailed toy boats in the summer and skated in the winter. As in many of her poems, she refers to the trials of life: sorrow on the sea, the deaths of friends, the acceleration of the passing years. In these lines, however, she expresses her gratitude for 'this peaceful scene / Where all is evermore serene'. Implicit here is the tension between the physical confinement imposed by age and the imaginative freedom inspired by an ordinary park: 'This tranquil pleasure charms my sight, / And wakens thoughts of calm delight.'

In his classic study of nationalism, *Imagined Communities*, Benedict Anderson posits that the most vivid figure for a community and its citizens is the daily ceremony of the simultaneous reading of the newspaper. 'Each communicant is well aware that the ceremony he performs is being replicated simultaneously by thousands (or millions) of others, of whose existence he is confident, yet of whose identity he has not the slightest notion.'[31] This same principle of cultural connection was anticipated in 1920 by Donald Carswell, the Scottish journalist and biographer, when he observed how readers in the nineteenth century had construed the *Glasgow Weekly Mail*:

> It was a stoutly Radical organ, closely packed with crime and local news and enjoying an immense circulation among the working classes of the West. Sabbatarian Scotland not permitting of that evil thing a 'Sunday' paper, this purveyor of information and sensation was religiously published on Saturday, but it was on the Sunday that the working man found time to read it as he lay in bed—whence it acquired its nickname of 'The Working Man's Bible'. The working man himself called it simply the 'Bluidy *Mail*'.[32]

The notion of a body of citizens reading the paper simultaneously on Sunday afternoons literalises Anderson's
imagined community and materialises the context in which
Bernstein engaged the readers of the *Weekly Mail* for nearly
a decade.

In the late 1870s the editorial policies of the *Glasgow
Weekly Mail* and the *Glasgow Weekly Herald* changed
abruptly. Alexander Murdoch, 1843–1901, joined the staff
of the *Weekly Mail*, presumably as poetry editor, and dis-
continued the 'response' column.[33] For several months the
poetry column was headed by a curt notice: 'We cannot
undertake to correspond with persons who send us poetry
for insertion. If pieces sent to us do not appear in our
columns within a few weeks after they are received, our
correspondents may understand that they are rejected.'[34]
The good-natured bantering between the *Weekly Mail* and
its contributors ceased, and there was no further interaction
among the poets. There were also fewer poems by women.[35]
On the other hand, the number of poems written by
women increased in the *Weekly Herald*, and the new editor,
William Canton, 1845–1926, was inclined to accept poems
on subjects that reflected significant changes in the social
landscape of Scotland.[36] Marion Bernstein had already
begun to explore these themes, especially with regard to
the city, and now she was ready to consider them more
broadly.

Bernstein was intrigued by the various dimensions of
northern life. She was fascinated by accounts she read in
the Scottish newspapers of storms and of perilous voyages
(141, 148, 166). She was also attracted to the plight of the
emigrant and the toll that emigration was taking on Scotland (140). Above all, during this nascent period of the
women's movement in Scotland, she embraced concepts of
the natural equality of humanity. For example, in Bernstein's 'O Caledonia, Thou Art Fair' (61) she transacts with
James Hogg's 'Caledonia'—published in 1810—in which he
famously praised Scotland's martial past and natural
beauty. Where he had celebrated the valour of Scottish
forefathers who had repulsed invaders from without, however, she urges modern Scots to resist 'the rich and proud'
who oppress them from within.

Few topics in Scottish history have been debated and dis-

puted more persistently than the causes and effects of the
Clearances. There is general agreement, however, that by
the mid-1870s, after many years of evictions and forced
removals from the lands they had worked for centuries, the
displaced and dispossessed Highlanders began to agitate in
earnest for the restoration of their traditional farming and
grazing rights. According to Eric Richards, 'the crofters and
their leaders took the battle to the landlords and sought to
wrest control of the land from their masters.'[37] A result of
these protests was the appointment of a Royal Commission—chaired by Lord Napier—into the condition of the
crofters. The evidence taken in representative communities
was reported variously in the press. The *Scotsman* and other
allies of the landlord interests offered only general accounts
of the proceedings and expressed few opinions, whilst the
liberal papers published extracts from the evidence—many
sarcastic in tone and incendiary in substance—which
included recollections of violent dispossessions and dislocations. In early August 1883 several papers quoted the testimony of a clergyman who asserted that 'the management of
most Highland estates was despotic in its nature' and that
'one man's will ruled whole parishes'. Such statements
inspired 'The Highland Laird's Song' (151) in which Bernstein levels a radical indictment against the hereditary
landed classes. Her refrain—'all for me, all for me'—portrays the laird as greedy, arrogant, and contemptuous of the
'common people'.

   The title of Bernstein's 'The Scottish Marseillaise' (164)
is instructive. Burns's 'For a' That and a' That' and 'Scots
Wha Hae'—which express his antipathy toward rank and
his sympathy with the spirit of the French Revolution—
were occasionally compared to 'La Marseillaise', and a
number of contemporary accounts of the crofters' revolt
regarded the agitations of the 1880s as a great triumph of
popular protest. Richards asserts that the report of the
Napier Commission 'constitutes the greatest single document on nineteenth-century Highland society, economy and
history.'[38] As a work of collective oral testimony, much of
which was published in the popular press, it unleashed
literary and political forces in support of the crofters. On
17 October 1885 Alexander Murdoch had published a
poem titled 'Give Back the Land!' in the *Glasgow Weekly*

Mail. Clearly, he and Bernstein shared a similar understanding of 'nature's plan', for he wrote: 'Up, Scotland! Tear the lie to rags! / Your birthright of the soil demand; / Are crofters less than grouse and stags? / Give back the land! Give back the land!' Marion Bernstein's reference to 'Alexander', however, is more than an instance of her interactions with her fellow poets. Where Murdoch addresses the lairds and pleads for the return of the crofters' lands, she addresses the crofters themselves and urges them to *take* action. Her verse is both radical and insistent. In its tone and in its substance, 'The Scottish Marseillaise' parallels the Crofters Act of 1886 as 'a decisive and unambiguous piece of class legislation on behalf of the common people.'[39]

A conundrum at the heart of Bernstein's poetry centres on the tension between her public and private identities. She signed her poems, as if to affirm the positions she avowed, and she addressed them, as if to invite correspondence from readers; in referring to herself as an invalid, however, she implied a distance and a difference between herself and the reader. In 1880, when D. H. Edwards invited her to submit two or three poems for inclusion in *Modern Scottish Poetry*, she composed 'Mirren's Autobiography' (132), in which she presents details of her youth, her illness, her disability, and her faith that she merely suggests elsewhere. Yet there is a surprising reticence in this 'life' and little of a self-reflexive nature. The many sources cited in her poems—from biblical, classical, English, and Scottish texts—reveal Bernstein's eclectic reading over the course of her career. Save for one, however, we are at a loss to name a poet with whom she identifies. That one is Robert Burns. In the first (147) of her two Burns Day poems, she associates intimately with him and with his travails: 'I think of the heart of a poet / Always unfit to bear / Sad poverty's heavy burden / Of sordid, ceaseless care.' We know that her mother died in 1896[40] and her brother in 1905;[41] that, after these losses, she became increasingly dependent upon her sister;[42] and that, as her health deteriorated and she was no longer able to teach, she was reduced to subsisting on paltry pensions from charitable sources. It is not surprising, then, that she came to regard Burns as a kindred spirit and expressed both sympathy for and empathy with his circumstances: 'Poor Burns! how thy sensitive nature / Fretted beneath the strain / Of want and debt and dependence, / A three-fold, galling chain.'

Time & Disability

The themes of time and of disability are distinct, but in Bernstein's poetry they tend to overlap, and there is a temptation to trace them to the tragedies in her childhood. In each case, she embraces familiar Victorian tropes. With time she invokes the discourse of melancholy, and with disability she adopts the discourse of invalidism. Both are capable of producing the sentimentality associated with Victorian literature and of eliciting sympathy in the reader.

Bernstein's treatment of time, however conventional its sentiments may be, is surprisingly complex. Indeed, in testing the limitations inherent in construing time as a linear configuration of past, present, and future, she anticipates postmodern constructions that often defy our understanding of chronology and of wholeness.[43] She obscures customary temporal dimensions in many of her poems; and she occasionally truncates or extends representations of time, so that the past flows to the present or the present to the future by literary sleight of hand. For example, in her lines 'On the Closing Year' (28), she fashions a triple analogy to equate the passing of time with the passing of life with the passing from Earth. Similarly, in her first-person poem 'On New Year's Day' (29), she centres herself briefly in the present between the regrets of the past and the uncertainties of the future. In 'Forward March!' (172) the transition from past to present occurs within the first couplet— 'There was a time when years seemed long, / But now how short they seem!'—and the remainder of the poem is an extended injunction to persevere in the present along the 'path we tread' to a future in 'that Land of Bliss'.

Several of Bernstein's poems on time are inspired predictably by particular occasions, and these seem calculated to summon the reader's sympathy. In 'On Hearing "Auld Lang Syne" ' (1)—probably composed at the start of 1874— she speaks sadly in the voice of one grown prematurely old and wistfully recalls 'the vanished joys of bygone years'. In another New Year's poem (29)—first published on 2

January 1875—she positions herself in the present moment
with 'little of hope' and 'much of fear'. 'Birthday Musings'
(121) was published five days after her thirty-second birthday; here she situates herself in the present between a contentious past and an ominous future, between 'another year
of earthly strife' and 'still another year of life'. In 'A Birthday Meditation' (158)—published shortly after she turned
thirty-eight—she sustains a mournful tone throughout; she
views life as a succession of 'schooldays' with 'hard lessons'
and 'little play'. In 'The Christmas Party' (153)—which she
attends in 'the mirth of a dream'—she awakens to the
reality that the friends and family she has gathered are 'the
ghosts of a bygone day' and that she is 'left with remembrance only / Of those dear ones, so kind and true'.
These melancholic pieces struck sympathetic chords in Bernstein's readers, two of whom composed poetic responses to
her.[44]

At first glance, these compositions on the theme of time
would seem to be the ones in which Bernstein most comfor-
tably constructs and represents her personal identity. In
'Home Music' (130)—published shortly after her thirty-
third birthday—she muses on the power of 'a homely
ballad' to evoke memories of 'life's happiest dreams':

> When the singer is a mother
>   With her children list'ning round;
> When the sister and the brother
>   Blend their tones in tuneful sound,
> While the husband and the father
>   Sits to listen and admire;
> Of all concerts, I would rather
>   Hear that sweet domestic choir.

This stanza *appears* to recall a scene from the poet's childhood with her father, mother, sister, and brother gathered
around her. The 'sweet and simple' moment created here,
however, is curiously impersonal, and the remembered 'fireside circle' is a familiar sentimental trope of domestic ideology. Bernstein's treatments of time are frequently crafted
as tiny melodramas, like this one, in which the illusions of
linearity and reality engage the reader.

Bernstein's preoccupation with time continued through-

out her career. In 'Too Soon Forgotten' (69) she grimly
treats time as an agent of forgetfulness. In her sonnet on
'Life's Sunny Summer Time' (75) she represents life in two
stages: the 'golden prime' of youth and 'all the after time'.
In 'Thoughts' (36) she treats the mercurial nature of time:
'What was Future is now Present, / What was present now
is Past.' In her more philosophical poems she often appropriates conventional metaphors and traditional tropes. In
'The River of Time' (15), for example, distinctions among
past, present, and future blur, and the 'mighty river' rolls
on through life to a 'vast eternity'. The first two lines of
'Changes' (19) repeat the initial couplet of a romantic poem
by the melodist Thomas Moore—'All that's bright must
fade— / The brightest still the fleetest'—but the tone shifts
abruptly as Bernstein introduces a series of realistic images
to convey the cruel passage of time, including the 'bright
abundant curls' which 'grow scanty and turn grey' and the
'smoothest, whitest brow' which 'soon shows time's
wrinkles'. These abrupt transitions from youth to age
underscore the illusion of temporal unity. So it is that in
several poems, on this theme of time, the speakers reflect in
fleeting present moments, recall dreary pasts, and await
uncertain futures.

When Bernstein's poems began to appear in the *Glasgow
Weekly Mail*, their sentimental strains evoked a number of
inquiries. The references to 'bygone years' and to 'vanished
joys' belong to the discourse of melancholy, and the allusions to her extended illness and confinement signify the
discourse of disability. Both discursive formulations drew
letters of sympathy from readers, and these in turn elicited
a cautionary note from the editor:

> The latest object of our epistolary poets' admiration is
> our clever correspondent, Marion Bernstein, who can
> write smart epigrams and merry rhymes even in her sick-
> bed. It was perhaps natural that Marion's discovery of
> her condition should awaken in the breast of many of
> our poets a feeling of warmest admiration and sympathy
> for one so young, so unfortunate, and yet so genial and
> brave. But we wish that they should make a distinction.
> Marion merits the sympathy of all our readers; but she

needs nobody's pity. It is only crushed and abject natures that are sustained by pity.[45]

In distinguishing between sympathy and pity in readers' responses to Bernstein's poetry, the editor also mediates between the feelings stimulated by lived experience and the 'emotional excess' created by melodrama.[46] His negotiation anticipates the manner in which the poet herself would enable and disable her personal figure in her work.

In representing her disability, Bernstein is most transparent in her preface to *Mirren's Musings*:

> The following 'Musings' have been, in a great measure, at once the solace and the result of a long period of physical affliction, during which I was hardly capable of any greater exertion than that required for occasional reading, writing, and conversation. In consequence of this feebleness, my mind was chiefly occupied in *musing* over what I read or heard of the world from which I was shut out, or what I remembered of my own past experiences.
>
> At times I feel deeply thankful for those calm and thoughtful years, which were not the least happy of the years I remember, in spite of physical suffering, and the natural longing for health that no human heart can quite suppress, even though able to say with the Psalmist of Israel, 'It was good for me to be afflicted.'
>
> I have to thank many stranger friends in various parts of the world for their kind letters expressing so much sympathy and good will. I am sure they will be pleased to know that my health has much improved lately. Although still quite unable to walk, I am no longer confined to my bed; but for many months past I have been well enough to resume my former occupation as a teacher of music, and I hope in that capacity to make the acquaintance of some of my readers.[47]

The diction in this passage is the discourse frequently adopted by the Victorians in their disability narratives. The picture that emerges here—of a woman 'afflicted' and 'longing for health', 'no longer confined' but 'still quite unable to walk'—parallels the complex representation of herself that Bernstein constructs in her poems. She is at once an

invalid and a thriving poet, a recluse and an artist engaged
with the world.

When Bernstein first announced her intention to publish
her collection of poems and songs—in 'My Book' (80)—
she also promised: ''Twill contain my own portrait, that
readers may see / What I look like, and feel well acquainted
with me.' That etching, reproduced as the frontispiece to
this present collection, is the only extant image of the poet.
The unidentified artist has situated her in a conventional
portrait pose, a three-quarter view intended implicitly to
disclose more of the sitter's nature than either a profile or a
full-faced attitude would reveal. Around her neck she wears
a lace collar, a bow, and a locket attached to a necklace.
Her most arresting feature, her long hair, is parted in the
middle and secured by a ribbon. Wearing her hair loosely
and draped over her shoulders gives her a girlish affect,
whilst reducing her to a bust precludes any hint of sexuality
and obviates any suggestion of her disability. Literally rising
above her body, the portrait dematerialises her physical
limitations and celebrates instead her artistic and intellectual accomplishments.

In various poems Bernstein presents herself—as many
Victorians portrayed disabled characters—as an object of
pity. She refers to herself as 'this poor invalid' (81), as 'a
lonely invalid' (66), as 'this poor nervous invalid' (35). She
strikes a stoical pose, in 'Musings' (72), but she acknowledges that her 'life's employment' has devolved into idleness. She refuses to dwell on her disability, per se, but she
affirms her immobility. In an epistolary poem she addresses
an admirer: 'Alas! be it said, I've been long ill in bed, /
And several years have passed over my head / Since last
o'er the floor of my room I could tread' (14). She expresses
her appreciation as well to other writers of sympathetic
notes, reports that her 'health seems rather better', but
admits that she 'still can't walk' (77). Most poignant of all
are the lyrics in which Bernstein laments her confinement.
'Calm, and unknown, I've lived alone' (73). 'O, how sweet
must freedom be / After long captivity!' (170). In 'A Meditation' (90) she reflects: 'I can but look upon the world / As
something far away.' She also identifies with a captive bird:
'If thou singest, thy songs must be / The songs of a sad
captivity' (177). Bernstein's sense of imprisonment persisted

until the end of her life. In 'Song of a "Shut-In"' (196)—
published in her final summer—she imagines a sensory catalogue of nature's gifts; kept within the 'gloomy walls' of
her flat in Ibrox, however, she can neither hear 'the murmur of the sea' nor smell 'the perfume of a thousand
flowers' nor feel 'the wild breeze blowing free'.

In her application for a grant from the Royal Literary
Fund, submitted in October 1904, Bernstein reported that
her annual sources of income were a pension of £10 from
the Indigent Gentlewomen's Fund, and another of £6 10s
from Colquhoun's Bequest for Incurables. The Royal
Society for the Relief of Indigent Gentlewomen of Scotland
awarded annuities to claimants who were 'broken in
health',[48] and Colquhoun's Bequest provided grants for
Glaswegians 'so destitute and helpless as to be proper
objects of charity'.[49] Bernstein's plea for support from the
Royal Literary Fund was not successful, but her hand-
written application and the letters of recommendation she
requested have survived. A reference from Margaret Braid,
assistant headmistress of the Park School for Girls,
described her as possessing 'considerable literary gifts' but
'much hindered by physical pain and weakness'; a testi-
monial from the Reverend Robert Armstrong, Minister of
St Matthews Parish, certified that she was 'a person of irre-
proachable character' but 'in necessitous circumstances
and enfeebled by bodily infirmity'; and, in her own letter,
Bernstein explained that her literary productivity had been
impeded by 'illnesses', 'chronic infirmity', 'physical weakness', and 'anxieties arising from my harassing circumstances'.[50]

Faith

Halfway through 'Mirren's Autobiography' (128), Bernstein
recalls a turning point in the course of her illness when,
after languishing 'through the first years of youth' with the
future looming 'helpless and drear' before her, an *inner light*
rose to cheer' her and to signal 'the Presence of God'.
Several scholars have ascertained a divide in literary works
by invalids between the corporeal and religious spheres,
and Maria Frawley has observed that, as in Bernstein's case
here, many 'invalids were empowered by Christian dogma,

or empowered themselves through it, in order to take control of their physical and spiritual destinies.'[51]

Bernstein's faith was a vital part of her life and work. She was a Christian, but a specific denomination is difficult to ascertain.[52] She was baptised, the year after her birth, in the Church of England, and at her death in Glasgow she was a member of the St Matthews Parish Church of Scotland.[53] In 'The Great Passover' (87) she references the Eucharist in the Anglican tradition, and in 'The First Paraphrase' (94) she quotes from a popular hymn published by the Kirk. Throughout her poetry, however, she reveals few ideological connections either with Anglicanism or with Presbyterianism. The various religious citations signal Bernstein's wide reading of biblical texts more clearly than they reflect a pattern of spiritual connections. Some of the most consistent themes in her religious poems address paradise, judgment day, and the loving nature of God.

References to Bernstein in the *Advent Review and Herald of the Sabbath*, published in America, reveal her early devotion to the Saturday Sabbath and intimate a brief flirtation with the Seventh Day Adventist Church. In 1874, on a mission to establish that church in Britain, J. N. Andrews called on her in Glasgow and conducted a 'Sabbath Conference' in her parlour.[54] Thereafter, in addition to printing two of her poems, 'Servants of God, Awake!' (64) and 'The Sabbath of the Lord' (106), the *Review and Herald* also published a notice of *Mirren's Musings*, in which a church stalwart described Bernstein's poems as 'lively and racy' and identified her as 'one of those who have recently embraced the Sabbath in Scotland'.[55] Five years after his first visit, Andrews returned to Glasgow, and in his journal, quoted in the *Review and Herald*, he recorded: 'We also visited Miss Marion Bernstein and her mother, at 5 Dunrobin Place, Paisley Road. Miss Bernstein has observed the Sabbath many years; her mother commenced its observance only a few years since. We found them in circumstances of distress.'[56] Although there was no Adventist congregation in Glasgow until the 1920s, it is clear from several of her poems—including 'Friday Evening Hymn' (96), 'At Sabbath Sunset' (97), 'Sabbath Eve' (102), 'The Seventh Day' (105), and 'Apotheosis' (176)—that Bernstein advocated most of her life for the Saturday Sabbath.

Much of Bernstein's religious poetry, however, embraced conventional Christian beliefs. Many of her spiritual pieces are didactic in tone, and most of her instructions on Christian life refer to common claims. In 'Beatitudes' (143) she echoes biblical cadences and preaches honesty and sincerity as well as good thoughts and deeds. In 'To An Atheist' (11) and 'A Question' (39) she debates imaginary adversaries and weighs their flagging faith against her own steady convictions. Her religious sentiments are chiefly 'musings' that reflect her search for peace in times of physical and spiritual distress.

Whilst Bernstein composed religious verse throughout her literary career, as time passed her spiritual motifs intertwined increasingly with other themes. From her belief in a loving and forgiving God, she found respite from the deaths of friends and comfort from her failing eyesight and declining health. Her belief that suffering preceded paradise was not a pessimistic view but a gift. In her late poems she quotes scriptural passages, cites them as footnotes, and relates them to ordinary lessons she gleans from the newspapers. In 'Coffining the Pauper' (161)—a poem inspired by a grim incident reported in the *Glasgow Weekly Mail*—she invokes phrases from Proverbs and from Matthew to elevate the 'wasted frame' of a poorhouse woman to a place beside Christ. Eventually, she came to apply Christian principles to figures difficult to treat as religious subjects. This change appears most clearly in her poems regarding Robert Burns. Her first poem, 'On Hearing "Auld Lang Syne"' (1), transacts with Burns's song to express loss and to lament the passage of time, but it does so without religious language. By way of contrast, one of her late poems, 'Robert Burns' (169), translates the popular image of the Scottish Bard into a Christian figure defamed but deserving of forgiveness. During the nineteenth century, moreover, ideal qualities associated with religiosity came to be gendered as feminine, according to Callum Brown, and 'the nature of womanhood was represented as highly dependent on religious qualities'.[57] By expressing her views in moral terms, Bernstein both affirms her Christian convictions and establishes her personal identity as a woman. 'Heartfelt religious beliefs'—asserts Valentina Bold—'underpinned Bernstein's desire for social change.'[58]

Rather than adhere to a strict and authoritative religious doctrine, Bernstein sought the comfort and joy that her belief in God provided. In 'A Dream' (53) she awakens to a utopian religious state: 'All the churches attended a conference / At which every sect agreed / That an erring opinion was not so bad / As a false word or wicked deed.' Similarly, in 'A Meditation' (198) she imagines the 'perfect truth' and the 'perfect unity' that might be realised if all denominations were accepted as equals: 'If all the churches would agree / To walk in all the light that's given / By Him who giveth light from heaven, / How many changes we should see!' She was deeply invested in the spiritual life and in a simple faith that would sustain her to the end.

Social Justice & Gender Equality

Although her reputation now rests on her poems on women's rights, Marion Bernstein recognised little distinction between gender equality and social equality. She had no patience for those who claimed privilege over others. In 'A Song for the Working Man' (22) she celebrated 'simple fare' and 'humble life'. She valued her fellow poets, many of whom were from the working classes, and she populated her poems with an array of ordinary citizens: postmen (37), policemen (42), fishermen (141), street musicians (54), an overworked pointsman (144), riveters out on strike (122), even a victim of intemperance (129). In her enlightened poem on 'Human Rights' (108), in which she advocated for universal equality, she foretold how women would treat men if the relationship between the genders were reversed: 'We'd give fair play, let come what might, / To he or she folk, black or white, / And haste the reign of Human Right.'

Bernstein was especially critical of those who abused power and position. In one of her most dynamic monologues, 'The Highland Laird's Song' (151), she constructs an ignoble nobleman who elevates himself above the 'common people'. In 'Move On!' (42) she describes how 'that useful man in blue' bullies harmless gatherings of 'loungers' and forces them to scatter. In 'The Music of the Streets' (54) she identifies 'a selfish class of people' who enjoy access to 'operas and concerts' but try to abolish the vernacular

forms of music that the 'little gutter children' love. Similarly, she condemns arrogance and pettiness in the work-
place. In 'The Pointsman' (144) she describes the 'scene of
terror' that results after the directors of the railway companies had declined to confer with the railway servants on
concessions proposed to protect the travelling public. In
'Light the Furnace Again' (124) she urges 'masters and men'
to set aside their differences and reminds readers that 'love
knoweth no class'.

One measure of Bernstein's commitment to social justice
is her interrogation of the Fugitive Slave Circulars of 1875
and 1876 published almost seventy years after the passage
of the Slave Trade Act and forty years after the passage of
the Slavery Abolition Act. In June 1875 the Admiralty had
issued instructions to its captains ordering that the navy
return to their masters any fugitive slaves who escaped to
her majesty's ships. These new procedures were seen as a
reversal of traditional policy towards slavery, and the
public and the press alike protested demonstrably against
the original circular, which was suspended in October
1875, cancelled in November 1875, and revised in January
1876. The public response to the instructions issued by
the Admiralty marked the first significant opposition to
Disraeli's imperialist programme, and the outrage revealed
that the abolitionist achievements of 1807 and 1833 continued to be recognised as central to humanitarian ideals
in Britain. Bernstein likewise took umbrage at the decree.
In 'An Appeal' (65) the depth of her sympathy is neatly
summarised in one couplet: 'Never by me should man or
maid / Be into slavery betrayed.' Together with 'The
Fugitive Slave' (74)—with its echoes of Elizabeth Barrett
Browning's 'The Runaway Slave at Pilgrim's Point'—these
poems address tensions between humanity and inhuman-
ity. In Bernstein's narrative the crew successfully shames
the captain, and together they defy the order issued in
the circular by agreeing to 'guard all human liberties'.

Three weeks after Bernstein voiced her opinion on a
labour dispute, in 'The Govan Riveters' Strike' (122), the
Glasgow Weekly Mail published a response in verse from
an unpractised poet—M. M'M—who acknowledged her
earlier 'strains' in support of working men but admon-
ished her to 'abstain' from matters 'quite out of the

range' of her 'knowledge, experience, or pen'.[59] His intention notwithstanding, the effect of his poem was to bait
her into a composition on one of her favourite topics—
feminism. In 'Marion's Reply to M. M'M' (123), she
retorts:

> As a woman, I'll say
> It is womankind's way
> To heed all the affairs of our brothers:
> Very ill would men fare
> Without counsel or care
> From their wives, sisters, daughters, or mothers.

Less important than her attitude toward the strike is the
fact that she was willing, as a woman, to express a political
position on an issue claimed as the province of men. She
was, as Elspeth King has asserted, 'a feminist some twenty
years before the term was in general use'.[60]

Bernstein's poems on gender matters may be conveni-
ently divided into three topics: domestic violence, domestic
inequality, and women's suffrage. She was not the only
woman in Glasgow, between 1874 and 1906, who was writing and publishing poems on these themes, but she was the
one who most effectively combined anger and humour in
expressing her views. Her witty rhymes and clever stanzas,
together with her feisty tone, made her poems popular with
readers of all classes. On 21 March 1874, the editor of the
Glasgow Weekly Mail declined a poem submitted by a contributor from Dumfries and declared that 'Women's Rights
is a topic we are specially desirous of avoiding' (p. 3).
Why, then, was he willing to publish Bernstein's feminist
poems? 'So far as Marion is concerned'—he later explained—'we have no objection to insert anything which
may provoke a smart retort from her. We like to strike fire
from our correspondents.'[61]

One of the most contentious issues in nineteenth-century
Britain was the problem of domestic violence. As King
comments:

> In the mid-1870s wife-beating in Britain had reached epi-
> demic proportions, and a parliamentary report on the
> state of the law relating to brutal assaults in 1875 recom-

mended that offenders should be lashed. There was much
debate and discussion on the proposal, which, inevitably,
because women had no representation in parliament,
was quietly dropped.[62]

The proposal also failed because some men believed they
had a 'right' to beat their wives and others viewed the practice as the 'habit' of the working classes. Bernstein railed
repeatedly against domestic abuse. In 'The Wetched Sex' (3)
and 'A Woman's Logic' (86), she spars with the editor of
the *Glasgow Weekly Mail*, whose responses to an incident of
wife-beating were, first, to quote an insensitive caption from
a *Punch* cartoon and, secondly, to offer his own condescend-
ing remark on women and women's rights. She holds her
anger in check, however, and wryly invites the editor to
imagine himself as the abuser: 'If *you* had been a collier,
now, / In some black mine or other, / *You* might "pwefer"
the right to kick / To death *your* wife or mother.' In other
poems she addresses her fellow women. In 'A Rule to
Work Both Ways' (17) she encourages her 'sisters' to turn
the tables on their attackers: 'If beating can reform a wife /
It might reform a husband too.' She advises those engaged
in 'husband-curing' to 'let each blow / Be given with the
kitchen poker!' In 'Married and "Settled"' (47) she laments
the increasing frequency of 'wife-murder' and urges 'ye
unhappy wives' to unite 'for mutual defence / Against assassination'. The rising force of these poems reflects Bernstein's growing confidence in speaking out against domestic
violence.

Because Marion Bernstein never married, readers are
often surprised to discover that she wrote a handful of
poems in response to questions posed in verse by bachelors
and spinsters in pursuit of marital advice. In 'Advice to
Anxiety' (58) she urges a 'poor youth'—who fancies 'a
happy home and loving wife'—to take the plunge and 'take
my blessing'. In 'The Best Kind of Wife' (32) she encourages
a lad seeking a wife who excels in domestic economies to
marry instead for love. In 'A Reply to "Twenty-Eight"' (67)
she responds to a query from a maiden who has bided her
time and who now—'with empty coffers'—'must take the
first who offers'. Bernstein's reply reflects her disdain for
the Victorian ideology of domesticity:

We're not all willing to be sold—
Maidens there are in plenty
Who'd rather work than wed for gold,
Though over eight-and-twenty.

In an increasingly urbanised society, in order to survive,
men and women alike sought employment outside the
home, so that the concept of separate spheres of home and
work was foreign to them. Eleanor Gordon acknowledges
that 'the degree of sex segregation of the labour force was
particularly pronounced in Scotland', but she also observes
that 'towards the end of the nineteenth century there was
a widening sphere of employment for single middle-class
women.'[63] Speculating on Bernstein's attitudes toward men
and marriage, Elspeth King asserts—in her reading of
'Wanted a Husband' (27)—that the poet 'had a very low
opinion of marriage as an institution'.[64] As we construe the
poem, however, we note that the quality she values most
in a man is his willingness to cooperate in the marriage
compact:

Wanted a husband who's tender and true,
Who will stick to his duty, and never get 'fou,'
But when all his day's work he has blithely gone
    through,
Help his wife, 'set to rights', till her work is done too.

We read the surprising coda, in which she rejects the very
'lad' she seeks, as a declaration of her independence both as
a woman and as a poet.

All her poetic life, Bernstein was outspoken on the rights
of women, especially the right to vote, and one of the most
distinctive qualities of her feminist project is the earnest
expression of her opinions in the public sphere. She uses
the dramatic openings and closings of 'A Woman's Plea'
(146) and 'Onward Yet! Upward Yet!' (114) as strategies to
engage her readers. In the former she sounds the call that
would become an established feminist agenda. In the latter
she addresses her 'sisters' in strains that cast the right to
vote as a religious imperative. In her poem 'On the Franchise Demonstration of the 6th Inst' (157), she addresses

her female readers and scolds them for failing to participate: 'Women of Glasgow, / What do you mean? / Why were you idle / All through such a scene?' 'Prove your right to the vote', she pleads, 'To ask is to have it.'

'Woman's Rights and Wrongs' (40) was written and published in response to 'Woman's Rights *versus* Woman's Wrongs' by Jessie Russell, 1850–1923, a fellow contributor to the *Glasgow Weekly Mail* and a poet whom many regard as a foil to Bernstein.[65] True, the editor of the paper wrote pointedly of Bernstein's 'sarcastic acidity'[66] as opposed to Russell's 'tender domestic sentiment'.[67] On some significant issues, though, the two were sympathetic, especially in their criticism of the division of work and wages by gender. Russell shied away, however, from Bernstein's political agenda. In her poem she eschews 'Woman's Rights' and 'Woman's Wrongs' as topics for poetic expression and declares that 'Parliament, Council, or Congress could never be womanly themes'. One week later, Marion Bernstein replied:

> Pray, in what way is wrong redressed,
>   But by conceding right?
> And Woman Suffrage is the best
>   For which our sex can fight.
>
> Why should we put our trust in men,
>   Who oft betray our cause?
> Let women vote away their wrongs,
>   And vote for righteous laws.

Eventually, Jessie Russell accepted the wisdom of this argument. She composed 'A Recantation'—dedicated to Bernstein—in which she admitted that she had been wrong and pledged to 'vote for none but Marion'.[68]

Bernstein's first lines on the theme of women's suffrage, 'Oh! I Wish that All Women Had Power to Vote' (76), appeared in the *Glasgow Weekly Mail* early in 1874. She confidently announces her candidacy for political office, predicts a meteoric rise to prominence, and promises to 'right all wrongs'. Only ten lines of this 'declined' text, which may be just a fragment, were published. Below the lines the editor quipped: 'Marion Bernstein is becoming as ambitious as the man who wanted to get into the pulpit just to know how the minister felt when he preached.' If the poet was annoyed by this comment, she did not show her displeasure. Instead, it would appear that she bided her time, pursued an alternative tack, and expanded this premature version into one of her most polished and popular texts, 'A Dream' (53). This poem draws upon a number of literary conventions and embraces the agendas that the poet advances elsewhere, including: the imposition of stringent punishments for wife-beating; the admission of women to the judiciary and the legislature; and the extension of the franchise to women. Florence Boos reads the poem as a 'utopian-feminist fantasy',[69] and Valentina Bold construes it as a reworking of 'the visionary tradition of Ramsay, Burns, and Hogg from a feminist perspective'.[70] In advancing her public protest advocating for political power for women, moreover, this piece is amongst the most radical that Bernstein ever composed:

> There were female chiefs in the Cabinet,
>   (Much better than males, I'm sure!)
> And the Commons were three-parts feminine,
>   While the Lords were seen no more!

Bernstein's 'dream' may be a fantasy, but her poem sets forth her true 'vision' of social justice and gender equality.

Poetic Craft

In the first notice of *Mirren's Musings*, the reviewer for the *Glasgow Weekly Mail* described Marion Bernstein as 'our versatile poetical correspondent'.[71] Like the diverse themes she pursued, the various elements of her poetry reward close reading. In 'Musical Reflections' (60)—with its allusion to Milton's *L'Allegro*—she wrote: 'It is in solitary hours / I best can feel sweet music's powers, / And wake the living spirit pent / Within the lifeless instrument.' A maker of music and a teacher of music, she was also 'a forthright woman of musical gifts'.[72]

Bernstein cast most of her poems in quatrains in predictable rhyming patterns, characteristic of newspaper verse, which facilitated composition and comprehension alike. A

considerable number, however, departed from convention
in form, rhyme, and metre. One she arranged in five-line
stanzas (86), one in eight-line stanzas (22), one in twelve-line
stanzas (23). Many she did not divide at all. There are four-line
epigrams (88 and 92), and there is a sixty-line paraphrase of a
Scottish Gaelic lament (85). 'On Hearing "Auld Lang Syne" '
(1) she inscribed in traditional ballad stanzas, whereas she
composed 'Wanted in Glasgow' (2) in twenty-four lines all of
which end in a rhyme with 'Clyde'. She wrote 'Cremation'
(4) in closed triplets. She sustained 'Mirren's Autobiography'
(132)—a long, self-reflexive effort—almost wholly in couplets
and chiefly in anapestic tetrameter. A poem in two stanzas,
'Teach Me How to Keep Thy Way' (95), is structured as a
dialogue between a speaker who wanders through 'life's
perplexing maze' and God who promises to light 'the path'.
There are scornful lines addressed to huntsmen (16), angry
lines addressed to wife-beaters (3, 17, and 86), and patriotic
lines addressed to the monarch (193). A poem about a local
hero is peppered with epic diction (30). In 'The Best Kind
of Wife' (32) each stanza concludes with a rhetorical maxim
(32).

Bernstein's versatility, in microcosm, is demonstrated in
the eight poems she denominated as sonnets. There have
always been variations on and departures from the traditional parameters by which the form is defined—fourteen
lines, with a 'turn' between octave and sestet, chiefly in
iambic pentameter—but she recurs to the pre-Petrarchan
notion of a sonnet as a 'little song' with changeable rhyme
and metre. For example, in both 'Fade not! oh, autumn
flowers' (59) and 'Life's sunny summer time' (75)—with
only four repeated end rhymes and short lines chiefly in
iambic trimeters—the economy of her verse parallels the
simplicity of her subjects. Her sonnet on 'The Rainbow'
(197) celebrates the covenant signified by the 'memorial
arch' and fulfils the principal expectations of a sonnet; but
the rhyme—ABBACDDAAEECEE—confounds the Petrarchan and Shakespearean patterns. Similarly, the rhyme
schemes of the two first-person sonnets—'To the Stars' (103)
and 'On the Prediction of Extraordinary Darkness, &c'
(127)—play recklessly with convention. The turn between the
two stanzas of her sonnet 'To Mary Cross' (160) marks the
transition between grief and consolation, and the arrange-

ment of the rhymes—ABBAABB ACCDEED—duplicates the pattern of Dante Gabriel Rossetti's 'Lovesight'. 'On Receiving a Bouquet' (66) also presents a traditional turn but an unconventional rhyme scheme—ABBACDDCEFFEBB— and measures of chiefly trochaic and occasionally dactylic trimeters; moreover, here Bernstein fashions a dramatic interaction between the speaker who received the flowers and the 'gentle unknown friend' who sent them. Finally, her tribute to Elizabeth Mouat (166) praises her subject's resolve and illustrates her own poetic discipline both by responding to the demands of an acrostic and by conforming to the traditional Petrarchan rhyme scheme—ABBAABBACDECDE— in iambic pentameter.

Arguably, the most sophisticated element of Bernstein's prosody is the witty use of enjambment by which she surprises and engages the reader. This strategy urges each poem forward, with little or no pause from one line to the next, and enhances its internal rhymes:

> Some love at first sight; but your love must be reckoned
> Not first sight, but second: and Justice has beckoned
> To me with her finger, and bade me set right
> Your dim second sight. I am told I'm a fright
> By my brother; but every girl, somehow or other,
> Seems a fright to her brother, and belle to her mother.
> Now, I really don't think myself one or the other. (14)

Notice, in this passage, the bold repetition of 'first sight' in the first and second lines. Observe also how the word 'second'—rhyming with 'reckoned' and 'beckoned' at the ends of the first two lines—rhymes with itself, internally, in the second and fourth lines; similarly, how the word 'brother' rhymes both with itself, internally, in the fifth and sixth lines and with 'other' and 'mother' and 'other' again at the ends of the fifth, sixth, and seventh lines. The verse delights by its intricacy. Whether the works are comic or serious in tone, lyrical, dramatic, or narrative in form, this enjambment fosters a conversational quality that one associates with the best nineteenth-century English and Scottish poetry, including the dramatic monologues of Browning and Tennyson, Joanna Baillie's *Fugitive Verses*, and Elizabeth Barrett Browning's *Aurora Leigh*.

Celebrated chiefly—and appropriately—as a radical feminist and social commentator, Marion Bernstein also deserves
recognition as an accomplished poet. In her best poems, in
language rich in lyrical expression and dramatic situation,
she escaped the constraints and expectations placed by
readers of her time upon women writers. In spite of her
confinement, she was admired for her energetic engagement
with her readers and with the issues of her day. Her best
work was characterised by an ardent moral sensibility
modulated by humour. Writing on a variety of subjects—
social and spiritual—she crafted her public persona and
achieved a reputation as a woman of letters in Victorian
Scotland.

Notes

[1] Bernstein, then living at 15 Kildonan Terrace, Ibrox, succumbed to
breast cancer on 2 February. NRS: Statutory Register of Deaths (1906)
No. 646/02 0176, p. 4.

[2] In 1898, in her application for a pension from the Indigent Gentlewomen's Fund, Bernstein acknowledged that she was not a 'Scotch-
woman' but stated that she had 'lived in Scotland for over twenty-four
years.' Records of the Royal Society for the Relief of Indigent Gentlewomen of Scotland, Summary Sheets of Applications to the Trustees of
the Fund for the Year 1898, Application No. 51.

[3] Bernstein's commitment to the arrangement of the prefatory material,
to the inclusion of her portrait, and to the expense of the gilt-edged
leaves and handsome cloth binding suggests that she regarded the book
as an artistic product. Her aesthetic expectations may have been partly
responsible for the delays in production to which she refers in 'He
promised that either by hook or by crook' (83).

[4] Bernstein's critical reception has been augmented by the efforts of
scholars who were endeavouring in the 1990s to locate the place of
women in the Scottish literary canon. See Douglas Dunn, 'The Representation of Women in Scottish Literature', Scotlands 2 (1994); Christopher Whyte, 'Introduction', Gendering the Nation: Studies in Modern
Scottish Literature (Edinburgh: Edinburgh University Press, 1995); and
Douglas Gifford and Dorothy McMillan, 'Introduction', A History of
Scottish Women's Writing (Edinburgh: Edinburgh University Press, 1997).
Gifford and McMillan observed that Scottish women's writing 'suffers
from the double bind of being Scottish and being by women' (pp. ix–x).
Whyte asserted that 'the texts in question are almost exclusively by
male authors' (p. x). The need to correct this gendered imbalance in
Scottish literature explains in part why Bernstein's poems, in the past
two decades, have been engaging a diverse and growing population of
readers.

[5] GRO: England and Wales Civil Registration Indexes; Index of Births, 1846: Bethnal Green, London; Vol. 2, p. 19. London Metropolitan Archives, Saint John, Bethnal Green, Register of Baptisms, P72/JN/Item 004.

[6] UK Census Enumeration Returns for Lancashire, 1841: Liverpool. PRO: folio ref. HO107/561/~F10.

[7] Lydia Pulsford was born in 1819 and baptised on 20 August. London Metropolitan Archives, Saint Anne, Soho, Register of Baptisms, DL/T/087/Item 027.

[8] GRO: England and Wales Civil Registration Indexes; Index of Marriages, 1843: Marylebone, London; Vol. 1, p. 166. London Metropolitan Archives, All Souls, Langham Place, Register of Marriages, P89/ALS/Item 058.

[9] GRO: England and Wales Civil Registration Indexes; Index of Births, 1844: Wandsworth, London; Vol. 4, p. 535. London Metropolitan Archives, Holy Trinity, Clapham, Register of Baptisms, P95/TR11/Item 069.

[10] GRO: England and Wales Civil Registration Indexes: Index of Births, 1852: Marylebone, London; Vol. 1a, p. 412. London Metropolitan Archives, Saint Marylebone, Register of Baptisms, P89/MRY1/Item 055.

[11] There is evidence that this relatively rare illness had been endemic in the human population from antiquity. In the second half of the nineteenth century, however, its transformation into an epidemic disease spread by the infectious poliovirus was experienced in a number of advanced societies.

[12] UK Census Enumeration Returns for London, 1851: Marylebone. PRO: folio ref. HO107/1490/~F899.

[13] *The London Gazette*, No. 21727 (12 June 1855), p. 2287; No. 21731 (19 June 1855), p. 2388.

[14] London Metropolitan Archives, Surrey County Asylum, Admission Register Male Patients, Vol. 3, 1859–71, H46/SP/B/01, p. 110.

[15] London Metropolitan Archives, Middlesex County Lunatic Asylum, Colney Hatch, Admission Register Male Patients, Vol. 1, 1859–67, H12/CH/B/02, p. 175. Male Patient Case Books, Vol. 7, H12/CH/B/13, p. 95. GRO: England and Wales Civil Registration Indexes: Index of Deaths, 1859: Barnet, London; Vol. 39, p. 78. The cause of death was 'General Paralysis of the Insane' (GPI).

[16] UK Census Enumeration Returns for Sussex, 1861: Burgh of Hastings. PRO: folio ref. RG9/0562/~F111.

[17] After they relocated to Glasgow, the sisters advertised lessons in voice, piano, theory, harmony, and counterpoint in the local newspapers. Lydia occasionally called herself 'Madame Bennett' and once identified herself as a past pupil of Sir Julius Benedict. A German-born musician who immigrated in 1835 to London, Benedict, 1804–85, enjoyed great success as a composer and conductor.

[18] The nature and extent of Marion's education are uncertain. Valentina Bold suggests that she occupies a 'place within the Scottish autodidactic tradition' (Bold, *James Hogg*, p. 262). Florence Boos insists, however, that 'she almost certainly received some formal education' (Boos, 'Cauld Engle-Cheek', p. 68).

[19] UK Census Enumeration Returns for London, 1871: Marylebone. PRO: folio ref. RG10/0149/~F60.

[20] GRO: England and Wales Registration Indexes: Marriages Registered in January, February, and March 1873, Sunderland, Index p. 16 and Index p. 127, Vol. 10a, p. 864.

[21] Eleanor Gordon and Gwyneth Nair, *Public Lives: Women, Family and Society in Victorian Britain* (New Haven: Yale University Press, 2003, p. 9.

[22] *Glasgow Post-Office Directory for 1874–1875* (Glasgow: Post Office, 1875), p. 504. The Bernsteins' inclusion in this volume suggests that they had arrived in Glasgow some time before the end of 1873. Meanwhile, Marion's sister Lydia and her husband were also settling in Glasgow; in the earliest extant record of Benjamin Malyon's printing business, he is listed as a 'ticket publisher' at 74 Argyle Street (*Glasgow Post-Office Directory for 1876–1877* [Glasgow: Post Office, 1877], p. 329).

[23] Dunrobin Place, now long lost to urban renewal, was identified in the 1871 census as located in Enumeration District 14—'along the north side of Paisley Road to the west side of Avondale Place'—and would have been positioned near the boundary between the municipal district of Tradeston and the police burgh of Kinning Park.

[24] See D[avid] Walker Brown, *Clydeside Litterateurs: Biographical Sketches, Portraits, Etc.* (Glasgow: Carter and Pratt, 1897) and George Eyre-Todd, *The Glasgow Poets: Their Lives and Poems* (Edinburgh: William Hodge, 1903). However, Hamish Whyte's recent collection of Glasgow verses— *Mungo's Tongues: Glasgow Poems 1630–1990* (Edinburgh: Mainstream, 1993)—reveals that 'condition of Glasgow' poems had gained considerable currency by the time when Marion Bernstein arrived in the city.

[25] Contrary to convention, Cameron (1841–1924) identified himself as the editor in a headline that ran across all eight columns of the first page of the issue for 31 January: 'Dr Charles Cameron Editor Weekly Mail Will Meet the Glasgow Electors in Scotia Music Hall This (Saturday) Afternoon at Half Past Three.' He would serve in the House of Commons for twenty-seven years, and in 1900 he was lauded as the most prominent amongst the contemporary Scottish radicals.

[26] Manners, 1837–1920, had achieved success in journalistic positions in Stirling and Liverpool. He was identified as the editor of the *Weekly Mail* in one of the many sketches composed and compiled by Alexander G. Murdoch, *The Scottish Poets: Recent and Living* (Glasgow: Thomas D. Morison, 1883), p. 195.

[27] *Newspaper Press Directory* (London: C. Mitchell, 1877), p. 213.

[28] Natalie Houston, 'Newspaper Poems: Material Texts in the Public Sphere', *Victorian Studies* 50.2 (2008), p. 239.

[29] Alexis Easley, *First-Person Anonymous: Women Writers and Victorian Print Media, 1830–1870* (Aldershot: Ashgate, 2004), p. 1.

[30] See Joan Lightwood, *The Park School 1880–1980* (Glasgow: Park School and MacLehose, 1980). According to Lightwood, the school was established by prominent Glasgow citizens whose interest in the cause of advanced learning for women 'led them to work for the academic education of girls' (p. 9). Bernstein was not a regular member of the staff

but was recommended as an adjunct instructor to students who desired private music lessons. Her connection with the school is confirmed in letters from the head mistress, Georgina Kinnear, and the assistant head mistress, Margaret Braid, in support of Bernstein's application for a grant from the Royal Literary Fund.

[31] Benedict Anderson, *Imagined Communities: Reflections on the Origin and Spread of Nationalism* (London: Verso, 1983), p. 35.

[32] Donald Carswell, *Brother Scots* (New York: Harcourt, 1920), p. 162.

[33] See Brown, *Clydeside Litterateurs*, p. 156, and Eyre-Todd, *The Glasgow Poets*, p. 423. Both sources report that Murdoch, a prize-winning poet who had laboured as a marine engineer, gave up his trade in 1878 to accept a permanent position on the staff of the *Weekly Mail*.

[34] *Glasgow Weekly Mail*, 7 February 1880, p. 7.

[35] This decline in the number of poems by women published in the *Weekly Mail* is not surprising. In the late 1880s, Murdoch contributed fifty sketches of 'Recent Scottish Poets' to the paper; only two of his subjects, Mary Cross and Jessie Russell, were women.

[36] For a biographical sketch of Canton and a notice of his appointment as editor of the *Weekly Herald*, see Brown, *Clydeside Litterateurs*, pp. 27–32.

[37] Eric Richards, *The Highland Clearances: People, Landlords and Rural Turmoil* (Edinburgh: Birlinn, 2008), p. 356.

[38] Richards, p. 381.

[39] Richards, p. 376.

[40] NRS: Statutory Register of Deaths (1896) No. 644/10 0663, p. 221.

[41] NRS: Statutory Register of Deaths (1905) No. 644/09 0215, p. 72.

[42] Lydia and Marion continued to advertise their services as music teachers into the 1890s, when they shared lodgings at 224 West Regent Street. Although they were plagued by personal difficulties, neither sister lost her sense of humour. In the 1891 census, Lydia gave 'Professor of Piano and Singing' as her occupation, whilst Marion gave 'Professor of Theory and Harmony' as hers; both under-represented their ages by six years (UK Census Enumeration Returns for Glasgow, 1901: Blythswood. PRO folio ref. ED 644/09 042/09, p. 13). Demented and suffering from bronchitis, Lydia died on 30 December 1916 (NRS: Statutory Register of Deaths [1916] No. 644/12 0011, p. 4. GGHB Archives Case Records of Gartnaval Royal Asylum; Ref: HB 13/5/171, pp. 85–90).

[43] See Paul Ricoeur, *Time and Narrative*, I, trans. Kathleen McLaughlin and David Pellauer (Chicago: University of Chicago Press, 1984), pp. 65–68.

[44] See the notes on 'Birthday Musings' (121) and 'Forward March' (172).

[45] *Glasgow Weekly Mail*, 12 September 1874, p. 7.

[46] A number of scholars have called attention to the way the Victorians embraced the 'melodramatisation' of disability. See, for example, Peter Brooks, *The Melodramatic Imagination* (New Haven: Yale University Press, 1976) and Martha Stoddard Holmes, *Fictions of Affliction: Physical Disability in Victorian Culture* (Ann Arbor: University of Michigan Press, 2004).

[47] *Mirren's Musings*, pp. [iii]–iv.

[48] Doris Havatny, *The Royal Society for the Relief of Indigent Gentlewomen of Scotland: A History, 1847–1997* (Edinburgh: Royal Society for the Relief of Indigent Gentlewomen of Scotland, 1997), p. 21.

[49] *The Medical Institutions of Glasgow: A Handbook*, ed. James Christie (Glasgow: MacLehose, 1884), p. 169.

[50] Royal Literary Fund, Form of Application for an Author, File No. 1686, 4 October 1904.

[51] Maria H. Frawley, *Invalidism and Identity in Nineteenth-Century Britain* (Chicago: University of Chicago Press, 2004), p. 162. See also Miriam Bailin, *The Sickroom in Victorian Fiction: The Art of Being Ill* (Cambridge: Cambridge University Press, 1994).

[52] Some years ago Elspeth King wrote of Bernstein: 'It is obvious from her surname and the allusions in her poetry that she was of Jewish origin' (*The Hidden History of Glasgow's Women: The Thenew Factor* [Edinburgh: Mainstream, 1993], p. 84). In this century, however, Linda Fleming has observed that 'Marion Bernstein's religious beliefs appear from her writing to be more Christian in orientation, so her relationship with possible Jewish ethnicity is elusive' (*The Biographical Dictionary of Scottish Women from the Earliest Times to 2004*, ed. Elizabeth Ewan, Sue Innes, and Sian Reynolds [Edinburgh: Edinburgh University Press, 2004], p. 34). Florence Boos concludes: 'Whatever her ancestry, several affirmations in *Mirren's Musings* suggest that she was a Christian' (*Working-Class Women Poets in Victorian Britain* [Petersborough, ON: Broadview, 2008], p. 338).

[53] St Matthews—later St Matthews-Blythswood and now Renfield St Stephen's—stood at the intersection of Bothwell Street and North Street. The minister, who wrote several letters attesting to Bernstein's eligibility for pensions, was Reverend Robert Armstrong, 1876–1914. See Andrew Herron, comp. *Historical Directory to Glasgow Presbytery* (Glasgow: Presbytery of Glasgow, 1984), pp. 176–77.

[54] John Nevins Andrews, 1829–83, was one of the leading figures in the new church and its first official missionary to Europe. Not long afterward, the *Review and Herald* quoted an account of this conference from a 'sister in Scotland': 'You will doubtless be pleased to hear that we have held prayer meetings here every Sabbath evening since then. These meetings are usually attended by six persons, including my mother and myself. Five of us have decided that the seventh day is the true Sabbath' ('Sabbath Keepers in Scotland', *Advent Review and Herald of the Sabbath*, 1 January 1875, p. 6).

[55] *Advent Review and Herald of the Sabbath*, 30 November 1876, p. 176. The notice was written by U[riah] S[mith], 1832–1903, editor of the paper and an advocate for religious liberty and the abolition of slavery.

[56] *Advent Review and Herald of the Sabbath*, 17 July 1879, p. 28.

[57] Callum G. Brown, 'Religion', in *Gender in Scottish History since 1700*, ed. Lynn Abrams, Eleanor Gordon, Deborah Simonton, and Eileen Janes Yeo (Edinburgh: Edinburgh University Press, 2006), p. 101.

[58] Valentina Bold, 'Beyond "The Empire of the Gentle Heart": Scottish Women Poets of the Nineteenth Century', in *A History of Scottish Women's Writing*, ed. Douglas Gifford and Dorothy McMillan (Edinburgh: Edinburgh University Press, 1997), p. 257.

[59] M. M'M, 'To Marion Bernstein', *Glasgow Weekly Mail*, 4 January 1879, p. 7.

[60] King, p. 84.

[61] *Glasgow Weekly Mail*, 12 September 1874, p. 7.

[62] King, p. 86.

[63] Eleanor Gordon, 'Women's Spheres', in *People and Society in Scotland*, II, *1830–1914*, ed W. Hamish Fraser and R. J. Morris (Edinburgh: John Donald, 1990), p. 216.

[64] King, p. 85.

[65] In her youth Russell had begun to prepare for a situation as a teacher, but she was orphaned when she was eight years old and was forced to pursue positions in domestic service and dressmaking. Eventually she married a Clydeside shipwright and settled with him in the working-class district of Partick. Her book of verse—*The Blinkin' O' the Fire and Other Poems* (Glasgow: Cossar, Fotheringham & Co., 1877)—was published with the encouragement of 'shipbuilders connected with every yard on the Clyde'. Her principal topics include the pleasure of courtship and the 'labour of love', the satisfaction of being a wife and a mother, and the enjoyment of domestic life. She also addresses such social problems as intemperance, spouse abuse, and the high rate of child mortality among the working classes. For a biographical sketch, see Alexander Murdoch, 'Minor Scottish Poets: Jessie Russell', *Glasgow Weekly Mail*, 18 June 1888, p. 3.

[66] *Glasgow Weekly Mail*, 24 June 1876, p. 7.

[67] *Glasgow Weekly Mail*, 9 September 1876, p. 7.

[68] *The Blinkin' O' the Fire and Other Poems*, p. 31.

[69] Boos, *Working-Class Women in Victorian Britain*, p. 339.

[70] Bold, 'Beyond "The Empire of the Gentle Heart"', p. 257.

[71] 24 June 1876, p. 7.

[72] Boos, *Working-Class Women in Victorian Britain*, p. 340.

THE COLLECTED POEMS
OF MARION BERNSTEIN

Poems Published 28 February 1874 to 8 April 1876 and Collected in Mirren's Musings

1. ON HEARING 'AULD LANG SYNE'

Oh! tell me not of auld lang syne,
   For I would fain forget
Those bygone days, whose memory
   Brings nothing but regret.

For I have far outlived the time   5
   When thoughts of days gone by
Could call the smile upon my lip,
   The light into mine eye.

Ah! now 'tis not with smiles, but tears,
   That I can call to mind   10
The vanished joys of bygone years,
   The years of auld lang syne.

The joys of auld lang syne are fled.
   My early hopes have flown,
The friends who have not changed are dead,   15
   And I am left alone.

2. WANTED IN GLASGOW

Wanted a filter, to filter the Clyde,
   After some hundreds of people have died,
Chancing to fall in its poisonous tide;
Those who fall in there are likely to bide,
And if they have opened their mouths very wide   5
   They may as well stay, for when dragged out and dried
   'Twill be found that although they're not drowned they
      have died
Merely by trying the taste of the Clyde.
Wanted a corner in which one may hide
Away from the smoke that is spread far and wide;   10
From the factory chimneys on every side,
   By which folks in Glasgow like herrings are dried.
   To cure the smoke nuisance has nobody tried,
Of all the good folks that in Glasgow abide?
   'No smoking allowed!' might be here well applied.   15
Wanted a little more national pride
To sort this great city on every side;
To sweep up the streets and the rubbish to hide.
Wanted more street cars. It's awful to ride
Jammed down the middle and crammed down each side,   20
   'Twouldn't be very much worse to be fried!
   Wanted to know when some means will be tried
   By which all those wants can be quickly supplied,
That Glasgow may flourish, her citizens' pride.

3. 'THE WETCHED SEX'

As *Punch*'s swell puts it, we decidedly 'Pwefer the wetched sex with all
its wongs.'—*Weekly Mail*

I'm quite distressed by what you've said;
   Can I have read aright?
What, rather see the fair sex wronged
   Than see their wrongs set right!

Oh, fie, for shame! I'm quite surprised—   5
   I don't believe it's true.
No, really, sir, I can't believe
   Such shocking things of you!

If you had been a collier, now,
   In some black mine or other,   10
You might 'pwefer' the right to kick
   To death your wife or mother;

And triumph in their helplessness,
   And take delight in 'wonging'
The 'wetched sex,' and scorn the rights   15
   Of those to you belonging.

Oh, what a recreant knight, to say
   Such things!—we'll all resent it!
But, after all, 'twas said in play—
   You never could have meant it.   20

4. CREMATION

All those who have in contemplation
The poisoning of some relation
Will vote in favour of cremation.
They naturally think consuming
A better method than entombing,   5
Which still leaves chances of exhuming.
The fire's a much more faithful keeper
Of secrets than the earth, and cheaper;
And cannot hurt the lifeless sleeper.
Throw daggers to the savage cruel,   10
Leave pistols for the stage-play duel,
And settle your accounts with fuel!
In these cold, cautious northern climes
Murders will be, in modern times,
Entirely undiscovered crimes.   15
Doubtless, the system of cremation
Will save some necks from strangulation,
And prove a blessing to the nation!
But 'twill scarce suit some friends of ours,
Who like to spend their leisure hours   20
Decking their loved ones' graves with flowers.
Let these, if rich, indulge their yearning
By burying instead of burning,
Till love's completely quenched by learning.
The poor may feel anxiety,   25
But to their guardians it will be
A boon, as e'en the blind may see.
Paupers can be disposed of cheap;
Burn them by scores, then you can sweep
Up all the ashes in a heap.   30
No nonsense then! No friends need go
Where they are laid, for none can know
Nelly from Jane, or Tom from Joe.
You need not mind the consternation
Of any tearful, poor relation—   35
Sentence the paupers to cremation.
Or else deal with them in the way
Dean Swift suggested one fine day
For Irish children—so they say.
He said the only way to treat 'em   40

Was not to feed, and teach, and beat 'em,
But just to kill, and cook, and eat 'em.
But I'll suggest a plan still better,
Which, if adopted to the letter,
Will make each taxpayer your debtor.   45
Now don't be shocked, good guardian father,
For though it looks like murder, rather,
You've gone so far you might go farther—
You've severed children from their mothers,
Husbands from wives, sisters from brothers—   50
Kill half and cook them for the others!
No butcher's bills then! no vexation
With either burial or cremation,
'Tis sure to meet with approbation.

5. THE SULKY MAN

Oh! a terrible plague is a sulky man,
Just looking as glumpy as ever he can—
Though he speaks not a word, yet his grim looks say,
'I always am put upon, every day;
But whatever you do, I shall still forbear,   5
And I'll not speak my mind—though a saint might swear!'
Oh, an angel might swear at the sulky man
When he gives himself airs, as such creatures can—
By complaint without words, contriving to teach
How silence can be more provoking than speech.   10
Poor Job had three friends, and they all had a way
Of speaking their minds to him every day;
'Twas trying, but still he was patient enough
We know, by the way that he answered their 'stuff.'
He'd soon have lost patience, and changed his plan,   15
Had one of those friends been a sulky man.

6. TO THE EDITOR OF THE 'WEEKLY MAIL'

To sentimental bards you say,
  In terms to make them quail, sir,
'We grant no amatory lay
  Admission to the *Mail*, sir!'

Perhaps Dan Cupid knows this, too,   5
  And it would serve you right, sir,
If he some day should shoot at you
  An arrow out of spite, sir!

Methinks if somebody should send
  A lovesong to yourself, sir,   10
You never would be stern enough
  To lay that on the shelf, sir!

I don't know if you're dark or fair,
  With tresses black or white, sir,
Or if your eyes are brown or blue,   15
  Or grey, or dull, or bright, sir!

I don't know if you're short or tall,
  Young, middle-aged, or old, sir,
Or fat or lean, or large or small,
  I never have been told, sir!   20

But if I knew, I'd quickly try
  A way that scarce could fail, sir,
To get a sentimental strain
  Admitted to the *Mail*, sir!

And I should laugh on reading there   25
  So soft a kind of song, sir;
I'd write again, then, to declare
  I thought it very wrong, sir!

7. FASHIONS AND FOLLIES

I wish you would decide between
The women and the men, sir,
And say which sex you think displays
The greatest common sense, sir.

Girls waste their time with fancy work,   5
They like to dress and flirt, sir,
But if such things can do no good
Whoever can they hurt, sir?

The men delight to shoot and fish,
More fond of 'sport' than flirting;   10
All 'manly sports' display a wish
To show their skill in *hurting*!

But ladies' fashions are no joke—
Absurd from shoe to hat, sir;
But, then, most men will drink and smoke,   15
And where's the sense of that, sir?

In ev'ry house we're arguing,
The sister and the brother;
Pray judge us, Mr Editor,
We cannot judge each other!   20

8. SQUARING THE CIRCLE

You give one way of squaring the circle,
    But a better, I think, I've found;
Yes, the best way of squaring the circle
    Is to 'act on the square' all round.

9. LOVE AND DEATH AND THE 'WEEKLY MAIL'

I lately dreamt that Love and Death
    Met in a storm of hail,
And taking shelter at an inn,
    They read the *Weekly Mail*.

Love, being fond of poetry   5
    (So oft by him inspired),
Read the poetic column first,
    And soon with anger fired.

'How's this,' cried he, 'insulting me;
    The poet's pride and glory!   10
Refusing to print poetry
    On subjects amatory!'

Death lightly glanced the column down,
    And smiled at Love's vexation;
But soon *his* brow displayed a frown   15
    Of sternest indignation.

'Obituary poems are
    Rejected too!' he cried,
'This is insulting *me* as well';
    'It is,' young Love replied.   20

Said Death, 'I'll shoot that editor!'
    Said Love, 'I hope you'll not;
At least, I hope you'll wait for me—
    I must have the first shot;

If I should shoot him when he's dead,   25
    Of course he'd feel no pain;
But when *my* arrow's in his heart,
    Yours will not come in vain.'

'Bravo!' said Death, 'your plan's the best,
    He first threw down the glove;   30
Because he slights both Love and Death,
    We'll make him *die of Love!*'

This vision, Mr Editor,
  Is absolutely true;
So change your tactics, or be sure   35
  'Twill happen so to you!

(We'll be shot if we do. —ED. *Weekly Mail.*)

10. A ROMANCE OF THE MORGUE

To the cold chamber of the dead
Were many curious gazers led
To look upon a form so fair—
None like it ere had rested there.
Beauty, alas! bereft of breath,   5
In the still majesty of death:
Life scarce could give such wondrous grace
As death had thrown o'er form and face.
And one came there who ne'er had known
Love's tenderness—for none had shown   10
A thought of tenderness for him.
His dreams of love were few and dim;
He felt that it would be his fate
To live and die without a mate.
And hither were his footsteps led;   15
He stood and gazed upon the dead,
Whose awful presence filled the place,
And for a while he could not trace
The meaning of the vague, wild pain
That thrilled at once through heart and brain.   20
His soul unto its depths was stirred;
And soon it seemed as if he heard
Unearthly sounds from far away,
And spirit voices seemed to say,
'This was thy soul's predestined mate;   25
Beyond death's portal she doth wait
Thy coming. Wherefore dost thou stay?
Haste to the bridal—haste away!'
He turned away; but ev'ry word
That he had heard, or dreamed he heard   30
Those voices say, come back again,
Still echoing through heart and brain
All the long day. But at the time
When church bells pealed their vesper chime,
From home—from earth he stole away;   35
And long before another day
His corpse was floating on the tide—
His soul, perchance, had joined its bride,
At morning twilight's first faint gleam,
They found him floating on the stream,   40

And bore him to the Morgue, where lay
So many a self-slain castaway,
And laid him next to her whose grace
Had drawn him to that resting-place.

11. TO AN ATHEIST

And is this world thy only hope?
   Thou canst not stay for many years;
And has thy life no wider scope
   Than earth's brief wishes, toils, and tears?

And is there nothing in thy mind   5
   That feels it cannot cease to live,
And sighs for joys it cannot find
   In anything this world can give?

And hast thou no capacities
   That have no place or fitness here,   10
Like fettered wings that long to rise
   And bear thee to a higher sphere?

And dost thou never think of Death
   With terror or with eagerness,
And almost wish to yield thy breath   15
   Life's last great secret to possess?

If thou hast looked upon the dead,
   Did nought within thee seem to say,
'Oh! whither can the *man* have fled?'
   He is not in this lifeless clay.   20

Have life's dark riddles waked no thought
   About the spirit's future goal
Within they heart? If they have not,
   It may be thou hast not a soul!

12. THE DONKEYS' DUEL

Two donkeys quarrelled one fine day,
And aggravating things did say:
I don't know what it was about,
But they agreed to fight it out,
And took two donkey friends to see   5
How very valiant they could be.
Then loudly at each other brayed
For fear of being thought afraid:
And having kicked each others' hide,
Declared 'their honour satisfied.'   10
Then said their donkey friends, 'Mon Dieu,'
What noble deeds can donkeys do.

13. REPLY TO J. B. M.

Oh! 'J. B. M.,' you must be stupid,
    Or else you'd clearly see
That I should not speak up for Cupid
    Had Cupid wounded me.

Your soft impeachment, Sir, is founded   5
    On something less than sand.
And being so unstably grounded,
    It can't expect to stand.

I wrote on 'Love and Death.' I know it;
    But logic sternly saith,   10
'If that proves love against the poet,
    'Tis equal proof of death.'

But, 'by return of *Mail*,' replying,
    I humbly hope to prove
That I am yet this side of dying   15
    And quite at peace with love.

14. TO D'ODEURS

Dear Monsieur D'Odeurs, I quite opened my eyes,
And stared with surprise, and no doubt I looked wise,
To see such nice verses in honour of me.
Ah! poor little me! but methinks could you see
Poor Marion you'd certainly alter your mind,   5
Although you're so kind, and to softness inclined.

Some love at first sight; but your love must be reckoned
Not first sight, but second: and Justice has beckoned
To me with her finger, and bade me set right
Your dim second sight. I am told I'm a fright   10
By my brother; but every girl, somehow or other,
Seems a fright to her brother, and belle to her mother.
Now, I really don't think myself one or the other.

But alas! be it said, I've been long ill in bed,
And several years have passed over my head   15
Since last o'er the floor of my room I could tread.
So, you see, your affections must take a new start
And at once I must part with your sensitive heart.
But I wish you good luck to the end of your life
With an amiable wife, and no shadow of strife;   20
And when you have read this I hope that you, too,
Will wish luck to me, as I've wished it to you.

15. THE RIVER OF TIME

Roll on, thou mighty river,
　　Roll onward to the sea,
The ocean of for ever—
　　Immense eternity.

Thou bearest on thy bosom   5
　　All things that live and die;
The hopes that bud and blossom,
　　And all too soon must fly;

The cares of kings and nations,
　　The woes that war imparts;   10
The hidden desolations
　　Of broken homes and hearts;

The joy, the fear, the trouble,
　　The envy, love, and strife,
That colour this vain bubble   15
　　That mortal men call life.

Roll on, thou mighty river,
　　Resistless in thy course;
For nought can stem thy current,
　　Nor aught oppose thy force.   20

Roll on, thou mighty river;
　　At last thy fate will be
To lose thyself for ever
　　In vast eternity.

16. MANLY SPORTS

How brave is the hunter who nobly will dare
On horseback to follow the small timid hare;
Oh! ye soldiers who fall in defence of your flag,
What are you to the hero who brings down a stag?

Bright eyes glance admiring, soft hearts give their loves   5
To the knight who shoots best in 'the tourney of doves';
Nothing else with such slaughtering feats can compare,
To win manly applause, or the smiles of the fair.

A cheer for fox-hunting! Come all who can dare
Track this dangerous animal down to its lair;   10
'Tis first trapped, then set free for the huntsmen to follow
With horses and hounds, and with heartstirring halloo!

The brave knights on the moor when the grouse are a-
     drive,
Slay so many, you'd think, there'd be none left alive;
Oh! the desperate daring of slaughtering grouse,   15
Can only be matched in a real slaughterhouse.

The angler finds true Anglo-Saxon delight,
In trapping small fish, who so foolishly bite,
He enjoys the wild terror of creatures so weak,
And what manlier pleasures can any one seek?   20

17. A RULE TO WORK BOTH WAYS

Suggested by a 'Wife-Beater's' Letter.

If beating can reform a wife
 It might reform a husband too,
Since such are the effects of strife—
 My sisters, I advise that you

Should try it, not with fists—Oh, no!   5
 For that would seem like some weak joker;
In husband-curing let each blow
 Be given with the kitchen poker!

When flagellating, let them see
 That you are not afraid to try   10
The very worst 'extremity';
 Then they must yield, lest they should die.

And if you cannot cure them, 'kill!'
 As coolly teaches the 'Wife-beater';
In widowhood, no doubt you will   15
 Find your existence somewhat sweeter.

When thus bad husbands cure bad wives,
 And wives cure brutes to whom they're mated,
Soon will the plagues of many lives
 Be safely buried, or cremated.   20

A wife or husband 'in the way'
 You need but beat to death, or smother;
And then you may at any day
 Find better fortune with another!

18. QUITE BEWILDERED

We're told that earth, sea, skies, and all
    Were hatched out from an egg of night;
An egg most infinitely small,
    Smaller than egg of any mite.

How it was hatched has not been stated,   5
    But the Tyndallian inference
Is, that it can't have been created,
    So it requires uncommon sense

To have the slightest comprehension
    Of how creation came about—   10
No, not creation, but *extension*—
    It's what 'no fellow can find out'!

19. CHANGES

'All that's bright must fade—
  The brightest still the fleetest';
Blue eyes can change to grey,
  Though blue would seem the sweetest.

The golden hair sublime,   5
  That all men must admire,
To sandy turns in time,
  Which no one would desire!

The bright abundant curls
  Grow scanty and turn grey;   10
And teeth that shone like pearls,
  Discolour and decay.

The smoothest, whitest brow
  Soon shows time's wrinkles there;
And withered grows the cheek   15
  That once bloomed bright and fair.

The tall and stately form
  Stoops 'neath the weight of years,
And brightest eyes grow dim
  With time, if not with tears.   20

Even warm hearts grow cool,
  As youthful hopes decay;
'Tis Time's unvaried rule
  To snatch all sweets away.

20. REPLY TO J. B. M.

Dear J. B. M., I was but joking,
   That time I called you stupid,
But then you threw out hints provoking
   That I'd been shot by Cupid.

And now you must be stupid, truly,   5
   To say such things again, sir,
Excuse my telling you so coolly,
   It is so very plain, sir!

You think my logic, like a feather,
   Will shiver at a breath, sir,   10
Since you can write of both together,
   Feel Love and not feel Death, sir.

Are all in love who chance to write
   Of Love and Death together?
Now really don't you think one might   15
   Name both, and not feel either?

You say Love's victims are so stupid
   That, when he's shot them through, sir,
They only sing in praise of Cupid.
   That may be true of you, sir.   20

But if they are so gentle to him
   Who have most cause to blame him,
Surely one who ne'er suffered through him
   With courtesy may name him?

21. THE THUNDERSTORM

The skies are lowering, dark and gray,
  The smoke from chimney tops beats down,
The birds are flying far away—
  All nature wears a sullen frown.

No breath of air sighs through the trees,   5
  Their leaves are drooping faint and still;
And stirred by no refreshing breeze
  The pond is waveless on the hill.

Where all was bright one hour before
  Dark clouds in heavy masses form,   10
And peal on peal with dreadful roar
  Begins the awful thunderstorm.

The trembling beasts to covert fly,
  Still heavier grows the sultry air,
While from the dark and angry sky   15
  Forked lightnings flash with lurid glare.

Hark, how the awful thunder rolls!
  As if it were the dread reveil
Sounding to waken sleeping souls
  To meet their fate in heaven or hell.   20

Will it sound thus on that great day
  When fires shall flash, and thunders roll,
And heaven and earth shall pass away,
  And vanish like a shrivelled scroll?

Oh, day! oh, hour! When shall it be?   25
  Not many years can pass before;
And *after* comes Eternity—
  The long unknown Forevermore.

22. A SONG FOR THE WORKING MAN

Oh! there's nothing in life so gay
  As labour and simple fare,
If you're able to pay your way
  Untroubled by cank'ring care.
But labour beyond one's strength
  Turns work from a joy to pain,
And tasks of a cruel length
  May well make the brave complain.

Ye friends of the working man,
  Who have brightened so many lives,
Now bid them do all they can
  In striving to help their wives;
It were sin to oppress the strong—
  But why should weak woman bear
A day's task, for man too long,
  And seldom his leisure share?

Much good has been surely done,
  But much still remains to do;
Then join in it every one,
  And carry the good work through.
When the working man and his wife
  Spend together their leisure hour,
The contentment of humble life
  Will be sweeter than wealth or power.

23. A SONG OF GLASGOW TOWN

I'll sing a song of Glasgow town,
That stands on either side
The river that was once so fair,
The much insulted Clyde.
That stream, once pure, but now so foul,   5
Was never made to be
A sewer, just to bear away
The refuse to the sea.
Oh, when will Glasgow's factories
Cease to pollute its tide,   10
And let the Glasgow people see
The beauty of the Clyde!

I'll sing a song of Glasgow town:
On every side I see
A crowd of giant chimney stalks   15
As grim as grim can be.
There's always smoke from some of them—
Some black, some brown, some grey.
Yet genius has invented means
To burn the smoke away.   20
Oh, when will Glasgow factories
Cease to pollute the air;
To spread dull clouds o'er sunny skies
That should be bright and fair!

I'll sing a song of Glasgow town,   25
Where wealth and want abound;
Where the high seat of learning dwells
'Mid ignorance profound.
Oh, when will Glasgow make a rule
To do just what she ought—   30
Let starving bairns in every school
Be fed as well as taught!
And when will Glasgow city be
Fair Caledonia's pride,
And boast her clear unclouded skies,   35
And crystal-flowing Clyde?

24. OH, SCENES OF BEAUTY!

Oh! scenes of beauty, hid from me,
  What longing thoughts ye raise,
While Fancy sings to Memory
  Sweet songs of other days—
Of happier days while yet mine eyes   5
  This glorious earth could see,
And look up to the azure skies,
  And o'er the sun-lit sea.
Oh! earth and sea, Oh! sun and moon,
  And every shining star,   10
I still remember in my gloom,
  How beautiful you are!

I've loved to watch the sunbeams bright
  Stream from the summer skies,
Flooding the world with joyous light,   15
  Cheering the saddest eyes.
But better still I've loved the night,
  Lit by a softer ray;
For moonlight made things beautiful
  That were not so by day.   20
Oh! earth and sea, Oh! sun and moon,
  And every shining star,
I still remember, in my gloom,
  How beautiful you are!

25. THE DANGER OF DELAY

When one in need would beg or borrow
    It is not well to say
'Go now, and come again to-morrow,'
    Nay, give him aid to-day.
Help which would come too late to-morrow   5
    May save a life to-day;
And wilt thou wait to learn in sorrow
    The danger of delay?

If thou hast ever wronged thy neighbour,
    And in self-discontent   10
Thou to redress that wrong wouldst labour—
    'Tis well thou dost repent—
But where there's wrong to be set right,
    Oh! set it right to-day!
'Thy soul may be required to-night,'   15
    And lost should'st thou delay.

Turn from the wrong which thou hast done,
    And better paths pursuing,
Pause not one hour, because that one
    Would add to thy wrong-doing.   20
Some with repentence half-begun,
    Yet wavering to-day
Will mourn while endless ages run,
    The danger of delay.

26. SIGH NOT FOR YESTERDAY

Sigh not for yesterday—
   'Tis vain to dream of things
   Which Time's too rapid wings
Have carried far away.

What hath been could not last.   5
   Joys that have passed away
   We miss still more to-day,
If brooding o'er the past.

Then let us talk no more
   Of friends estranged or dead,   10
   Of hopes that long have fled,
Or pleasures that are o'er.

The bright sun shines to-day,
   And life hath sweetness yet;
   Then breathe no vain regret   15
For what hath passed away.

27. WANTED A HUSBAND

'Baking and cooking, scrubbing and dressing—
Accomplishments grand, well worth possessing;
Economy too, with wisdom discreet,
My wife must practise to make all ends meet.'
—Eleve.

Wanted a husband who doesn't suppose,
That all earthly employments one feminine knows—
That she'll scrub, do the cleaning, and cooking, and
    baking,
And plain needlework, hats and caps, and dressmaking.
Do the family washing, yet always look neat,   5
Mind the bairns, with a temper unchangeably sweet,
Be a cheerful companion, whenever desired,
And contentedly toil day and night, if required.
Men expecting as much, one may easily see,
But they're not what is wanted, at least, not by me.   10

Wanted a husband who's tender and true,
Who will stick to his duty, and never get 'fou,'
But when all his day's work he has blithely gone through,
Help his wife, 'set to rights,' till her work is done too;
Who will not absurdly, and helplessly go,   15
And trouble the wife about 'buttons to sew,'
On his shirt, or his gloves, or his coat, or his vest,
But will sew them himself, and not think he's oppressed.
Now, if such a lad you should happen to see,
He's wanted by many, but yet—not by me!   20

28. ON THE CLOSING YEAR

Minute by minute, and hour by hour,
    And day by day,
In joy and sorrow, in sun and shower
    Time flies away.

And when a week or month has fled,   5
    'Time flies,' we say,
Yet 'tis not time, 'tis life, instead,
    That flies away.

And now one more short year is gone,
    Then let us say—   10
What hopes fulfilled, what duties done,
    Blest its brief stay.

Alas! no hope fulfilled hath cheered
    A single day;
Alas! our course hath not been steered   15
    In Duty's way.

Neglected was the Word Divine
    Day after day;
To worldly thoughts we did incline—
    From God did stray.   20

Oh, bygone year! what was thy worth?
    Are we to-day
No nearer Heaven, although from Earth
    Passing away?

29. ON NEW YEAR'S DAY

I enter on another year,
  Not knowing what 'twill bring;
Little of hope, and much of fear,
  Doth from remembrance spring.
For years gone by have left with me   5
  Little except regret,
And in the future I can see
  No light before me yet.

But there is always light above,
  Though clouds obscure the sky;   10
The presence of our Father's love
  In darkest hours is nigh.
Then, oh, my soul, be not afraid,
  Though thou must journey o'er
The gloomy path, with thorns o'erspread,   15
  Thy Saviour trod before.

Thou too must sorrow, and become
  Acquainted well with grief;
But He at last will guide thee home,
  And give thee sure relief.   20
Then trust in Him, and banish fear,
  Howe'er thy lot be cast;
And strive to spend the coming year
  More nobly than the last.

30. THE HERO OF THE CLYDE

Hence! Envy and Detraction pale,
    Your frowning faces hide;
You need not listen to my tale—
    The Hero of the Clyde!

No names of warlike victors bring   5
    To dazzle by his side.
A more than warrior I sing—
    The Hero of the Clyde.

I need but simply name his name,
    'Tis echoed far and wide,   10
For Jamie Lambert all proclaim
    The Hero of the Clyde.

Now old, and weak, and blind is he,
    An almshouse doth provide
A scant reward for such as he,   15
    Brave Hero of the Clyde!

The chill that robbed him of his sight
    Came from cold Clutha's side,
While he for others' lives did fight—
    Brave Hero of the Clyde!   20

Raise forty pounds a year—he may
    Be glad and satisfied;
But thrice that sum would not repay
    The Hero of the Clyde.

Stint not your gifts, for twoscore lives   25
    He rescued from the tide;
Let Glasgow see that nobly thrives
    The Hero of the Clyde.

31. TO AMATORY POETS

I address every amorous poet
    Who may read, or may write to the Mail,
Just to warn some who don't seem to know it,
    'Gainst a course that is certain to fail.

If you'd make love in stanzas poetic,   5
    Many people your lays may admire;
But the Mail is too unsympathetic,
    And will put your soft songs in the fire.

For the Editor thinks love alarming,
    And for lovers professes disdain;   10
He'd deny that there's anything charming
    In 'Sweet Jessie, the Flower o' Dunblane.'

He would sternly refuse 'Annie Laurie,'
    Drive the bold 'Duncan Gray' to despair,
And quite scornfully scoff at the lassie   15
    Who is pining for 'Robin Adair.'

I don't even believe 'Highland Mary'
    His frigidity ever could move;
He has shown himself wond'rously wary
    In avoiding 'The Power of Love'!   20

So endeavour your passion to smother
    Or (if your endeavour should fail)
You can send the account to another,
    And not to this terrible Mail!

32. THE BEST KIND OF WIFE

'O where shall I search for a suitable wife?'
   Said Cœlebs one day, with his lantern in hand;
And he searched, and he searched through the world all
   his life—
   He hunted on sea, and he hunted on land.
But he never found one that would suit him—and why?   5
   The reason is plain—that he tried the wrong way.
You can all of you find a good wife if you try,
   And you need not be searching all night and all day,
For this is the truth. It will yet be confessed
The best kind of wife is the lass you love best.   10

II

You may marry a wife who can cook and can sew,
   And have all other virtues a woman can claim;
But if she can't love you you'd far better go
   And wed one who knows nothing but love's gentle
     name.
You might marry a wife with a long pedigree,   15
   And riches, and beauty that none could excel;
But if you don't love her, it's easy to see
   You'd best wed the rustic you could love too well.
For this is the truth. It will yet be confessed
The best kind of wife is the lass you love best.   20

III

All those who will marry must marry for life,
   And therefore beware lest your choice should be wrong;
For where there's no love there is sure to be strife—
   And strife matrimonial can last very long.
But all joys will be brighter, all sorrows less deep,   25
   In the heart where a true love doth constantly dwell.
Then still let your mem'ry this true proverb keep—
   'He loveth most wisely whose heart loveth well.'
For this is the truth. It will yet be confessed
The best kind of wife is the lass you love best.   30

33. AN ABLE ADVOCATE

Once a lawyer defended his client so well
    That no one could listen unmoved to his pleading,
Such a sorrowful narrative he had to tell,
    It was really enough to set every heart bleeding.

The poor client listened with wondering ears,   5
    And struggled for calmness—but struggled in vain—
Till he sprang to his feet, and protested with tears
    He had never before known the half of his pain!

34. THE WELL OF TRUTH

I have read an old tale that the storybooks tell—
    And so doubtless, dear reader, have you—
How the bright lamp of Truth has been hid in a well,
    And I really believe it is true.

But the Mountain of Error is piled o'er that well,   5
    We shall have to dig deep for the light;
And long we may labour—how long, who can tell?—
    Ere its radiance rejoices our sight.

But the labour of clearing old errors away
    Brings honour to age or to youth,   10
Though it may not reveal till some far-distant day
    The long-buried light of the truth.

35. 'ENDING IN SMOKE!'

To this poor nervous invalid
It seems quite terrible to read
The queer things that are lately said
About disposing of the dead.
I get the horrors when reflecting,   5
Not upon death, but on dissecting;
And I confess my consternation
Is worse when thinking of cremation!
I don't object so much to die,
And that must happen by-and-by;   10
But, be it most distinctly stated,
I do object to be cremated,
For I would lie where those who love me
Can (if they choose) place flowers above me.
Methinks, e'en when 'asleep,' 'twould cheer me   15
If some fond heart were hovering near me.
    Of course, this is but foolish dreaming,
Only an idle fancy's scheming,
Yet it seems like a cruel joke
To think that I may 'end in smoke'—   20
Oh, horrible imagination!
But all who aid in my cremation
Shall see results they never wanted—
I promise them they shall be haunted!

36. THOUGHTS

Day by day Life's scroll unfoldeth—
    Slowly is our fate revealed;
Every eye the Past beholdeth,
    But the future is concealed.

Moments mournful, moments pleasant,   5
    Come and go, and none can last;
What was Future now is Present,
    What was present now is Past.

It, perhaps, may soothe our sorrow
    Thus to think 'twill pass away: 10
Life must change. Perhaps to-morrow
    May be brighter than to-day.

And sweet scenes of bygone gladness
    Are not altogether fled;
Mem'ry, lighting up our sadness,   15
    Half restores the lost and dead.

When Life's joys seem lost for ever,
    We can *dream* them o'er again;
All Time's changes cannot sever
    One bright link in Mem'ry's chain.   20

And the Future—none can know it
    Until Time the truth reveal.
Fancy may pretend to show it;
    Time still proves her scenes unreal.

Radiant Hope, for ever smiling,   25
    Speaks of happier days in store,
Many simple hearts beguiling,
    Though they've found her false before.

Hope and Fancy oft deceive us,
    But they make our days more bright;   30
May they never, never leave us,
    Or withdraw their cheering light.

37. COURTSHIP ON VALENTINE'S MORNING

I loved a fair maid,
But I was afraid
To tell her how much I adored her,
So I purchased a fine
Pink and gold valentine,   5
As expensive as I could afford her.

It was covered with doves,
And little winged Loves,
And pansies and white and red roses,
With some verses between   10
The best I have seen,
In which love all his ardour discloses.

I sealed it with blue,
To show it was true,
And 'twas posted at four in the morning;   15
So 'twould reach her at eight
If it's truth that they state
In the rules the Post Office adorning.

I took care to get dressed,
In my superfine best,   20
And I went just as daylight was dawning,
And watched in her street,
In hopes I might meet
Her first glance on St Valentine's morning.

I had but to wait   25
Precisely till eight,
When the postman went there with my letter;
The verses she read,
And she afterwards said
That they caught her young heart in love's fetter.   30

She drew up the blind,
For fortune was kind;
She looked over to me and said 'Harry!'
And at the sweet sound
My heart gave a bound—   35
I rushed over and asked her to marry.

She drooped her bright eyes,
Affected surprise,
But so far the idea from scorning,
Said she felt inclined,   40
If I didn't mind,
To get married next Valentine's morning.

38. COME AGAIN, COME AGAIN, BEAUTIFUL SPRING

Come again, come again, beautiful spring,
Freshness of youth with thy sweet presence bring;
Thy smiles have a light from the sunshine apart;
While they dazzle the eyes they can gladden the heart.

II

Come again, come again, beautiful spring!   5
Bid the buds blossom, the forest birds sing;
Joyous the face of all nature will be,
Beautiful spring, when enlivened by thee.

III

Come again, come again, beautiful spring!
E'er round thy name dearest memories cling,   10
Calling up thoughts of those innocent hours,
When, in our childhood, we culled the spring flowers.

IV

Come again, come again, beautiful spring!
Then shall the greenwoods with melody ring;
Hasten thy coming, full soon may it be,   15
Beautiful spring! we are waiting for thee.

39. A QUESTION

'The fool hath said in his heart there is no God.'

What will you give if you take away
My faith in the God whom I trust to-day—
If to religion I bid farewell,
What can you give me (Oh! quickly tell)?—
For the blessed peace that pervades my life,   5
That soothes its sorrows, and calms its strife;
That makes all duties, though hard, seem sweet,
And rough paths smooth to my weary feet;
That teaches me to be kind and just,
And worthy always of love and trust;   10
That wakens bright hopes of joy unseen,
Brings peace in grief, and makes joy serene;
That can banish terror when Death draws nigh
(Sawest thou ever a Christian die—
Praising his God with his latest breath,   15
And saying, 'Where is the sting of death?')—
What shall I have if I yield all this—
What can you give me of equal bliss—
That shall cheer my spirit in woe or strife;
Bless all the sorrows and joys of life;   20
And give, when I draw my latest breath,
A happy hope 'mid the pangs of death?

40. WOMAN'S RIGHTS AND WRONGS

'I may be wrong in opinion, but still to my mind it seems
As if Parliament, Council, or Congress could never be womanly
    themes,—
Touching the so-called Woman's Rights, such discussion belongs
To the tender and true in a less degree than the subject of Woman's
    Wrongs.'
—Jessie Russell

Pray, in what way is wrong redressed,
    But by conceding right?
And Woman Suffrage is the best
    For which our sex can fight.

You'd give the lash to wifebeaters,   5
    But surely you should know,
If women legislated, they'd
    Have had it long ago.

You speak of women's wages
    Being scandalously small;   10
Believe me, Woman Suffrage
    Soon would find a cure for all.

Our claims are oft misunderstood;
    We would but share with man
The human right of doing good   15
    In any way we can.

Why should we put our trust in men,
    Who oft betray our cause?
Let women vote away their wrongs,
    And vote for righteous laws.   20

41. RULES FOR HOUSE-HUNTING

At this season of the year
People come from far and near
Seeking houses, cheap and dear;
Now, house-hunters, will you hear
Good advice?   5

It's unwise to rent or buy
Any house that stands too high,
For when next door to the sky,
Leaky roofs may make you sigh—
That's not nice!   10

But a house that stands too low,
Where the breezes cannot blow,
Would cause suffocation slow,
And it might be damp also,
My dear friend!   15

And a dwelling in the middle
Is like frizzling on a griddle;
But deciding is a riddle;
Worse than studying the fiddle—
So attend!   20

An idea I have got,
Which you'd better try than not,
Just decide the thing by lot,
Some addresses throw 'hotchpot'
In a hat.   25

Then farewell to care and doubt,
Drink success in double stout,
Give the lots a shake about,
And the first address drawn out—
Stick to that!   30

42. 'MOVE ON!'

SONG FOR MUSIC

When a throng of loungers meet
At the corner of the street,
Gossiping through half the day,
Just in everybody's way;
Then the guardian of the peace,   5
Comes to bid such nonsense cease,
Telling them to go their ways,
In decided tones he says,
          'Move on!'

II

When some idle crowd at night,   10
Seem as if they meant to fight,
And begin to swear and shout,
Hardly knowing what about;
Then that useful man in blue
Gives the storm no time to brew;   15
Scatters them in different ways,
And with needful sternness says,
          'Move on!'

III

Now in many scenes of life,
Scenes of idleness or strife: 20
When some storm begins to brew,
When we've nothing good to do;
Then we need a friend who will
Kindly bid us not stand still;
Duty's path is never wide,   25
Loiterers get pushed aside.
          'Move on!'

43. REFLECTIONS

With all his faults and all his folly,
   Man bears the stamp Divine;
And some are true, and some are holy,
   As guiding lights they shine.
Wreaths of thorns the world may weave us,   5
Friends we've trusted may deceive us,
But some true hearts will not leave us
   When our joys decline.

II

With all its cares and all its sorrow
   Life still hath much of joy.   10
If dark to-day 'tis bright to-morrow—
   Half gold and half alloy.
Murmur not when fortune's changing—
Only faithless friends estranging
Leaves the love that never ranging   15
   Nothing can destroy.

44. LOOK FORWARD AND LOOK UPWARD

Look forward and look upward,
  Though dark thy path may be;
Some light still shines from heaven
  To guide and comfort thee.
Though the past has brought but sorrow,   5
  And the present brings despair,
Yet the sunshine of to-morrow
  May disperse all clouds of care.
    Look forward, and look upward,
      Where comfort may be found;   10
    There's always light above us,
      Though gloom may reign around.

II

Oh! learn to think all sorrows
  But clouds that pass away;
Though long these clouds may linger,   15
  They cannot always stay.
Every night must have a morning,
  And dawn will seem most bright
When its beams dispel the shadows
  Of a dark and stormy night.   20
    Look forward, and look upward,
      Where comfort may be found;
    There's always light above us,
      Though gloom may reign around.

45. A DOUBTFUL STORY

I heard a tale the other day
    From somebody or other;
If true or false I cannot say,
    And neither can my mother.
'Tis all about young Bessie Jones,   5
    The blacksmith's pretty sister,
The story runs that Joseph Bunce
    Met her in the lane and kissed her!

The washerwoman heard it from
    The mangle-woman's daughter,   10
And she was told by her young man,
    Who lives across the water.
He heard it from two girls he knows,
    Named Jane and Betsy Marler
(Housemaid and cook at Mrs Row's),   15
    And they heard it in the parlour.

Some friends went there to talk and smoke,
    And in their conversation
Of pretty Bessie Jones they spoke,
    And they said on that occasion   20
That Bessie had been walking home
    When Joseph chanced to meet her,
And as he saw she was alone
    He with a kiss did greet her.

Now, these young men who at the Row's   25
    Told this important story
Had heard it from old sailor Bowse,
    Who heard it from Meg Laurie:
She heard it at the chandler's shop,
    And said 'she didn't doubt it.'   30
But now I'll let the subject drop,
    For that's all I know about it.

46. COME BACK TO ME, YE HAPPY DREAMS

Come back to me, ye happy dreams,
   That cheer'd my heart in days gone by,
And lighted life with brighter beams,
   Than those that light the summer sky.

Visions of youthful hope and joy—   5
   Dreams of ambition's proud success;
Oh! why should time your power destroy,
   And mar such simple happiness?

Oh! ye bright visions, though unreal,
   Ye far excelled reality!   10
As youthful untried warriors feel
   The joy of certain victory!

So in these fair, false dreams of youth,
   Those hopeful hours before the strife,
We think not of the sombre truth   15
   We have to learn in later life.

47. MARRIED AND 'SETTLED'

Oh! I have sighed to read
   The trials of this season;
Wife-murder seems, indeed,
   An everyday transgression.

Too oft the marriage bond   5
   Is one of fear and pain;
Affection true and fond
   Should link that sacred chain.

Can home appear 'sweet home'
   When 'husband' means a foe   10
And 'wife' a slave?—for some
   Submit to have it so.

It seems to me such wives
   Act rashly, at the least,
Like men who risk their lives   15
   In taming a wild beast.

Beast-taming seems to be
   Not quite a woman's mission;
The brutes might stay for me,
   In bachelor condition.   20

But, since you choose to wed
   And risk your limbs and lives,
Consider what I've said
   All ye unhappy wives.

Exert your common sense   25
   And form a combination
For mutual defence
   Against assassination.

48. THE HEATHER AND THE BROOM

How I love the bonnie broom
   That upon the mountain grows!
To my eyes its yellow bloom
   Fairer seems than pink or rose.

I can think no scene so grand,   5
   Where the richest gardens bloom,
As the free wild mountain land
   Clad with bonnie, bonnie broom.

Oh, the moors are covered now
   With the heather's purple bloom,   10
And the hillsides brightly glow
   With the bonnie yellow broom;

And they look so well together
   In the springtime all in bloom—
The purple coloured heather,   15
   And the golden tinted broom.

All your cultured grounds are small,
   And though bonnie they may be,
Yet the heather-covered moor
   And the broom-clad hills for me!   20

Tell me not of gardens fair
   Filled with beauty and perfume,
For there's nothing anywhere
   Like the heather and the broom.

49. ON RECEIVING THE FIRST FLOWERS OF THE GARDEN FROM A FRIEND IN LONDON

You send to me the first sweet flowers
    That Spring has sent to you,
To blossom in a colder clime
    Than that in which they grew.

II

I thank you for the welcome gift;   5
    Sweet flowers I seldom see;
Though all things bright and beautiful
    Are ever dear to me.

III

So you have travelled, pretty flowers,
    Four hundred miles, to say   10
That I am not forgotten quite
    By friends left far away.

IV

Thrice welcome to your northern home,
    Well cared for you shall be;
Lift up your drooping heads and bloom   15
    A little while for me.

50. I REALLY DON'T KNOW WHAT TO SAY

I really don't know what to say,
  But will succeeds where wit would fail;
And I've made up my mind to-day
  To write some verses for the *Mail*.

My Muse has been some weeks on strike,   5
  And given me no end of bother;
Now, though she won't do all I like,
  I'll make her work some way or other.

And I must not forget the rules
  By which the prudent editor   10
His crowd of ardent poets schools,
  To write enough, and then no more.

Twenty or thirty lines at most
  (If I write more, I'm sure to rue it):
Then of forbidden themes a host,   15
  I must avoid—how can I do it?

So many rhyme about the spring,
  I must not try that theme again;
And no one to the *Mail* dare sing
  A sad or sentimental strain.   20

Love, death, grief, politics, the rights
  Of women, and sometimes of men, too,
Are themes in which the Muse delights,
  But which the *Mail* would not consent to.

Then shall I greet with friendly rhyme,   25
  A brother or a sister poet?
Ah, no; at this 'gey kittle time,'
  The *Mail* would neither print nor show it.

I am a silly goose to dream—
  But fancy's roving, who can bound it?   30
Before I've fixed on any theme,
  There's thirty-two lines done, confound it!

51. A SLIGHT INCONSISTENCY

To one correspondent the Editor says
    That 'Love needs encouragement!' wondrous confession!
To another he firmly declares that he lays
    His veto on every romantic expression.

A slight inconsistency here I might prove,   5
    For 'tis hard to distinguish 'twixt why, which, and
        whether;
But perhaps the dear Editor may be in love,
    And love and consistency can't live together.

Yes, that must be the case—now, ye poets unite
    To wish him good luck, and a quick acceptation;   10
Then sometime perhaps he'll permit you to write
    Sweet songs to objects of *your* adoration.

52. IN THESE STEAM-ENGINE DAYS

In these steam-engine days
Blest is the one who strays
'Among the untrodden ways,'
    Far from the great world's strife.
Blest are those regions lone,   5
Where change is yet unknown,
And travelling not yet grown
    The business of life.

Steamship and railway train
Make every friendship vain,   10
And break the silver chain
    Of home affections sweet.
Though they have loved each other,
Children leave sire and mother:
The sister and the brother   15
    Part, never more to meet.

Ere steamers were invented,
They stayed at home contented,
And early ties cemented
    With many a faithful heart.   20
Now all is altered quite;
Friendship's last delight,
And kindred love seems slight
    After long years apart.

Hearts that have once been fond   25
Can only correspond,
With those the seas beyond,
    In written words, and few.
Thus do affections die
Slowly, but certainly,   30
Shall we beyond the sky
    These broken ties renew?

53. A DREAM

I dreamt that the nineteenth century
   Had entirely passed away,
And had given place to a more advanced
   And very much brighter day.

For Woman's Rights were established quite,   5
   And man could the fact discern
That he'd long been teaching his grandmamma
   What she didn't require to learn.

There were female chiefs in the Cabinet,
   (Much better than males I'm sure!)   10
And the Commons were three-parts feminine,
   While the Lords were seen no more!

And right well did the ladies legislate,
   They determined to 'keep the peace,'
So well they managed affairs of State,   15
   That the science of war might cease.

Now no man could venture to beat his wife,
   For the women had settled by law
That whoever did so should lose his life,
   Then he'd never do so any more.   20

There were no more physicians of either sex,
   For the schools were required to teach
The science of healing to every child
   As well as the parts of speech.

There were no more lawyers—all children learned   25
   The code of their country's laws;
There were female judges, and truth became
   The fashion in every cause.

All the churches attended a conference
   At which every sect agreed   30
That an erring opinion was not so bad
   As a false word or wicked deed.

At this I felt sure there was some mistake,
   It seemed such a *strange* idea!
My eyes opened wide, and that made me wake,   35
   Now wasn't the vision queer?

54. THE MUSIC OF THE STREETS

SONG FOR MUSIC

There's a selfish class of people,
    One occasionally meets,
Who are trying to abolish
    All the music of the streets.

They have operas and concerts,   5
    They can go to play and ball,
And at home they have pianos,
    To amuse themselves withal.

So, of course, they don't consider,
    In the midst of all their treats,   10
How the little 'gutter children'
    Love the music of the streets.

Since it gives them harmless pleasure,
    I can never understand
Why they shouldn't sometimes listen   15
    To a roving German band.

There are clever street musicians—
    And, if not, the girls and boys
Can appreciate performers
    Who know how to make a noise.   20

If an organ hinders study,
    I believe one can postpone
The profoundest cogitations
    Till the outdoor tune is done.

And, if not—well, what about it?   25
    Leave your study, and, I'm sure,
Life will jog along without it,
    As it managed to before.

55. SONG

Oh, bring me a bunch of flowers to-day,
   For the summer time is flying,
Dead are the lilac and the may,
   And the roses are now dying.
Before the summer's sunny hours   5
   Have vanished all away,
Let me once more behold the flowers—
   Oh! bring me some to-day.

I fain would see them where they grow,
   But since that may not be,   10
Go, gather some, and you shall know
   How dear they are to me.
How well I love the meadows fair
   Where once I used to stray,
And the simple flowers that blossom there—   15
   Oh! bring me some to-day.

56. GAS ON THE STAIR

Oh! why are we left without gas on the stair,
In darkness and fear three months of the year?
It doesn't appear by any means clear
What the reason can be, for the gas is not dear.
Our way in the dark it's perplexing to steer,   5
Although one may be sober and taking good care.
It's dangerous too and it's very unfair!
I wish the Gas Company only could hear
The remarks that are made, they would have an idea
That their ways in the suburbs are thought very queer;   10
For we do not love darkness instead of light here.
Yet from May until August—oh, death and despair!
We are left in the dark without gas on the stair.

Between May and August, at night dark and drear,
What mishaps may you meet on the stairways, Oh, dear! 15
You may fall, break your limbs, or your nose, or your
     neck,
And be carried upstairs an unfortunate wreck,
As many a broken-limbed native declares
Through a long life lamenting his 'getting up stairs.'
But the time's drawing near when the gas will appear   20
The belated to cheer. By its light, bright and clear
They can see far and near, up and down, there and here,
And their course they can steer without danger, Oh, dear!
Let us hope all the suburbs next May will declare
That they will not be left without gas on the stair.   25

57. THE GIANT-KILLER

There were swarms of frightful beings
    In Jack Giant-Killer's days,
Such as ogres, giants, dragons,
    And ill-natured sorts of fays.

Who ate up little boys and girls,   5
    And didn't seem to mind
Even gobbling grown-up people,
    Or whatever they could find.

There are a few now in existence,
    But we hear of them at times   10
Quite out-dragoning the dragons
    In their most atrocious crimes.

That imp of Wantly was the last*
    To eat a church and steeple,
But modern dragons gulp down ships,   15
    And swallow scores of people.

But there still are giant-killers
    Who are not afraid to fight
With grim ogres in high places,
    Dragging their dark deeds to light.   20

And among them noble Plimsoll
    Holds a high and foremost place
In the family of heroes,
    Doing honour to the race.

Champion of the British sailors,   25
    Wives and mothers bless his name,
And a nation's warm approval
    Sets it in the rolls of fame.

May all rotten ships be 'Plimsolled!'
    But just one we might retain,   30
And with all the ogres in it
    Set adrift upon the main.

---

* 'The dragon of Wantly churches ate, &c,'—*Old Song.*

58. ADVICE TO ANXIETY

'But here lies the trouble, the exchequer's is toom
An' the broth in our poor's-house is said to be thin.
Tell me this, and wi' joy ower the moon I'd maist leap,
Hoo to wed her and keep her on a'e pound a week.'
—Anxiety

Poor youth, with but one pound a week,
With which you fondly wish to seek
A happy home and loving wife
To cheer you 'mid the cares of life.

You'll find, if you resolve to try it,   5
You'll have to live on a scanty diet;
Yet till you try you cannot know
How far your pound a week will go.

But I can tell you, without joking,
Drinking you can't afford, or smoking;   10
Little you'll taste of earthly pleasure,
Save in each other's love—a treasure

Unsaleable at any price.
If not quite sure this will suffice
You for your sole amusement, tarry   15
For better fortune ere you marry.

If this wet blanket does not smother
Your ardent wish to wed each other—
If youth, and health, and love possessing,
Why, wed of course, and take my blessing!   20

59. SONNET

Fade not! oh, autumn flowers!
  Linger a little while,
  And, with your cheering smile,
Brighten the fleeting hours.
Unconscious of the powers   5
  Of that bright loveliness
  Your blossoms all possess
Are ye, oh, innocent flowers!
'Neath sunbeam, or in showers,
  Ye always wear a smile—   10
  Like Faith, that knows no guile,
But, through life's changing hours,
  Deemeth both light and shade
  By faultless wisdom made.

60. MUSICAL REFLECTIONS

Oh, lovely music! of thy spell,
'Tis easier to dream than tell;
There lives a charm in every tone
To none but those who love thee known,
Sole pleasure shared by earth and heaven,   5
To raise our fallen nature given.
The lonely find a friend in thee,
And crowds, a bond of sympathy;
And thou art known in every land,
A language all can understand,   10
Comfort or courage to impart,
And melt, or soothe, or rouse the heart.
It is in solitary hours
I best can feel sweet music's powers,
And wake the living spirit pent   15
Within the lifeless instrument.
What pleasure in such hours I find,
Conversing with each master mind.
Of great musicians who have wrought
Vast systems of poetic thought,   20
'Untwisting all the chains that tie
The hidden soul of harmony.'
And scarcely less delight I feel
When I am called on to reveal
The secrets of the heavenly art—   25
For to acquire, or to impart,
Are both delightful tasks to me.
And since it is my destiny
To work, I fain that work would choose
Swayed by Euterpe—sweetest muse!   30

61. O, CALEDONIA! THOU ART FAIR

Oh, Caledonia, thou art fair,
   When summer sunshine smiles above thee,
And e'en in winter, bleak and bare,
   I wonder not thy children love thee.

Thou hast had foes, and known defeat,   5
   And who has not? among all nations
There's none whose sons did ne'er retreat—
   All have been crushed on some occasions.

I would not praise success in war,
   It seems to me so much more glorious   10
To keep from scenes of strife afar,
   And make the arts of peace victorious.

Forget thy old barbarian days—
   The dreadful deeds that have been done;
Let no one boast of blood-stained bays   15
   That can but tell of battles won.

Since Scots will always love to praise
   Their country, let them call her fair,
And let each do his part to raise
   The power of peaceful commerce there.   20

The rich and proud oppress thee still
   Fair Scotland! thy own sons oppress
Each other. Many a glen and hill
   For 'sport' is made a wilderness,

May time and commerce right this wrong;   25
   For deerparks, give thee fields and farms,
And send elsewhere for sport the throng
   For whom such butcher-work has charms.

62. OH, I WISH I WERE A SWALLOW!

Oh, I wish I were a swallow!
   I would know no winter time;
The sweet summer I would follow
   In her flight from clime to clime.
How I love the summer flowers,   5
   And the summer skies, so blue,
And the cheering sunny hours;
   And the birds' sweet music, too!
Oh, I wish I were a swallow!
   I would know no winter time;   10
The sweet summer I would follow
   In her flight from clime to clime.

When I see the leaves all shaded
   With dull tints of brown and red;
When the blossoms all are faded,   15
   And the singing birds are fled,
Then, how mournfully recalling
   Summer's sweetness passed away,
'Mid the wreck of beauty falling
   Into darkness and decay,   20
Oh, I wish I were a swallow!
   I would know no winter time;
The sweet summer I would follow
   In her flight from clime to clime.

63. BLAME NOT THE BROKEN-HEARTED

Be to the mourners tender,
   Blame not the tears they shed—
That sorrowfully render
   Love's tribute to the dead.

Do not rebuke the sighing   5
   Of the poor stricken heart;
Oft through a loved one's dying
   Life's dearest joys depart.

Wise words but mock the sadness
   Of those who grieve in vain;   10
No hope of future gladness
   Can banish present pain.

Can one at midnight borrow
   A ray of morning light?
The lonely mourner's sorrow   15
   Is like a long dark night.

How can one judge another
   Or prove a soul forgiven?
What heart its doubt can smother—
   Are our loved dead in heaven?   20

Shall we with rapture meet them
   Among the angels blest?
Oh! are we fit to greet them—
   There in the land of rest?

For some there's other greeting;   25
   Even the doomed can love,
What grief to think of meeting
    If it were not above!

Blame not the broken-hearted,
   Though deeming heaven despair   30
If their beloved departed
   Could not be with them there.

Slight not the deep dejection
   Of love less wise than strong,
In this cold world affection   35
   So seldom lasts too long.

64. SERVANTS OF GOD, AWAKE!

HYMN

Servants of God, awake!
   The Master draweth near;
Your careless slumbers now forsake
   For He will soon be here.

The tasks are still undone   5
   That he hath left to you;
Awake, and hasten everyone,
   Hasten your work to do.

In the declining day
   Pause not to mourn in vain   10
The hours that you have slept away,
   And cannot now regain.

But use the present hour
   With diligence and care,
And earnestly with all your power   15
   For His return prepare.

65. AN APPEAL

On the new Admiralty order requiring British sailors to surrender
fugitive slaves to their masters.

Oh England! Scotland! Ireland! ye
Will surely never, never, see
Your sailor sons so true and brave
Refuse to shield a hunted slave.
Why in the Book of books, 'tis said—   5
That if a slave to thee has fled,
Thou shalt not rivet his broken chain,
Or yield him up to his foes again.*

I wish I were a British tar,
I'd show you what my feelings are;   10
Though of a loyal heart I'd be
A rebel, Oh! Ward Hunt, to thee.
Never by me should man or maid
Be into slavery betrayed;
I'd sooner die to set them free,   15
For so I'd have done unto me.

Oh, it would be a great relief
For me to see each Tory chief
Fall from his misused power disgraced,
And be by Liberals replaced.   20
Whate'er they do seems weak and wrong,
At doing nothing they are strong,
And times to come will learn their glory,
In the byword 'a lazy Tory.'

---

*Deut. xxiii, 15

66. SONNET, ON RECEIVING A BOUQUET

Lovely flowers! are they mine?
Who did this sweet offering send?
'Oh, it was an unknown friend,
One whose name you'll not divine.'
'Twas a kindly thought, indeed,
Thus to send these smiling flowers   5
To enliven the dull hours
Of a lonely invalid.
Therefore, doubly sweet are they
And, for every blossom here,
May some brighter flowers appear,   10
Shedding fragrance round the way
Of the gentle unknown friend
Who this pleasing gift did send.

67. A REPLY TO 'TWENTY-EIGHT'

'When in my teens I vowed that I
    Would marry for affection;
At twenty-one I looked about
    For fortune and connection.

But now the case is altered quite,
    A maid with empty coffers,
If still a maid at twenty-eight,
    Must take the first who offers.'
                    —Lavinia

Oh, Miss Lavinia, fie for shame!
    You've scandalised the nation!
Old maidenhood's insulted name
    Cries out for vindication.

The solemn sacred marriage tie   5
    Could not have been intended
To be a trick of trade, whereby
    Ill fortune might be mended.

If eligible as a wife—
    If clever, young, and healthy,   10
You have enough for single life,
    Although you are not wealthy.

A maid who toils for daily bread
    Will always be respected;
But she who for mere cash would wed   15
    Deserves to be neglected.

I'd in a cavern make my home
    Ere ever I would do so;
Or on some desert island roam,
    Like that old hermit Crusoe.   20

We're not all willing to be sold—
    Maidens there are in plenty
Who'd rather work than wed for gold,
    Though over eight-and-twenty.

68. HOPE

No more, thou sweet deceiver,
   Shalt thou my trust betray.
I once was a believer
   In all that thou could'st say;
But now I scorn thy scheming,   5
   Thy subtle spells I break—
To trust thee was but dreaming,
   And now I am awake.

II

My words of Hope bereft me,
   But greater is my care;   10
I find since Hope has left me
   Her absence is despair.
Her soothing spells forsaking
   I have increased my pain;
How vain was my awaking!   15
   I fain would dream again.

69. TOO SOON FORGOTTEN

SONG, FOR MUSIC

When friends we loved to cherish
    Are numbered with the dead,
Then soon our love doth perish—
    Soon is their mem'ry fled.

How quickly our affections   5
    For other friends make room;
How dim our recollections
    Of those within the tomb.

Too soon, too soon forgotten,
    As if they ne'er were loved;   10
They lie in gloom and silence,
    From scenes of life removed.

And those who loved them dearly
    May mourn a while; but yet,
Although they loved sincerely,   15
    The fondest will forget.

70. FAR OUT AT SEA

Encircled by the shining sea,
O'erarchèd by the azure sky,
Our little ship appears to be
The centre of the world, and we
No other sign of life can see   5
Save the seabirds as they fly.

No trace of land can we descry;
The circular expanse of blue—
The deep blue sea, the bright blue sky,
Are all that now can meet the eye;   10
There's not a single cloud on high,
Or another sail in view.

71. SOARING UPWARDS TO THE LIGHT

SONG, SET TO MUSIC

Hark! the skylark gaily sings,
Waking in the morning bright;
With the dew upon his wings,
Soaring upwards to the light.
Upwards to the glorious sun,   5
Upwards through the radiant sky;
Singing with triumphant tone
As he wings his way on high.
Hail, sweet lark! each morning winging
Through the air thy joyous flight,   10
Greeting to the bright sun singing—
Soaring upwards to the light.

II

There's a flower below the earth
Blossoming in pallid white;
In the mine it had its birth,   15
And it never saw the light.
Still its face is upward turned
From the dull earth where it grew,
Just as if the flower had learned
To seek the light it never knew.   20
Birds, and flowers, and all things pure,
All things lovely, all things bright,
Taught by instinct, strive to soar—
Struggling upwards to the light.

III

There's an instinct few deny,   25
Striving in each human soul;
Though not winged, we long to fly,
Spurning this dull earth's control.
In our childhood, in our youth,
And when youth has taken flight,   30
Still our souls are seeking truth—
Soaring upwards to the light,

Though the way be long and high,
We will take no downward flight;
But a long Excelsior cry—   35
Soaring upwards to the light.

72. MUSINGS

If I could have had the choosing,
    Of my earthly destiny,
Something more than idle musing
    Should my life's employment be;
    But this was not left to me.   5

Long years, sick and helpless lying,
    I have sung with changeful strain;
Oft rejoicing, seldom sighing,
    Always dreaming—not in vain;
    Hopeful dreams can banish pain.   10

Now, though still to walk unable,
    From my window I can gaze;
Sit with friends around the table,
    At my piano teach, or raise
    Songs of mirth, or hymns of praise.   15

Yet what words can breathe my yearning
    For the freedom others know?
How I long for health's returning!
    Lord, on me this boon bestow,
    In this gift Thy mercy show.   20

Whether granting or refusing
    My importunate request—
Thine alone the right of choosing,
    And thou knowest what is best—
    Be Thy name for ever blest.   25

73. FAME

Oh, Fame! bestow thy wreaths of bays
   On those who such a crown desire;
Thou wilt not heed my simple lays;
   'Tis not for thee I tune my lyre:
I'll seek within this heart of mine   5
For honour purer far than thine.

For here an oracle doth dwell,
   That when I ask will surely say,
If I have used my talents well,
   Or idly wasted them away;   10
And if my heart proclaims me right,
I'll triumph o'er a whole world's spite.

Therefore, I will not wish for Fame,
   For worthless would its plaudits be
If praise were coupled with my name,   15
   While yet my heart could censure me.
Should my own heart condemn me, then
How false would seem the praise of men!

Oh, heart of mine! I scarce have known
   Of any other world but thee;   20
Calm, and unknown, I've lived alone,
   And thou art world enough for me.
In thee I'll seek just praise or blame,
Heedless how strangers name my name.

74. THE FUGITIVE SLAVE

Suggested by the celebrated and execrated 'Slave Circular.'

I dreamt I saw a hunted slave,
   With flying feet for miles she fled
Pursued by many a ruffian knave,
   And in her breathless flight she said,
Oh! if I can but find my way   5
   To British ship, or British shore,
Then will my fetters fall away,
   And I shall be a slave no more.
Onward with beating heart she flies,
   Right onward to the shining sea.   10
Oh! blessed sight that meets her eyes—
   'Tis Britain's flag of liberty!

II

At once she plunges in the wave—
   'Britain's brave sons will shelter me,
Or, if these waters prove my grave,   15
   Far better death than slavery!'
Exhausted by the swelling tide,
   Yet with the hope of freedom brave,
The swimmer gains the vessel's side—
   'Oh freemen! shield a hunted slave.   20
My foes are coming quick!' she cries,
   'But I am safe in British hands,
Oh help me from these waves to rise,
   Take me with you to happier lands!'

III

Then said the captain of the ship,   25
   'We dare not brave your master's claim.'
Among the tars, from lip to lip,
   Went muttered threats and cries of 'Shame.'
They lift the dusky maid on deck,
   'Captain, there's nought we *dare not brave!*   30
May heaven soon send our ship to wreck
   If we dare not protect a slave!'

'You're right, my lads!' the captain cries,
　'Now, come whate'er of this may come,
We'll guard all human liberties   35
　From foreign foes, or foes at home.'

75. SONNET

Life's sunny summer time
Is in the days of youth;
Of all our life in truth
Youth is the golden prime.
Warm as a southern clime,   5
Bright as Italian skies
It seems to Mem'ry's eyes
In all the after time.
Thoughts noble and sublime
Have stirred all hearts in youth—   10
A love of right and truth,
And scorn of fraud and crime.
Oh! may these nobler feelings stay
When bloom and brightness pass away.

Poems Published 25 April 1874 to 6 May 1876 but not Collected in Mirren's Musings

76. 'OH! I WISH THAT ALL WOMEN HAD POWER TO VOTE'

Oh! I wish that all women had power to vote,
And I wish they were voting for me!
I should just like a seat in the Parliament House,
And to add to my surname M.P.
And I would contrive to climb   5
To the Cabinet in time,
And then as the Prime Minister
You'd see what I would do!
I'll right all wrongs, indeed I will,
If e'er such dreams come true.   10

77. 'I AM VERY GLAD THAT I CAN SAY'

I am very glad that I can say
   In answer to your letter,
That—in spite of hope deferred—to-day
   My health seems rather better.

For years, both day and night, I lay   5
   In bed, but now I'm able
To get up nearly every day
   And take tea at the table.

Still I can't walk, which I regret,
   But thank my stars again, sir,   10
That, though I am so helpless, yet
   I seldom suffer pain, sir.

I've read these friendly letters five
   With great surprise and pleasure
I'm sure as long as I'm alive   15
   These letters I shall treasure.

Far sweeter than the voice of Fame
   Are words of kindly feeling,
Such sympathy for being lame
   Is half as good as healing.   20

78. WHAT THE POPE SAID

Said the Pope (so he did), if all Papists agree,
To be guided by me,
What fine times shall we see!
If they'll do all I tell them, set up I shall be.

We will soon have another Bartholomew's day;   5
Such slashing away;
As good as a play.
Best answer to Protestant logic, I say.

But if Catholics once for themselves dare to think,
I shall certainly sink: 10
For I'm close to the brink
Of that which might surely make any Pope shrink.

Then Catholics all, rally round at my call;
Let our enemies fall:
Send the Book to the wall.   15
Then we shall look big, and the truth will look small,
And long live myself, to grow fat by it all.

79. WHAT SOMEBODY SAID

Somebody said that I said something—
   Now what it was, I do not know;
But I am very sure 'twas something
   I never could have said—oh, no!

Somebody heard it and believed it,   5
   As people will believe, you know!
And having as the truth received it,
   Soon turned a friend into a foe.

Somebody said some more about me,
   Most mischievous, though very kind;   10
This caused another friend to flout me,
   And much disturb my peace of mind.

What things some folk delight in saying,
   Not wicked, but *mal apropos*;
And often dreadfully dismaying—   15
   I wish they wouldn't blunder so.

Poor Job found out that the vexations
   Caused him by each devoted friend,
Surpassed all other tribulations
   That ever Satan's spite could send.   20

And it would be a serious error,
   To think that modern wisdom tends
To make kind friendship less a terror
   Than in the days when Job had friends.

80. MY BOOK

I'm to publish a book—may my friends all remember!
It will surely be ready for sale by December,
In time for a Christmas, or New Year's Day present,
Among friends who find reading and poetry pleasant.
One hundred and twenty-eight pages I'll cram in it,   5
And I hope they may please all who choose to examine it;
'Twill contain my own portrait, that readers may see
What I look like, and feel well acquainted with me.
Now I'll tell you the price—gentle muses, don't frown! —
Every work has its price, and my book's half-a-crown.   10
And, dear readers, the sooner your orders come in,
The sooner the publisher's work will begin:
Send your names, and I'll send my prospectus to you,
Or the simplest of orders by letter will do,
If you'll just be so kind as to drop me a line   15
That you want Songs and Poems by
        Marion Bernstein.

81. AN AWFUL MISTAKE

Oh it's really too bad! It's distressing, indeed
It's enough to give fits to this poor invalid!
Pray fetch me the salts—and give me my fan,
And send for the doctor as quick as you can:
And open the window—oh let me have air!   5
For I scarcely can breathe—I'm quite killed, I declare!
Oh, give me some water, I'm going to faint,
'Twould be too much for Job, although Job was a saint.
Oh what do you think? Here's the *Mail*, only look
At the verses I've written announcing 'my book.'   10
Now, who could have imagined, whoever could guess,
That the printers would actually spoil my address?
They have been, and they've gone, and they've put
     Number *three*,
When it ought to be five—couldn't anyone see?
I had written as plainly as writing could be.   15
I don't think I'm quite murdered—I think I'll revive;
And I'll write to the Editor, he may contrive
To induce the *Mail* printers to print Number five—
F i v e, five, 5 Dunrobin Place.
Dear friends, this address in your memory trace.   20
Like a cramped Chinese damsel, unable to roam,
I'm obliged to transact all my business at home;
And a host of kind friends and assistants I'm needing,
To insure the success of my present proceeding.
I hope all my old friends so good-natured will be   25
As to take my prospectus and canvass for me.
Where's the gentle D'Odeurs? Where's that tease, J. B.
     M.?
I'm expecting a host of subscribers through them!
A. Strachan, H. E. Mosley, and funny D. C.,
T. L. H., who sent such a nice letter to me;   30
Mary R. of Kilbarchan, who once doubted whether
The heather and broom ever blossomed together;
And my Edinburgh friend, the Old Fogy, who took
Up the pen to advise me to publish a book.
Since I've followed his counsel, Old Fogy, I'm sure,   35
Should send in the names of his friends by the score.
Then there's— Oh this won't do! If I scribble too many
Such lines the good Editor won't publish any!

I'll wind up with a general rallying call
To my friends everywhere, rich and poor, great and small, 40
As book agents, for once lend a hand, one and all,
And I'm sure my new book will not go to the wall.

82. MY OWN DEAR NATIVE HOME

Oh! I left my heart behind me
    When I left my native land;
And love's subtle power doth bind me,
    With an ever strengthening band,
To the old home over yonder,   5
    Many hundred miles away.
'Absence makes the heart grow fonder,'
    As my heart can feel to-day;
Still whatever friends surround me,
    And wherever I may roam,   10
Love's enduring links have bound me
    To my own dear native home.

Though my destiny may sever
    Me from all I've loved of yore;
Oh, my country! though I never,   15
    Never may behold thee more—
Foreign scenes may glow with beauty,
    Foreign friends prove kind and true;
But, 'twill seem both joy and duty
    Still to leave my heart with you,   20
And whatever friends surround me,
    And wherever I may roam,
Love's enduring links have bound me
    To my own dear native home.

83. 'HE PROMISED THAT EITHER BY HOOK OR BY CROOK'

He promised that either by hook or by crook,
Ere the first month was out he would finish my book;
But the month is now past, and I see with regret
That the book's not half done—it may take six weeks yet.
He's made me quite ill with this needless delay,   5
And I can't make him hurry for all I can say.
Now, dear friends, if impatient, as doubtless you'll be,
Turn your wrath on the printer, and pity poor me.

84. COME BACK, SWEET MUSE

Come back, sweet Muse, no longer stay
From one who loves thee far away;
Once all the cares life brought to me
Were solaced by thy minstrelsy.

But lately thou hast ceased awhile   5
To cheer me with thy friendly smile;
And, oh, in many dreary hours
I've missed thy sweetly soothing powers.

Return, sweet Muse, return and sing,
And I'll forget thy wandering;   10
Quite happy when I hear thy strain,
And find thee at my side again.

Poems Collected in Mirren's Musings, June 1876, but not Previously Published

85. ROBIN DONN'S LAMENT

PARAPHRASE OF THE CELEBRATED GAELIC BALLAD.

(From Dr. Mackay's Translation.)

Sad seems the home of my childhood,
    and strange sound the once beloved voices,
For I miss the sweet voice I loved best, and
    the kind, ready-listening ear.
Though glad was my homeward-bound   5
    journey, no longer my spirit rejoices;
For unto the heart that once loved me,
    alas! I no longer am dear.
Ah me! what a sorrowful hour,
    was the hour that saw me returning!   10
What avails me to tell of the pain
    that then pierced through my heart like a spear?

II

I wandered o'er meadow and lane,
    and the woodpath with boughs interlacing,
I went over all the old places where   15
    I and my loved one have met;
But when I looked down from the crags,
    and beheld her my rival embracing,
Oh! the anguish that came o'er my
    spirit—that pang I shall never forget.   20
What I felt as that day's sun was setting,
    from my heart all its happiness ceasing,
Made existence seem weary and worthless,
    for nothing is left but regret.

III

'Oh, thou golden haired daughter of   25
   Donald, I cannot believe that thou knowest
How the strength I once boasted has vanished,
   through ill repaid passion for thee.
I have loved thee too fondly and truly,
   and still wheresoever thou goest,   30
My heart, that can never forget thee,
   where thou art will constantly be.
But this once, I beseech thee to hear me;
   the pride of my spirit is broken:
Since for ever I must be without thee,   35
   one last kiss refuse not to me.'

IV

Then proudly, in scorn and in anger,
   the maiden I loved looked upon me.
'No! never,' said she, 'will thy fingers
   the snood from my tresses unbind: 40
Is it strange that, when thou wert long absent,
   one equal to thee should have won me?
And did'st thou then think thyself better
   than all whom thou leaved'st behind?'
Then lightly she laughed at my sorrow—   45
   'Why, surely, if love hath undone thee,
Thou wert not to die by the foeman—
   tenderer death thou wilt find!'

V

But how can I hate thee, my darling? Not
    even thy pride and thy sneering   50
Can chill the warm fount of affection
    that springs in my bosom for thee.
E'en when I most bitterly blame thee
    then cometh thine image endearing;
And my anger is lost in my love when   55
    that dearly-loved vision I see.
The thought of the time when you loved
    me, e'en now to my spirit is cheering,
And seems like a tower of strength,
    and a harbour of refuge to me.   60

86. A WOMAN'S LOGIC

'Kicking never degrades a woman, however much it may injure her physically. Now, if she had what some call her rights, she would be very seriously degraded indeed.'—*Weekly Mail*

An injury cannot degrade us,
As you very properly say,
A compliment truly you've paid us,
A capital weapon you've made us,
For which with our thanks we must pay.   5

And yet I am tempted to using
This weapon against you to-day.
'Tis cruel, but then there's no choosing;
Fate drives, and 'twere useless refusing,
I must do the best that I may!   10

That injury cannot degrade us,
This argument plainly invites;—
Degraded you could not have made us,
E'en though for our sins you had paid us,
By wrongfully granting our rights!   15

87. THE GREAT PASSOVER

'Christ our Passover is sacrificed for us; therefore let us keep the feast.'

In the early hours of evening,
    When the light began to wane,
When the day was just beginning,
    The Passover lamb was slain.

(For 'tis not at dreary midnight   5
    That the Hebrew days begin,
But to-day goes out at sunset,
    And to-morrow then comes in.)

And the day of that Passover
    Was a morrow that should be   10
Through all after time remembered—
    Day of Faith's great mystery.

Then the Lord with his disciples,
    (Who so soon should lose their Head),
Shared together the Last Supper—   15
    Eating the unleavened bread.

And he spake of the Passover—
    Changed this ordinance must be,
When ye keep it, 'ye shall do so
    As in memory of me.'*   20

On Passover night, Oh Israel!
    Out of Egypt ye were led,
On this night the 'blood of sprinkling'
    By the Paschal lamb was shed.

But a lamb for the Passover   25
    Ye shall never kill again,
For to-day, once and forever,
    Shall the Lamb of God be slain;

---

*Luke 22; 15, 19

And the cup which ye are drinking
  Is the blood that he shall shed;   30
And the bread that ye are eating,
  As his body, is that bread.

When the Paschal feast returneth,
  And th' unleavened bread ye break,
Ever will the Lamb be present   35
  In the bread and wine ye take.

Then he gave his last commandment,
  'Love each other,' for my sake.
(When will all the Christian churches
  To themselves this lesson take?)   40

'Tis by love, not persecution
  That my gospel ye must preach—
Love each other; God's kind message
  Only loving lips can teach.

Then at dark and dreary midnight   45
  From them all he stole away,
And he went into the garden
  Of Gethsemane to pray.

And he groaned in mortal anguish
  As his doom drew near at length,   50
And his human heart did languish
  Till an angel gave him strength.

See, a band of soldiers coming—
  Ha! what treachery is this?
Yonder comes his own disciple,   55
  And betrays him with a kiss.

But he knoweth the deceiver,
  And in solemn tones he saith,
'Judas, dost thou then betray me
  With a kiss, unto my death?'   60

Those who love him now forsake him,
  Life is dear, each guards his own;
Those who hate him rudely take him
  Hence to meet his doom alone.

All that night until the morning,   65
  He is mocked and scorned by all,
And while yet the day is dawning,
  Born to Pilate's Judgment Hall.

Then from Pilate unto Herod,
  And from Herod back again,   70
Till at last, with cruel torments,
  'Christ our Passover is slain.'

Well may earth's foundations tremble,[†]
  And the sun withdraw his light,[‡]
And these hours, so near the noontide,   75
  Wear the darkness of the night!

While he lingeringly dieth,
  To his gracious nature true,
'Father, pardon them,' he crieth,
  'For they know not what they do.'[§]   80

Then to the repentant sinner
  Slain beside him, he doth say
Tenderly, 'Thou shalt be with me
  E'en in paradise, to-day.'[‖]

[†] Matt. xxvii, 51
[‡] Matt. xxvii, 45
[§] Luke xxiii, 34
[‖] Luke xxiii, 43

But at last the pang is over,   85
  And the light shines forth again,
For Redemption's work 'is finished,'
  And the Lamb of God is slain.

See, the day is almost closing,
  No such day hath been before;   90
There hath been a great Passover,
  Now the sacrifice is o'er.

Take him from the cross, and bear him
  Quickly to the grave away;
For it is the preparation,   95
  Sunset brings the Sabbath-day.

And it is a festal Sabbath,
  Nothing should be left undone;
Seldom do the weekly Sabbath
  And the Feast come both in one.   100

Sacred, henceforth and forever,
  To earth's latest history,
Far beyond all other Sabbaths
  Shall that festal Sabbath be.

Earth's *first* Sabbath saw Creation,   105
  Finished by the Maker blest.
Now the great work of Salvation
  Is achieved, and Christ doth rest.

Sealed within the silent tomb
  His pale corse in darkness lies;   110
But afar from all the gloom
  Rests his soul in paradise.

And the thief who sought his grace,
    Even in the grasp of death,
Rests with him in that bright place—   115
    Praising him with every breath.

Thus in spirit Jesus keeps
    Sabbath with the saints of light,
While his mortal semblance sleeps
    In the charnel's rayless night.   120

Shall the sacred Seventh-day,
    Thus divinely-doubly blest,
Be despised and cast away
    At the antichrist's behest?

No, let all who cry 'Salvation!'   125
    With the gospel flag unfurled,
Preach the Sabbath Restoration
    To the cold, forgetful world.

88. EPIGRAM

Love's a first-rate theme for rhyming,
Pretty words so sweetly chiming—
Loves and doves, and hearts and darts,
What a charm their sound imparts!

89. TO THE EDITOR

It would seem by the style of your recent reply
That a change in your tactics you don't mean to try.
You'll 'be shot if you do,' of course means that you won't;
Ah, well, you are sure to be 'shot' if you don't.
I should really be *frightened* to challenge such foes   5
As those two who still patronise arrows and bows,
By whose darts so much more execution is done
Than by French *mitraileuse*, or by Krupp's greatest gun.
But, 'The gods make men mad—' ahem! Perhaps 'twould
    be best
Just to leave one or two of my thoughts unexpressed!   10

90. A MEDITATION

Again I see the radiant skies
All full of golden light,
While floating o'er the ether blue
Are clouds of fleecy white.
I see the street, and gardens filled   5
With many a shrub and tree;
And every scene seems beautiful,
And new, and strange to me.
I longed to see the skies again,
I prayed by day and night;   10
My prayers have not been all in vain,
Once more I see the light.

II

And when the evening shadows fall,
And sunlight leaves the skies,
The lovely moon will shine, and all   15
The twinkling stars will rise.
'Tis long since I have seen the moon,
Or looked upon a star,
Except in dreams, and then they seemed
So cold, and oh! so far.   20
But moon and stars will shine to-night,
And I shall see them shine;
'Tis joy to see them, and once more
That happiness is mine!

III

But I am still a pris'ner here,   25
From home I cannot stray;
I can but look upon the world
As something far away.
Yet once I could not see the sun,
And now his radiance bright   30
Gives even to captivity
A solace and delight.
I will not mourn for what hath been,
Nor fear what yet may be,

But rather prize the happiness   35
That God still gives to me.

IV

And, since my prayers have once been heard,
I will not cease to pray,
But still send up appeals to Heaven
Unwearied, night and day.   40
I feel His promise cannot fail;
I know—I always knew,
That though it may be long delayed
Yet still it must be true.
Then by Thy truth, Oh! God of truth,   45
My health and strength restore;
Oh Lord, bow down thine ear to me,
And grant my prayer once more.

91. CREMATING A MOTHER-IN-LAW

'The crowning experiment of my life, the cremation of my wife's deceased mother. My wife and I were in my study, with the remains of our dear mother before us. I placed in the receptacle, with the body, about twenty pounds avoirdupois of sodium.'
—Dr Pelling

The first cremator
Great Britain e'er saw
Was a man who cremated his mother-in-law.
Ah! how many men
Before and since then 5
Would have liked such a task more than my little pen
Has the power to express;
But you'll easily guess
If you've one of your own, although nevertheless,
I think that I may 10
As well pause to say,
Other kinsfolk are often as bad, in their way.
Hurrah! for cremation!
The next generation
Will know how to treat an unwelcome relation! 15
We shall hear little more
Of the mother-in-law,
Or the husband or wife that is voted a bore;
For when once they are hid
Underneath the 'stone lid,' 20
They will do just as Pelling's mamma-in-law did,
By consent of her daughter
Whose love, like iced water,
Stood fire, as such anticombustibles *oughter*.
That lady, I fear, 25
When *her* time draws near,
Won't cremate, but just *thaw* in the heat of her bier;
And vanish she may
By *boiling away*,
But people of less *ice-cream-atory* clay 30
When they're left to their fate
And the sodium, cremate
Themselves. For their death it is needless to wait;
Because, be it said,
Whether living or dead, 35

The 'subject' is certain to be crematèd
Quite equally well,
And ashes don't tell
Any secrets, so far does this system excel
Any method yet shown,   40
Or to man ever known,
Of inducing inquiry to let one alone.
'Twill be bad for the *bore*,
But some others, I'm sure,
Will bless Dr. P. and his mother-in-law!   45

92. EPIGRAM

If a man has more malice than wit,
Then of course for a critic he's fit;
But if there's much wit in his pate
He's not in a *critic*-al state.

93. OH STAY, SWEET SUMMER, STAY

Oh! ye sunny summer hours,
Pass not so soon away,
With singing birds, and blooming flowers,
Oh stay, sweet summer, stay.

What though the singing bird   5
But seldom comes this way,
'Tis *sometimes* in the city heard,
Then stay, sweet summer, stay.

What though your flowers bloom
Alas! so far away,   10
The breezes waft me their perfume,
Then stay, sweet summer, stay.

Bright sunbeams on the wall
Make me feel blithe and gay;
And I should say, if this were all,   15
Oh! stay, sweet summer, stay.

'Tis dreary lying here
Through winter cold and grey;
But sunny skies my spirit cheer,
Oh! stay, sweet summer, stay.   20

Fair scenes, and birds, and flowers—
Ah! not for me are they,
Yet give me your bright sunny hours,
Oh! stay, sweet summer, stay.

94. FIRST PARAPHRASE

GENESIS I

From the collection used by the Kirk of Scotland, with ten additional
verses, which are distinguished from the original composition by being
printed in italics.

'Let heaven arise, let earth appear,'
    Said the Almighty Lord,
The heaven arose, the earth appeared,
    At His creating word.

Thick darkness brooded o'er the deep.   5
    God said, 'Let there be light.'
The light shone forth with smiling ray,
    And scattered ancient night.

Light shone forth without star or sun—
    God said, 'The day doth dawn.'   10
And thenceforth every day begun
    With night before the morn.

Before the evening shades descend,
    The waning of the light
Proclaims that day draws near its end;   15
    Now, once again 'tis night.

He bade the clouds ascend on high,
    The clouds ascend, and bear
A wat'ry treasure to the sky,
    And float upon the air.   20

God called the new created height
    Heaven. Soon fled away
The evening shade, and morning light—
    So passed the second day.

The liquid element below   25
    Was gathered by His hand.
The rolling seas together flow,
    And leave the solid land.

With herbs, and plants, and fruitful trees,
　　The new formed globe He crowned,   30
Ere there was rain to bless the soil,
　　Or sun to warm the ground.

And every plant before it grew,
　　Was formed at His command;
Before the soil its presence knew   35
　　'Twas fashioned by His hand.

So passed the darkness of that night,
　　The radiance of that day;
In its appointed shade and light
　　The third day passed away.   40

Then high in heaven's resplendent arch
　　He placed two orbs of light.
He set the sun to rule the day,
　　The moon to rule the night.

Night saw the moon and stars. The sun   45
　　Shone brightly through the day.
Thus the fourth eve and morn did run
　　In their appointed way.

Next from the deep, the Almighty King
　　Did vital beings frame;   50
Fowls of the air, of every wing,
　　And fish of every name.

While the fifth eve and morn begun,
　　Rolled on, and passed away;
The glorious setting of the sun   55
　　Marking the close of day.

To all the various brutal tribes
　　He gave their wondrous birth;
At once the lion and the worm
　　Sprang from the teeming earth.　　　　　　　60

Then chief o'er all His works below
　　At last was Adam made;
His Maker's image blessed his soul,
　　And glory crowned his head.

Fair in the Almighty Maker's eye　　　　　　　65
　　The whole creation stood.
He viewed the fabric He had raised,
　　His word pronounced it good.

E'en while he spake, the sun went down,
　　The sixth day passed away,　　　　　　　70
O'er God's completed work begun
　　At eve, the seventh day.

He worked not on that day. With joy,
　　His creatures He surveyed;
And angels praised Him solemnly　　　　　　75
　　For all that He had made.

And when that day had passed away,
　　Most solemnly God blest
Its hours, and called the seventh day
　　His Consecrated Rest.　　　　　　　　80

95. TEACH ME HOW TO KEEP THY WAY

Teach me how to keep Thy way
Threading life's perplexing maze;
Guide my footsteps, lest they stray
Into the forbidden ways.
Do not Thou thine aid refuse: 5
Pathways cross on every side;
And the way I can but lose,
If Thou wilt not be my guide.

Tremble not, my child, for see
I am with thee evermore;   10
If thou wilt but follow me
All thy steps are safe and sure.
But lest thou thy guide forget
I will hold my lamp for thee,*
Then though strayed afar, thou'lt yet   15
Find the path by seeking Me.

---

* 'Thy word is a lamp to my feet.'

96. FRIDAY EVENING HYMN

Composed on Good Friday evening, 1874

The day is past, the sun goes down,
Let every care and labour cease.
The workday week is over now,
It is the time of Sabbath peace.

Thus, when creation's work was done,   5
The sunset brought the Sabbath blest;
And on a Sabbath eve begun
Our Saviour's great funereal Rest.*

Behold, in such an hour as this
His form within the grave they lay,   10
And by that solemn Rest of His
New-consecrate the Seventh Day.

While they who in His footsteps trod
Turn, weeping from the grave away,
And rest, obedient to their God,†   15
Through that most solemn Sabbath day.

Oh! may the setting of the sun
On each returning Sabbath eve,
Remind us of what Christ hath done,
And may our souls His grace receive.   20

May every Sabbath bring to us
New death to sin, new sense of rest,
Till Life's last sun shall set, and thus
Give us the Sabbath of the blest.

---

* Luke xxiv, 53–54
† Luke xxiv, 56

97. AT SABBATH SUNSET

The Sabbath sun is sinking low,
The day is nearly past;
Its peaceful hours too quickly go,
Too heavenly here to last.

The cares of earth come back again,   5
The weary, anxious strife,
And Satan's snares, which, not in vain,
Beset our daily life.

But one brief day of all the seven
The world no more prevails;   10
But one brief day we're nearer heaven,
And Satan scarce assails.

Then blessed be the Sabbath day,
Best proof that God is love,
It lends to earth a transient ray   15
Of glory from above.

98. TO ANNIE ON HER BIRTHDAY

This doleful, dismal time of year
When everything looks dark and drear,
Is not the most propitious time
To task one's brains to make a rhyme.
Had you been born in summer sweet   5
Your birthday I no doubt could greet
With some more freely flowing lay
Than these dull rhymes I write to-day.
It's much too cold for fancies bright;
I'm half asleep both day and night,   10
Feeling half dead, and half alive—
How can the muse poetic thrive?
Only one thing original now can I say—
May you have many happy returns of the day!

Nov. 2, 1873

99. THE THREE GUIDES

'Tis said that human reason
Is like a star's bright ray
That guides us well, but not so well
As doth the light of day.

'Tis said—God's word by Moses   5
Is like the moon's clear light
That guides us better than the stars,
Though still it is but night.

But now the Sun of Righteousness
Hath risen, and His ray   10
Absorbs the light of moon and stars
In bright and glorious day.

100. ON TOOTHACHE

Toothache will stay
Till it goes away,
No one who has tried can doubt it;
The very best way
To shorten its stay   5
Is to leave off thinking about it!

101. MOTHER, WEEP NOT FOR THY CHILD

Mother, weep not for thy child
  Laid to rest beneath the flowers,
By the world still undefiled,
  Saved from grief, and sin's dread powers;
  In life's earliest, sunniest hours   5
'Taken from the ills to come.'
  O'er thy head the storm-cloud lowers,
But thy child escapes its gloom
  In the shelter of the tomb.

II

Think of all the mournful years   10
  Thou thyself hast passed below,
Think of all the strifes and tears
  Which thy child will never know.
  Surely it was best to go
To the grave while life seemed fair;   15
  It was better not to know
How much pain the heart can bear
  Ere it longs for refuge there.

102. SABBATH EVE

From even unto even,
  At setting of the sun,
One day in every seven,
  The peaceful Sabbaths run.

Sweet days of hallowed leisure,   5
  Made sacred to the Lord,
No work, no worldly pleasure,
  Their solemn hours afford.

But there are higher pleasures
  Than earthly joys bestow,   10
And there are richer treasures
  Than can be found below.

If thou wouldst feel those pleasures,
  Learn to commune with God;
If thou wouldst find those treasures,   15
  Look up to his abode.

If thou hast eyes enlightened
  By Truth's far-reaching light,
Death's shadows shall be brightened,
  And Heaven revealed to sight.   20

Although to Godless mortals
  The grave seems wrapped in gloom;
Thou shalt behold the portals
  Of Heaven beyond the tomb.

By such high contemplation   25
  Thy wisdom shall increase;
Such solemn meditation
  Shall fill thy soul with peace.

Thus shalt thou gain the treasures
  That never can decay,   30
And feel life's purest pleasures
  Upon the Sabbath-day.

103. SONNET, TO THE STARS

Ye stars that shine so calm and bright,
Down glancing from above us;
I half believe you love us!
Who is there loveth not your light?
It maketh beautiful the night;   5
So sweetly mildly beaming,
Like radiant diamonds gleaming,
Bespangling yon cerulean height.
And yet there's something in your light
That's far more sweet and tender   10
Than any jewel's splendour.
Ye seem to me like spirits bright,
A loving vigil keeping
While all the world is sleeping.

104. A SLEEPLESS NIGHT

Oh come, sweet sleep, with all thy charms
Enfold me in thy downy arms;
My wearied spirit fain would be
Refreshed and soothed and cheered by thee.

'Tis weary watching through the night,   5
And longing for the dawn of light;
'Tis weary at the morn's first ray
To wish the daylight passed away.

Yet so they feel who cannot rest,
Who with sweet slumber are not blest   10
By thee our life and health we keep;
Oh! come to me, refreshing sleep.

105. THE SEVENTH DAY

God rested on the seventh day,
    When He the world had made,
And 'Be this day for ever blest
    And sanctified,' He said.

'Then let all children of the Lord   5
    Cast earthly thoughts away,
And think of heavenly things alone
    Upon the seventh day.

And therein shall no work be done,
    Either by man or beast,   10
Until the setting of the sun
    Proclaims my Sabbath ceased.

Six days have you to labour in,
    Then labour as ye may;
But 'tis your God's command that ye   15
    Rest on the seventh day.'

Christ rested on the seventh day
    From all his bitter woes,
When, after he was crucified,
    In death He sought repose.   20

And from this weary world the while,
    His spirit passed away,
And found sweet rest in Paradise,
    Upon the seventh day.

And on the first day of the week   25
    He rose to life again;
To let His sad disciples see
    Their hopes had not been vain.

Believers should the Sabbath keep
    In God's appointed way,   30
And from the cares and toils of earth
    Rest on the seventh day.

106. THE SABBATH OF THE LORD.

Our God a holy name hath given
To but one day of all the seven—
   The Sabbath of the Lord;
Then why despise the seventh day,
Why take its sacred name away,   5
   And why that name accord
Unto a day God hath not blest,
A day on which He did not rest:
   If children of the Lord,
Why think you His commandment strange,   10
Why strive His ordinance to change,
   And trample on His Word?

107. A SONG OF SUMMER

Sing, every little bird,
   The gentle summer reigns;
Now let each minstrel voice be heard
   In blithest, sweetest strains.

Wake, all ye flowers fair;   5
   Open your soft bright eyes;
Let your sweet incense on the air
   Float upward to the skies.

How bright the whole world seems
   When radiant with the blaze   10
Of the warm sunshine's golden beams,
   Through the long summer days!

How fair all nature seems
   Beneath the chastened light
Of Luna's soft and silvery beams,   15
   In the brief summer night!

Shine, every twinkling star;
   Smile on us from those heights
That seem to me not quite so far
   In these sweet summer nights.   20

The lovely summer-time
   Makes earth like heaven appear;
Methinks in the celestial clime
   'Tis summer all the year.

108. HUMAN RIGHTS

Man holds so exquisitively tight
To everything he deems his right;
If woman wants a share, to fight
She has, and strive with all her might.

But we are nothing like so jealous   5
As any of you surly fellows;
Give us our rights and we'll not care
To cheat our brothers of their share.

Above such selfish, *man-like* fright,
We'd give fair play, let come what might,   10
To he or she folk, black or white,
And haste the reign of Human Right.

109. REPLY TO THE FOREGOING

I thank the 'little unknown friend'
Who did this fragrant bouquet send,
And graceful cluster from the vine;
Accompanied by many a line
Expressing kindly sympathy   5
In very charming poetry.
The blossoms are not only graced
By 'crystal dewdrops,' but the taste
That blended their bright hues so well
Helps to increase their beauty's spell,   10
Queen of them all the yellow rose
A world of beauty doth disclose;
Methinks of all her species rare
I never yet saw one so fair.
But yet when deeming her the best   15
I seem ungracious to the rest,
For each appears too full of grace
To take a secondary place,
Indeed it gives me great delight,
To see these lovely blossoms bright   20
A sympathetic offering;
And yet less pleasure does it bring
Than those sweet verses that you send
To tell me you're an unknown friend
For what seems sweeter far to me   25
Than flowers or fruit is sympathy.

110. THE SWALLOW

'The swallow has aye been the type
    O' cauldrife heartless friends,
That share oor joys in summer hours
Then flee when summer ends.'
—Mary Inglis

Come tell me, pretty swallow,
    What must I think of you?
Do you good fortune follow—
A type of friendship hollow
    And hearts that are not true?   5

II

Then said to me the swallow,
    'For answer ask my mate.
He thinks my heart not hollow,
His fortunes do I follow
    Through good or evil fate.   10

III

We wander,' said the swallow,
    'Where sunshine smiles above;
But human hearts are hollow,
And know not how to follow
    The summertime of love.   15

IV

Who ever knew the swallow
    A second time to wed?
Nay, second love were hollow,
    Mourning we wait to follow
Our ne'er forgotten dead.'   20

V

Oh loving, changeless swallow!
  Constancy dwells with you,
No emblem is the swallow
  Of fickle hearts, or hollow,
But of affection true.   25

Poems Published 8 July 1876 to 6 January 1906, Subsequent to the Printing of Mirren's Musings

111. JUST HEAVEN, DEFEND US

From cruel shafts of envious spite,
  In which malignant hearts delight;
From truth's eclipse, from falsehood's night,
  From foes Thy servants scorn to smite,
    Just Heaven, defend us.   5

With steadfast courage to endure
  The wounds we have no balm to cure;
With faith in Thee, for ever sure,
  With patience, peaceable and pure,
    Just Heaven, defend us.   10

With all the panoply of right
  That arms Thy soldiers for the fight
Against the gloomy Prince of Night,
  From dire defeat, from coward flight,
    Just Heaven, defend us.   15

Then, when before the dawn of day
  The powers of darkness flee away;
Thou, who hast heard Thy children pray,
  Shalt hear their thankful voices say,
    'Thou did'st defend us.'   20

112. A LEAP-YEAR ROMANCE

Young William loved fair Rosalie,
Who dwelt upon the banks of Dee,
And quite as much in love was she,
But William loved so timidly.
He looked, and sighed, but nought said he.   5
Things went on thus for years just three—
The fourth year leap-year chanced to be,
And, tired of his timidity,
'How very shy you are,' said she,
'I'm sure you're not a bit like me!   10
I wish that we could change, for we
Are quite unsuited thus to be.
You'd be a gentler girl than me,
And I'd not fail in bravery
If I were you, and you were me,   15
How very different things would be!
I would go down on bended knee,
And say, "Miss, will you marry me?"
And you'd say "yes" undoubtedly,
And then how happy we should be!'   20
Young William stared at Rosalie,
As most men would, it seems to me,
And how it chanced I ne'er could see,
Or whether she proposed, or he,
But, 'tis a fact well known to me,   25
The middle of last February
Young William wedded Rosalie.

113. THE SUN SHINES ON FOR EVER

Some call the night the death of day,
  But daylight dieth never;
For though unseen, and far away,
  The sun shines on for ever.

When storm clouds veil the sunbeams bright,   5
  Yet sunshine faileth never;
Far, far above those clouds the light
  Is shining on for ever.

In vain the shadows of the night,
  Or stormy clouds endeavour,   10
To quench the sun's unchanging light—
  He shines undimmed for ever.

In life's dark hours you can but sigh,
  Yet be despairing never;
The time of darkness passes by—   15
  The light shines on for ever.

114. ONWARD YET! UPWARD YET!

What's in the power to vote?
  Ah! sisters, try it:
You'll keep the Right afloat,
  And drown Wrong by it.
Strive to increase your power;   5
  By its increasing,
Progress will be your dower—
  Progress increasing.
    Onward yet, upward yet,
      Higher and higher;   10
    Hopefully, fearlessly,
      Toil and aspire.

Aim high—yes, high as Heaven!
  You may attain it;
Only to those 'tis given   15
  Who strive to gain it.
Not only womankind
  Thus should endeavour,
But let all humankind
  Press on for ever.   20
    Onward yet, upward yet,
      Higher and higher;
    Patiently, earnestly,
      Toil and aspire.

115. NATURE'S ARISTOCRACY

Are all men equal in their birth?
    No, rather let it be confessed
That some are sent as lights on earth,
    Better and greater than the rest.

Honour dwells not alike in all;   5
    Some men are bad, some men are good.
Are those who 'neath temptation fall
    Equal to those who have withstood?

Some men are foolish, some are wise;
    Are those who idly waste their days   10
Equal to those whose energies
    Are spent in wisdom's noble ways?

Give pity to the worst you see;
    Give honour where you justly can;
Pity the thief, but say, is he   15
    The equal of the honest man?

Some men are cruel, some are kind,
    Their wives and children must decide
Which is the greatest—which shall find
    Most honour at his own fireside.   20

Oh! say not all are equal then,
    For nature has her ranks you see;
The wicked are her 'common men,'
    The good her 'Aristocracy.'

116. OUR CAT CAN SAY 'IM-PH-M'

I was reading James Nicholson's 'Im-ph-m' one day,
(And a capital poem it is, I may say),
And, when reading it over, it lately struck me,
That our cat can say 'Im-ph-m' as plain as can be.
    We sometimes say 'Im-ph-m,'   5
    And puss replies 'Im-ph-m!'
She understands 'Im-ph-m' you clearly can see.

Her language is chiefly the language of eyes;
She looks grave, she looks glad, she looks saft, she looks
    wise;
When she looks in our faces our feelings she knows,   10
Whether merry or sad, and her sympathy shows
    By her sweet coaxing 'Im-ph-m,'
    Her saft, soothing, 'Im-ph-m'—
There's more in that 'Im-ph-m' than you might suppose.

She sits on my knee, with her paw round my neck,   15
I can't find in my heart her caresses to check;
So I call her my darling, my dear pretty Jack;
And she has such a wise way of answering back,
    With her sensible 'Im-ph-m,'
    The tenderest 'Im-ph-m';   20
If you heard her say 'Im-ph-m' your sides you would
    crack.

I fear you will think me exceedingly flat,
To scribble three verses in praise of a cat;
But I wish you could see her, or hear her some day,
You would own she'd a most irresistible way   25
    Of murmuring 'Im-ph-m,'
    That musical 'Im-ph-m';
The simple word 'Im-ph-m' is all she can say.

117. ON THE DEATH OF 'RHYMING WILLIE'

Can it be that he is gone,
  Willie of the merry song,
Blooming face, and stalwart form,
  And so young, and blithe, and strong?

He was young for wedded ties,   5
  Yet a wife and children four
Looked to him with trusting eyes,
  As a guardian strong and sure.

Sadly will the widow weep,
  Of his faithful care bereft,   10
With the little ones to keep
  By their loving father left.

Did he feel his coming end,
  And for wife and children pray,
Who must lose their truest friend   15
  When his young life ebbed away?

Fear not, Willie! slumber thou,
  All life's cares in peace resign;
Heaven will guard thy loved ones now,
  With a mightier arm than thine.   20

118. CAPRICIOUS MAY

Oh! what do you mean, Miss May,
By coming to us this way?
  With snowy showers,
  Instead of flowers,
And gloomy instead of gay?   5

Are you losing your charms, Miss May?
Are you growing quite old and grey?
  Why, when skies were blue,
  We would think of you,
And say, 'It's like sunny May!'   10

And yet you are here to-day—
May here—while the snowflakes lay
  On the ground so chill,
  And the wind blows shrill;
Oh! it's much more like Hogmanay!   15

No more will I sing or say
In praise of the 'smiling May,'
  Of her sunny hours,
  And her scented flowers,
And her songbirds blythe and gay.   20

You have come to us now, Oh May!
Not to cheer, but to freeze and slay.
  You have made me ill
  With the awful chill
That you brought on your opening day.   25

So, since you behave that way,
You're more welcome to go than stay.
  May glorious June
  Console us soon
For the airs of capricious May!   30

119. JUSTICE, MERCY, AND TRUTH

Are there any yet on earth
   Who are just, and kind, and true?
Virtues of eternal worth,
   How I long to meet with you!
If all other hearts disown you,   5
Come and let my heart enthrone you.

Honest souls we sometimes meet
   Trading on the world's highway,
Scorning fraud and low deceit:—
   Such there are, but where are they?   10
Many seeming good and just
Win, and disappoint our trust.

There are hearts whose loving kindness
   Overflows on all around,
But 'mid human sin and blindness   15
   Such warm hearts are rarely found.
Many cold and selfish prove
Few, indeed, know how to love.

There are faithful souls and true:
   Lips that know not falsehood's stain;   20
But they are so few—so few!
   We may seek them long in vain.
Ah! how many will deceive,
And how few can we believe!

There is One whose justice fails not,   25
   Though His mercy long will wait;
Every soul that sins and quails not
   Proves that justice, soon or late.
Heaven is for God's children, who
Learn their Father's works to do,*   30
Learning to be like Him, too—
Just and merciful and true.

---

*John viii, 38

120. WELCOME TO MAY

Welcome again, sweet May!
  Welcome again!
Making the meadows gay,
Brightening the light of day
  O'er hill and plain.   5

How I have longed for you!
  Now you are here.
Sickness and sadness, too,
Weighed on my spirit through
  The winter drear.   10

Ah me! how drearily
  Passed each chill day—
Painfully, wearily,
But now so cheerily
  Comes the bright May.   15

Pain quickly vanisheth,
  Hope fills my heart
At the Spring's balmy breath;
And the grim shades of death
  Gently depart.   20

How could such shadows stay
  Where springtime smiles?
Thou ever winsome May
Chasest all gloom away
  With thy sweet wiles.   25

Queen of the seasons thou
  Art, lovely May;
Softly breathe o'er my brow,
Healthgiving breezes; now
  Blest be thy stay!   30

121. BIRTHDAY MUSINGS

Another year of earthly strife
    Above my head hath rolled;
And still another year of life
    Before me doth unfold.

Father in Heaven, teach my heart   5
    To choose Thy righteous way;
And though sharp thorns bestrew the path,
    Oh, let me never stray.

Let me not start at danger's frown,
    Or turn aside for pleasure's smiles;   10
But faithful in Thy path keep on,
    Unmoved by sin's alluring wiles.

And as each year rolls fast away,
    Let each one bring me nearer Thee;
Then I with joy shall meet the day   15
    That sets my weary spirit free.

And gladly from her bonds of clay
    Will my unfettered soul arise;
And soar on rapid wings away,
    To seek her Father in the skies.   20

122. THE GOVAN RIVETERS' STRIKE

Ye riveters of Govan,
   Who stay at home at ease,
And live upon the 'strike fund'
   As idle as you please,
While wiser men, and better,   5
   Who lazy ways don't like,
Must starve through keeping idle,
   Because you're out on strike.

In vain you hope to profit
   By spoiling Govan trade;   10
Ye riveters of Govan
   You're thoughtless, I'm afraid.
You hinder others' labours,
   To serve your selfish ends;
Behaving to your neighbours   15
   Like foes, instead of friends.

'No man can serve two masters,'
   And consequently you
Can't well obey trades-unions
   And serve employers too.   20
Cast off trades-union shackles,
   And work, or you must know
That all the trade of Glasgow
   To foreign lands will go.

By strikes you'll never profit.   25
   'Tis published far and wide
That strikes have nearly ruined
   The shipyards of the Clyde.
Be wise now, and reflect, lads,
   You've children to be fed;   30
And half a loaf is better
   Than not a bit of bread.

123. MARION'S REPLY TO M. M'M

You are welcome to say
(As perhaps you well may)
That my verses were quite unpoetic;
But you're very far wrong
If you think that my song   5
Was in any way 'unsympathetic.'

Men are eager to claim
Woman's int'rest, yet blame
One whose sisterly lecturings show it.
Inconsistent, I find,   10
Is the masculine mind,
Though the masculine mind does not know it.

As a woman, I'll say
It is womankind's way
To heed all the affairs of our brothers: 15
Very ill would men fare
Without counsel or care
From their wives, sisters, daughters, or mothers.

124. LIGHT THE FURNACE AGAIN!

Light the furnace again!
Now let masters and men
Shake hands, work together, and 'love one another.'*
'Love worketh no ill.'†
'Mistrust love doth kill.'‡   5
Love knoweth no class, but counts each man a brother.

Light the furnace again!
Many eyes long in vain
Have watched for that flame, with its glory and beauty;
Chilling famine, like frost,   10
In its warmth will be lost,
For it shines, like God's love, on men doing their duty.

Light the furnace again!
Sing a hopeful refrain;
Though frauds, famines, and wars stint the wages of
labour,   15
Fortune's frowns, bravely borne,
Will the sooner be gone,
Only keep Love and Trust between neighbour and
neighbour.

---

* John xiii, 84
† Rom. xiii, 10
‡ I. Cor. xiii, 5

125. HEARTSEASE

The simple, sweet heartsease,
    That blossoms everywhere,
Has oft more power to please
    Than any rival fair.

Because it seems to speak   5
    Of innocence and peace,
Of joy serene and meek,
    Of hope that will not cease.

Oh! many a weary heart
    For ease doth vainly sigh,   10
And think naught can impart
    That boon, except to die.

But these are fading flowers
    That blossom from the ground;
In high celestial bowers   15
    The true heartsease is found.

And angels scatter blossoms
    E'en on this earth of ours,
And plant in human bosoms
    Immortal heartsease flowers.   20

Seek them, and you will win them,
    Ask, and they will be given;
And they have power in them
    To make earth seem like heaven.

Whatever joys are wanted,   25
    Whatever hopes may cease,
Where heaven's heartsease is planted
    E'en pain becometh peace.

126. REST

It is the joy of Heaven,
   The comfort of the blest,
That unto them is given
   Eternal rest.

They toiled and suffered here,   5
   They wandered east and west;
There, free from care or fear,
   They are at rest.

Yet oh! we ill can spare
   Those whom we loved the best,   10
When they are taken there
   Unto their rest.

God comfort us, when left
   By grief and care opprest,
Of all we loved bereft,   15
   Far from our rest.

Like lambs strayed from the field,
   Or fledglings from their nest,
So yearn we to behold
   Our home of rest.   20

127. SONNET

ON THE PREDICTION OF EXTRAORDINARY DARKNESS, &c.

That prediction of darkness I think is a hoax,
Invented by some of those comical folks
Who always are thinking up practical jokes—
And the heat that's to follow, and leave none alive
Less than twenty, or more than about forty-five.   5
Now whether this awful prediction is true,
We shall know in some days, at the most very few.
In the meantime it seems to some folks and, to me,
That they state the doomed ages more positively
Than most men of science would venture to do,   10
And that's why I cannot believe it is true.
But whatever may come, whether darkness or light,
Though the changes on earth may the wicked affright,
There is peace for God's children who trust in His might.

128. A RAINY DAY FLITTING

Oh, the cares of a rainy day flitting!
I can scarcely find language befitting
   The state of the case,
To describe our misfortunes when quitting
   Five Dunrobin Place.   5

Now, of course, ere the lorry securing,
We had said, 'Should the rain come down pouring,
   We should wait till next day';
But a calm 'twixt the showers, most alluring,
   Made us hasten away.   10

Ere the lorry was half or a quarter
Filled with goods, there came down the rain water,
   Making everything wet;
Such a flitting day my mother's daughter
   Will not quickly forget!   15

We ourselves in a cab went off dry;
But about our wet things did we sigh,
   As I think we well might!
And we'd Puss in a bag, like to die
   With 'the nerves' in her fright!   20

In St George's Road, close to our door,
Number two hundred forty and four,
   Second close from the Cross
(When our troublesome journey was o'er),
   'Cabby' drew up his horse.   25

Then the rain ceased from falling awhile,
And the sun 'twixt the clouds seemed to smile,
   Quite amused by the fun,
Till the lorry gave up its wet pile,
   And our flitting was done.   30

129. THE VICTIM OF INTEMPERANCE

(Founded on an Incident in Real Life.)

Passed away, passed away from the earth—
  Died of starvation!
Not through negligence, sickness, or dearth;
  But through temptation.

'Twas strong drink lured him on to his death   5
  Too prematurely—
Stopped his quick pulse and feverish breath
  Swiftly and surely.

Oh! how dear to his mother was he!
  She had no other;   10
Oh! how fondly indulgent was she,
  Too tender mother!

Keeping food for him morn, noon, and night,
  Lying untasted.
Drink alone was his food and his blight—   15
  Thus his strength wasted.

Oh! what grief in his heart lay untold,
  Making life sadness;
Grief that God could have eased and consoled—
  Drink turned to madness.   20

Yet he strove to laugh sorrow away;
  Reckless and hollow
Was his mirth. When he tried to be gay,
  What gloom would follow!

But that gloom in his heart did he hide;   25
  He seemed uncaring,
While all faith and all hope he denied—
  Bold, though despairing.

Though he lived in rebellion, could he
　　Die in repentance?   30
Oh! all ye who live wisely, can ye
　　Dare to pass sentence?

By his reckless, extravagant mirth,
　　Springing from sadness;
By the waste of his talents and worth,   35
　　Pity his madness!
And oh! let not his passing from earth
　　Move you to gladness.

130. HOME MUSIC

When the busy day is over,
  And you rest at evening time;
O how sweet sounds simple music,
  Set to well-remembered rhyme.
Grander strains might prove less cheering,   5
  But a homely ballad seems
Sweet and simple, and endearing,
  Calling back life's happiest dreams.

When the singer is a mother
  With her children list'ning round;   10
When the sister and the brother
  Blend their tones in tuneful sound,
While the husband and the father
  Sits to listen and admire;
Of all concerts, I would rather   15
  Hear that sweet domestic choir.

We may praise the glorious voices
  Of the geniuses of song,
Whose celestial art rejoices
  Many and many a wond'ring throng;   20
But the songs that go the nearest
  To our hearts are always those
Sung by friends we hold the dearest,
  Friends our fireside circle knows.

131. NEW YEAR'S MUSINGS

The years roll on for ever,
    How fast they come and go!
Like waves on Time's long river
    That doth for ever flow
Right onward to the boundless sea   5
Of an unknown eternity.

They bear us past our childhood,
    And past youth's sunny shore.
They bear away our dear ones,
    And bring them back no more.   10
New friends, new scenes, they bring us to;
But, ah! the past they ne'er renew.

We cannot be forgetful
    Of all we leave behind,
Yet not with thoughts regretful   15
    Should they be called to mind.
Since we can ne'er turn back again,
Why should we grieve our souls in vain?

When we are looking onward,
    We look towards the light;   20
The river floweth sunward,
    But steer your bark aright.
How can you reach the cloudless clime
If shipwrecked on the stream of Time?

It is a treach'rous river;   25
    Then ever watch and pray,
Lest by some hidden whirlpool
    You should be drawn away—
Drawn down into eternal night,
And never reach the land of light.   30

Another wave has passed us,
    Another wave draws near;
What angels call a moment
    Is unto us a year.
Heaven guide us safely to that shore,   35
Where happy souls count years no more.

132. MIRREN'S AUTOBIOGRAPHY

I was born the sixteenth afternoon of September,
In a year that's too long past for me to remember;
And what does it signify *where* I was born?
It might have been under some wild hedgerow thorn,
Or perhaps in a palace, perhaps in a cot,   5
Or among the small fairies, in some unknown grot,
In England, Wales, Ireland, or land of the Scot,
France, Germany, Russia, or Turkey; but what
Does it matter about the particular spot?
I was born in some one of these places, if not   10
In another; and that's about all I have got
To say of that highly blest part of the earth
Distinguished by little Miss Marion's birth.
I look back to the days that rolled o'er my young brow,
When the sun brighter shone than it ever shines now;   15
When my strength and activity won me the name
'Little Sturdyboots,' long ere my first trouble came.
Oft the north wind in summer-time piercingly blows,
And it blights ere its blooming some half-opened rose.
So the cold breath of sickness prevented my prime,   20
And caused me to fade ere my blossoming time.
The weakness too surely increased day by day,
Till no more I could join my companions at play,
And I'd wistfully watch them while sitting alone,
And build for my solace a world of my own,   25
Filled with bright airy castles, while Hope whispered long
Of the grand things I'd do when I grew well and strong.
But alas! though long hoped for, that time never came,
And I grew up to womanhood feeble and lame.
Oh! womanhood, sweet is thy blossoming time,   30
Of a whole life the summer, the joy, and the prime.
But thou camest to me without sunshine or bloom,
Thou camest like winter with coldness and gloom,
No more from the threshold of home I could stray
To feel the warm sun on a bright summer day;   35
Thou did'st bring to my frail limbs a heavier chain,
And for years on my couch I was doomed to remain.
Oh! 'twas sad through the first years of youth thus to
    languish
And how bitter and sore was my physical anguish!

And helpless and drear loomed the future before me,   40
While darker and darker the cloud lowered o'er me;
But though gloom reigned around, *inner light* rose to cheer
   me,
For the Presence of God ne'er had seemed half so near me.
And to feel that blest Presence was sweeter than health,
It was brighter than sunshine, and better than wealth;   45
It was joy amid sorrow, and peace amid pain
Perfected; and never before or again
Have I felt thus the power of our Father to cheer
The soul 'mid the worst that can trouble it here.
For still as pain lessened, and health would improve,   50
That gladdening Presence would farther remove.
'Twill return, I doubt not, if I need it again,
But 'twould make earth too bright were it now to remain.
Now no more I'm bedridden, or pain-racked, or ill,
Yet, too feeble to walk, I'm a prisoner still.   55
As the wounded in battle are borne from the plain
Inactive to languish, while comrades are slain,
So am I laid aside from the battle of life,
While stronger ones struggle and fall in the strife.
But my life now is peaceful, and little of pain   60
Comes to ruffle its calmness, or make me complain;
And the worst glooms that darken its sunshine I find
When the sorrows of others o'ershadow my mind.
Like a flower confined to its stem, I have stayed
Long confined to my home; like a flower I fade;   65
And as withered flowers crumble to dust where they lay,
And the wind passes over and sweeps them away,
So I wither, and so, soon, my memory must
Pass away, when my form shall lie mould'ring in dust.

133. LEAP YEAR VALENTINES

It's Leap Year, so I think I'll jump
   At somebody to marry;
I'll pop the question, plain and plump,
   To that conceited Harry.

I'll write it in a valentine—   5
   Yes, that's the way to do it;
I'll say 'Dear Hal, will you be mine,
   And you shall never rue it.

I'll make you happy if I can;
   Believe my declaration,   10
There really is no other man
   I'd wed in all creation!'

Now such a tender billet-deux
   Should leave no chance of choosing;
He would be less than human who   15
   Could think about refusing.

But still I may as well make sure,
   And if I fail with Harry,
I'll try my luck with Thomas Mure,
   He's good enough to marry.   20

Yet Thomas might refuse me, too;
   Then Cadwallader Coffer
Can certainly be trusted to
   Accept a lady's offer.

I'm sure of one among the three,   25
   I'll write to all together;
And if they all accept, you see,
   I have my choice of either!

Each maiden who for marriage pines
   Should act on this suggestion,   30
In half-a-dozen valentines
   Let Cupid pop the question!

134. THE RESURRECTION OF THE FLOWERS

Come out of your graves, O ye slumbering flowers,
    For the Winter of Death is o'er,
And the advent of Spring, with her wondrous powers,
    Recalls you to life once more.

Ye have died at the North wind's chilling breath,   5
    And your petals strewed the ground;
Ye have slept by the icy hand of Death
    In a long oblivion bound.

Ye seemed as if ye had never bloomed,
    Or never would bloom again,   10
For all your beauty the worms consumed
    And let not a leaf remain.

But now, with the coming of the Spring,
    Comes your resurrection day;
Ye are slowly and surely awakening   15
    For the festival of May.

As yet, though the hedges are not green,
    And drear are the leafless bowers,
Your tiniest, earliest buds are seen,
    And they'll soon be leaves and flowers.   20

As you have died, so must we die
    When our winter time shall come,
And through the days of darkness lie
    In a cold and silent home.

But, as you revive and bloom again   25
    In the sunshine of the Spring,
So we hope to burst Death's icy chain
    At the coming of our King.

Then shall sorrow pass from earth away,
    And sweet Eden be restored;   30
And immortal flowers shall bloom for aye,
    In the garden of the Lord.

135. AN EVENING SONG

Day is o'er. Softly the flowers
   Close their eyes, falling asleep.
Slumber reigns through all their bowers,
   Still a few night flow'rets peep
   At the stars, which nightly keep   5
Watch above, in yonder skies.
   And the moonbeam on the deep
   Seems across the waves to sweep
Like a fairy bridge that lies
'Twixt this world and Paradise.   10

Hour of dreams, bringing again
   All the past back to my view;
Hopes of joy, mem'ries of pain,
   Your soft spell still can renew.
   Haunting dreams! wherefore do you   15
Throng my soul at evening's hour?
   Far away all the day through,
   Yet at eve falling like dew
On my soul, that, like a flower,
Thirsts for your refreshing power.   20

136. TOILING UPWARDS

O, sorrowful soul, art thou weary
    Of this life with its trial and care?
Does thy way seem too dismal and dreary,
    And thy burden too heavy to bear?
Cherish hope that the way may grow brighter,   5
    And have faith in the wisdom and love
That appointeth thee burdens no lighter
    While thou strivest for mansions above.
There are thorns in the rough part of duty,
    But it leads to the garden of God;   10
And the path has its own rugged beauty,
    Looking back on the way thou hast trod.
None of those who that path have ascended
    Ever counted their labour as lost;
Growing strong by the way that they wended,   15
    They have almost forgotten the cost.
And oh, at the end, when the portal
    Of glory is opened for thee,
When thou viewest the pleasures immortal
    Where the faithful rewarded shall be,   20
Thou wilt know why thou now art enduring
    So much pain in thy rugged ascent,
And perceiving what thou art securing,
    Then will rest from thy labours content.

137. HAPPY DREAMING

Oh, Lady Fortune, smile on me,
  And do not tread me down;
I've borne your coldness patiently,
  And smiling met your frown.

I've dreamed the dream of girls and boys   5
  Who airy castles build,
And furnish them with future joys
  And fancies unfulfilled.

In some, such dreams are seeds of fate
  That yet shall upward spring,   10
And show to those who trust and wait
  A glorious blossoming.

Oh, never was the dream in vain
  That waked a poet's lyre;
Or, 'mid the throes of earth-born pain,   15
  Could heavenly thoughts inspire!

And never did that hope betray
  Which taught the soul to sing
The glories of a happier day
  Than Time shall ever bring!   20

And if we dream of joys below
  That ne'er can be our own,
In dreaming that they may be so
  Their sweetest joy is known.

So I will dream and hope and toil,   25
  Whate'er my lot may be;
Grim disappointment cannot spoil
  Sweet hope's felicity.

And still, though Fortune coldly seems
  Ambition to deny,   30
I have a wealth of golden dreams
  That kingdoms could not buy.

Then, Oh, my soul! lift up thy voice
   In glad and hopeful song,
While in thy dreams thou can'st rejoice   35
   All joy to thee belongs.

138. TO THE GREAT INVENTOR

Respected Mr Edison,
　　Wherever you may be,
I wonder if you'll condescend
　　To take a hint from me.

They say you are inventing things　　　　　5
　　From morning until night—
Queer microphones, and megaphones,
　　And that electric light.

One thing you've not invented yet
　　Which would surpass the rest,　　　　　10
And cause you to be canonised,
　　As more than ten times blest.

We want a kind of telephone
　　That needs no string or wire,
And can be kept in every house　　　　　15
　　For use when we require

To speak to people miles away,
　　Or out upon the sea,
Or in balloons, or where'er
　　A living soul can be—　　　　　20

A kind of spirit telegraph.
　　I leave you to decide
The way to make it, and find out
　　How it should be applied.

And when you've made it, use it first　　　　25
　　To call across the sea,
And tell me that you'll send one by
　　The next balloon to me.

Pray let me have the first you make,
　　Then I shall be contented;　　　　　30
And to myself the credit take
　　Of getting it invented.

139. SONG

In the morning sunlight
　All the world is gay,
Merry hope awaking
　With the op'ning day.
But sweet hope, grown weary,   5
　Ends her singing soon;
Toil seems hard and dreary
　In the heat of noon.

Afterwards the shadows
　Gather round us fast,   10
Over towns and meadows
　Evening falls at last.
With the dewy even
　Comes the time of rest,
And the gates of heaven   15
　Open in the west.

For the sunset splendour
　Comes before the night,
Like a deathbed vision
　Of the world of light.   20
O, my Father, grant me
　Such a dream sublime;
Let life's dull day end in
　'Light at evening time.'

140. THE SCOTTISH EMIGRANT

They meet, they love, they wed;
  And now life's cares begin.
He toils for daily bread,
  But bread he scarce can win.
Soon comes a little child   5
  Their poverty to share;
Her eyes, so sweet and mild,
  See love, but see not care.
Yet care is in the home,
  The wolf is at the door;   10
Thence must the husband roam,
  Such sorrows have the poor!
They part with many fears,
  Though hope shines bright above
And smiling on their tears,   15
  The baby coos of love.
Across the stormy sea,
  Ten thousand miles away,
The lonely man must be
  Prepared for toil or fray: 20
Watchful both day and night,
  For many a savage foe
Is lurking out of sight,
  To aim a treach'rous blow.
At last in savage hands   25
  He finds himself a prey,
And through their pathless lands
  They lead him far away.
He sees no white man's face
  While days and weeks roll on,   30
He hears no white man's voice—
  One long, dull year is gone;
And still the months roll by,
  And no one comes to save:
Then must he live and die   35
  'Mong savages a slave?
No! Who would prize mere breath
  If he may not be free?
Better the risk of death
  Than long captivity.   40

He takes the chance of flight—
   Escaping from his foes.
But where are those he loved,
   For whom he crossed the waves?
Have they forgetful proved,   45
   Or are they in their graves?
There's One who knoweth all,
   And time the truth will tell;
Whatever may befall,
   God doeth all things well.   50
Commit to Him your care,
   And trust the mighty Mind
That ruleth everywhere
   The lives of all mankind.

141. THE EAST COAST FISHERMEN

Though there's sorrow on the sea,
  Though there's mourning on the shore,
There are some from care set free
  Who shall sorrow nevermore;
Now they slumber peacefully,   5
  All their toils and trials o'er.

You on whom affliction's rod
  Falls so heavily to-day,
Question not the love of God
  Who has called your friends away;   10
'Neath the waves, as 'neath the sod,
  Just as calmly slumber they.

All must yield at last to death.
  Would you rather die alone
Or while death enfranchiseth   15
  Souls of friends to join your own?
Happy band that entereth
  Hand in hand the world unknown!

Mourners, weeping on the shore,
  You can soothe each other's tears;   20
Grief so shared is soonest o'er—
  Sympathy sustains and cheers.
You will love each other more
  From this time through after years.

Though to you the ceaseless surge   25
  Of the waves along the shore
Only seems a dreary dirge
  For the friends you see no more,
Does it not your spirits urge
  To new hopes scarce felt before?   30

Does not Heaven seem more dear
  With so many loved ones there?
Surely its bright scenes appear
  Nearer now than once they were,
E'en while falls the mourner's tear   35
  Does not hope rebuke despair!

Though bereavements rend the heart,
   Love is neither lost nor vain,
There is hope for those who part
   That they all shall meet again.   40
Faith gives peace 'mid sorrow's smart—
   Peace divine that conquers pain.

142. THE FLOWER SERMON

Oh, shall I read the Word of God
   This sunny Sabbath day?
Or gaze upon the works of God,
   That still more plainly say—
How great the skill that made them all,
   How exquisite the powers   5
That gave such glowing life and grace
   To these sweet summer flowers?

Preach to me, Oh ye roses!
   Your lovely looks can preach
With mute, resistless logic   10
   More eloquent than speech.
Tell of the hand that made you—
   That same that spread the skies,
And decked the earth with beauty
   To cheer His children's eyes.   15

Tell of the One who giveth
   The sunshine and the rain;
Who loveth all that liveth,
   And doth all life sustain.
None can dispute your teaching   20
   Or its sweet truth disprove;
The text of all your preaching
   Saith only 'God is love.'

143. BEATITUDES

Blest be the tongue that speaks no ill,
    Whose words are always true,
That keeps the 'law of kindness' still,
    Whatever others do.

Blest be the ears that will not hear   5
    Detraction's envious tale;
'Tis only through the list'ning ear
    That falsehood can prevail.

Blest be the heart that knows no guile,
    That feels no wish unkind,   10
Forgetting provocation, while
    Good deeds are kept in mind.

Blest be the hands that toil to aid
    The great world's ceaseless need—
The hands that never are afraid   15
    To do a kindly deed.

Blest be the thoughtful brain that schemes
    A beautiful ideal;
Mankind grows great through noble dreams,
    And time will make them real.   20

Do good in thought. Some future day
    'Twill ripen into speech;
And words are seeds that grow to deeds,
    None know how far they reach.

Like thistle-down upon the breeze,   25
    Swift scattered here and there,
So words will travel far, and these
    A fruitful harvest bear.

Where goodness dwells in heart and mind
    Both words and deeds will be   30
Like cords that closer draw mankind
    In peace and charity.

144. THE POINTSMAN

AN EVERYDAY STORY

The pointsman stood at the crossing
  For eighteen hours in the day,
Watching the trains fly past him,
  And turning the points each way.

He was blithe, alert, and watchful   5
  The first twelve hours of the day.
The last six hours he grew drowsy,
  And so would you, I should say.

But the drowsiness creeping o'er him
  He strove with and kept at bay,   10
Yet shapes came flitting before him
  From Dreamland, not far away.

For eighteen hours, with precision,
  He was turning the points that day,
And then came a dread collision,   15
  For the pointsman mistook the way.

O what a scene of terror,
  What terrible forms of pain!
All through a moment's error
  Of an overwearied brain.   20

Why was that brain o'er-wearied?
  Why? Let his masters say;
Why was the pointsman working
  For eighteen hours that day?

Most people are selfish and foolish,   25
  And so such a system thrives;
Too selfish to care for the pointsman,
  Too foolish to think of their lives.

And so we see death and disaster,
   With anguish, affliction, and tears,   30
And want is the poor man's master,
   And oppression goes on for years.

They will keep to their heartless system,
   And many such scenes will cause,
As long as the law permits them;   35
   How long shall we bear such laws?

145. THE LIGHT-GLINT ON LOCH LOMOND

(Lines suggested by the article with this title in the *Helensburgh Times* on 3 December.)

The boatman's son crossed o'er the loch,
   There seemed no cause for dread.
Next morn they found his boat adrift,
   And knew that he was dead.

They dragged the loch, they searched the strand,   5
   And islands here and there,
To bring his body to the land,
   And ease his father's care.

At last all ceased the search save one,
   He said, 'I'll never give o'er   10
Till I have found my darling son
   And buried him on shore.

But O, to find my bonnie bairn,
   I cannot tell the place,
Wilt thou not help me, O my God,   15
   In thy unstinted grace!'

Up from his aching heart the prayer
   Had scarcely time to rise,
When, startlingly, an answer rare
   Descended from the skies.   20

A light that was not of this world,
   Nor yet of sun or star;
A glimmer of celestial light
   Flashed downward from afar.

It stood a moment on the wave,   25
   Above the wat'ry bier,
And to the mourner seemed to say,
   Behold, thy son lies here.

He knew it came from God's own hand,
　　His pious heart believed,   30
Taught by pure faith to understand
　　The answer he received.

He marked the spot. He came again
　　And found his lost one there:
And found the blessings that remain,   35
　　After an answered prayer.

146. A WOMAN'S PLEA

To do our duty is our right,
    A right we'll never yield,
For duty done is virtue's might
    And honour's shining shield.
To vote for all that's right and just,   5
    To vote down all that's wrong;
These are our rights. For these we must
    Cry out in speech and song.

To be a safeguard to the weak,
    To curb the pride of power,   10
To give just honour to the meek,
    And poverty to dower;
These are the aims of righteous laws;
    But if the laws are wrong
Our votes must right them. That's our cause,   15
    Our work, our prayer, our song.

Though oft oppressed, our steadfast hearts
    Will never be afraid,
The strength a righteous cause imparts
    Will keep us undismayed.   20
For O! the world is full of need,
    The world is full of wrong;
For freedom to do good we plead
    With pen, and speech, and song.

147. ROBERT BURNS

While others will tell of thy triumphs,
 Thy genius, and thy fame,
I can only think of thy sorrows
 Whene'er I hear thy name.

I think of the heart of a poet   5
 Always unfit to bear
Sad poverty's heavy burden
 Of sordid, ceaseless care.

Poor Burns! how thy sensitive nature
 Fretted beneath the strain   10
Of want and debt and dependence,
 A threefold, galling chain.

It crushed the strength of thy spirit
 With more than Arctic cold,
It froze thy heart into stillness   15
 Ere forty winters old.

Ah! the price of thy meanest statue
 Might then have changed thy fate;
Dost thou see the wealth that is lavished
 Over thy grave, too late?   20

Dost thou witness how oft the poet
 Is deemed of little worth
Till the voice of the minstrel is silent,
 And the spirit passed from earth?

Nay, methinks thou hast brighter visions   25
 Than the passing shades of Time;
Thou seest the things eternal
 The realities sublime.

Where thou art they think not of sorrow,
 Such thoughts have passed away,   30
As the shadows of morning twilight
 Flee at the dawn of day!

148. SHIPWRECKED

I went forth to sea in a fragile bark,
   I toiled against wind and wave;
I am shipwrecked now on the ocean dark,
   That is like to be my grave.

Like seaweed, tossed by the restless tide,   5
   And hopelessly drifting on,
So I am adrift on the waters wide,
   All hope of deliverance gone.

O, for the glorious light of day!
   But the night frowns dark o'erhead,   10
And not one star doth its cheering ray
   On the storm-tossed struggler shed.

O, for a rock on some desert shore,
   Where this buffeting might cease,
And, my weary strife with the tempest o'er,   15
   I could fall asleep in peace.

149. FAR AWAY IN THE WEST

Far away in the west,
　　Far beyond the waves,
Far from all he loved best,
　　In a field of graves
On a foreign shore   5
　　He is laid to rest—
He'll come home no more
　　From the far, far west.

Far away to the west,
　　Ah, how many roam,   10
Far away, far away,
　　Far from friends and home!
Tho' 'tis wealth they seek,
　　Oft 'tis woe they find,
And the hearts are weak   15
　　That they leave behind.

If they come from the west
　　To their own again,
Like a stab to the breast
　　Is the deadly pain.   20
Older grown and changed,
　　To return and find
All the love estranged
　　That they left behind.

There are hearts that are true,   25
　　There are faithful eyes,
That keep watch long years thro'
　　Toward the western skies,
With expectant gaze,
　　Looking o'er the wave;   30
But their loved one stays
　　In his far-off grave.

150. THE STAR OF BETHLEHEM

Suggested by the flower of that name.

Sweet white starlike little flower,
Thou canst preach with subtle power;
Thy sweet name recalls the time
When from Midian's sultry clime
Wise men brought their offering   5
To Judea's new-born King.
Like an angel guiding them
Shone the star of Bethlehem.

Once again that star will shine,
Heralding the King divine.   10
Kings and great men will be blind
Till it bursts o'er all mankind;
But the poor and lonely gaze
Heavenward, watching for its rays.
Quickly may'st thou dawn for them,   15
Glorious star of Bethlehem!

O to see earth's troubles cease!
O to greet the Prince of Peace
When upon His shining throne
He descends to claim His own,   20
With unnumbered saints of light,
Quite eclipsing day and night!
In the new Jerusalem
Shines the Star of Bethlehem!

151. THE HIGHLAND LAIRD'S SONG

I have a very large estate,
  All for me, all for me;
My cares are small, my wealth is great,
  All for me, all for me.
Once other people shared my land,   5
And rented holdings far from grand;
But I have made them understand
  It's all for me, all for me.

The common people I do not
  Like to see, like to see;   10
A vulgar village is a blot
  On propertie, propertie.
Although they say their homes are dear,
I'll have no vulgar peasants here;
I'll keep my land for sheep and deer,   15
  All for me, all for me.

The dirty creatures now complain,
  Blaming me, blaming me;
They say, 'We're anxious to remain,
  Let us be, let us be.'   20
I'll harass them by night and day
Until I drive them all away,
Upon my land not one shall stay,
  It's all for me, all for me.

152. NEARER TO THEE

When sunshine smiles serene
   Over our way,
When not a cloud is seen,
   But all seems gay;
When the glad soul should raise   5
Each day new songs of praise,
Too oft, O Lord, it strays
   From Thee away.

Glad hearts forget their need
   Even of Thee,   10
Though from Thy hand indeed
   Their joys must be.
To purge away our dross
Thou sendest grief and loss,
Raising us by the cross   15
   Nearer to Thee.

Why should I be afraid
   Though I should see
Sunshine exchanged for shade
   Dark'ning o'er me?   20
Lord, through the darkest days
Teach me to sing Thy praise,
Send me in Thine own ways
   Nearer to Thee.

153. THE CHRISTMAS PARTY

I gathered a Christmas party
　Of the ghosts of a bygone day—
The friends, aunts, uncles, and cousins
　Who have passed from the earth away.

How I welcomed their well-known faces,   5
　And how glad did our meeting seem!
We were many, and well could be merry,
　But 'twas only the mirth of a dream.

And when I awoke they vanished
　As I opened my eyes to the light,   10
For the beams of the morning banished
　The spirits that came in the night.

I am left with remembrance only
　Of those dear ones, so kind and true;
They have left me, alas, how lonely!   15
　Now my friendships are cold and few.

Ah, when we shall meet in heaven
　Now glad will our gathering be!
And the ties that have long been riven
　Will be bound for eternity.   20

154. NEW-YEAR THOUGHTS

Pass away, O, years!
Let the flight of time be faster, faster,
   Put an end to tears,
Haste the longed-for coming of the Master!
   Long doth He delay,   5
And the time of waiting is so dreary!
   Time, fly fast away,
Mother Earth is growing old and weary.
   After all her grief,
All her centuries of guilt and sorrow,   10
   Let the blest relief
Come at last, the never-ending morrow.
   Lo, our longing eyes
Fail with watching till our Lord returneth,
   Yet, as time still flies,   15
Still the light of hope more brightly burneth.
   Will he come this year?
Will our souls with joyous welcome greet Him?
   When He shall appear
Shall we not be 'unprepared to meet Him!'   20
   O, my soul, be sure
That thou buildest on the Rock Foundation,
   There to rest secure,
'Mid dissolving worlds, in His salvation;
   For the Lord, our Rock   25
Will not fail when earth is rent asunder.
   Safe amid the shock
Will His own be kept in joy and wonder.

155. THE DEATH OF DOUGLAS

You've heard the Douglas singing
  Of Annie sweet and fair,
His Annie's praises ringing
  Wi' love beyond compare—
  Wi' love beyond compare,   5
For fond and true was he,
  And he trusted Annie Laurie
Wherever he might be.

The Douglas went to battle
  Across the stormy wave;   10
He sought for wealth and glory,
  He found a foreign grave—
  He found a foreign grave,
And Annie, where was she?
  Oh, her heart was not wi' Douglas   15
When he lay doon to dee.

Afar frae Annie Laurie,
  He thought o' her each day;
For her, by night an' mornin',
  He ne'er forgot to pray—   20
  He ne'er forgot to pray,
A faithful heart had he,
  An' his prayer was still for Annie
When he lay doon to dee.

The love o' Annie Laurie   25
Was love that couldna' hide;
Forgetful o' the absent
  She soon became a bride—
  She soon became a bride,
An' Douglas o'er the sea;   30
  An' he dreamed not she was faithless
When he lay doon to dee.

156. A DREAM OF REST

At eve, when the light has faded
   Out of the sunset sky,
And the night's dim curtain shaded
   The landscape far and nigh;
When, instead of the glowing sunlight,   5
   The beams of moon and star
Shine with a pale, cold radiance
   Seen dimly from afar;
I call not the darkness dreary,
   I think not the daylight best;   10
For sweet to the heart that's weary
   Are the shadowy hours of rest.

After fair childhood's springtime,
   After youth's summer hours,
After life's golden autumn   15
   With fruits instead of flowers;
After the cloudy winter,
   With its frosts and with its snows,
Before the eternal springtime
   Comes death with its deep repose.   20
After earth's sorrow and sinning
   That every soul oppressed,
Ere the better life's beginning,
   Is it not good to rest?

Sometimes my eyes grow weary   25
   As if dazzled by the light,
Sometimes the day seems dreary,
   And I long for the quiet night;
For the sleep that knows no dreaming,
   And the shades no morn shall break,   30
Till the morn of heav'n is beaming,
   And the rested dead awake!
Then no more will the dead be dreary,
   Or a dreamless sleep seem best;
We shall never again grow weary   35
   After that long, long rest.

157. ON THE FRANCHISE DEMONSTRATION
OF THE 6TH INST

Women of Glasgow,
   What do you mean?
Why were you idle
   All through such a scene?

Where were your banners?   5
   Where were your trades?
Have women no need
   Of political aids?

Much work for small wages,
   Great wrongs, which few note,   10
Are yours, till you right things
   By getting the vote.

Now, when are you going
   To make such a show
For feminine franchise,   15
   I'm anxious to know?

Lay sewing and cooking
   Aside for one day;
Assemble by thousands
   In splendid array.   20

I don't mean in dresses
   Of costly expense;
I mean in the splendour
   Of bright common-sense.

Prove your right to the vote   25
   By the thousands who crave it;
And with steady persistence—
   To ask is to have it.

158. A BIRTHDAY MEDITATION

How many once-loved friends are gone
   Unto the land of light,
Where I, perchance, may follow soon,
   And bid this world 'Good night!'

This busy world! It seems to me   5
   That here I have no place,
No courage for the battlefield,
   No strength to run the race.

This world is all a battlefield,
   Where heroes win the day;   10
And where the weak must die, or yield,
   And wounded pine away.

This world is like a swift run race,
   The swiftest gains the prize;
And he who runs with feeble pace   15
   In vain the issue tries.

This world is like a training school,
   Hard lessons, little play;
With many a strict, unvaried rule,
   And chastisements each day.   20

And I am like a weary child
   Wishing my schooldays o'er,
With all life's lessons learned, and I
   Set free for evermore.

159. ANSWER TO M. A. SMITH

Dear M. A. Smith,
Who are you joking with,
And what about?
I've taken endless trouble to find out.
Would you wish women-folks to stay at home,   5
And never roam;
Ever to church, or just a friend to see,
And take a cup of tea?
Iron machines, we know, need rest for oiling,
Can wives be always toiling?   10
E'en hard-worked wives contrive some time or other
To spend a day with mother.
What I propose is, that, instead of going
To mother, you'll be showing
Your interest in laws, as well as labours,   15
Both for yourselves and neighbours.
And when we get the vote,
I wish you all to note
It takes no longer to vote members in
To Parliament than School Boards. Did you win   20
The School Board vote for nothing? No; you use it,
And none say you abuse it.
Your votes will have a different effect
To votes of fools and drunkards, I expect.
We women need to use our strength of mind—   25
Strong-minded men we very seldom find;
And feeble-minded voting is the cause
Of all unrighteous laws.
You heard of that poor outcast lately found
Dead on the open ground?—   30
A little child, homeless, unaided. Note
The cruel wrong. Each widowed mother's vote
Would tend to change the laws which now we see
Suffering such things to be.
Pure principles and tenderness of heart   35
Should in our laws have part.
I say, 'tis woman's right to make this so.
And who can answer, No?

160. SONNET—TO MARY CROSS

Grief will not last forever;
   Time brings a cure for every pain,
   And wounded hearts grow strong again.
'Twere useless to endeavour
To conquer grief. You never   5
   Could silence thought; you'd strive in vain
   The sick heart's aching to restrain.

You could not check the river;
   But drought can make the stream run dry,
   And sorrow's fountain, by-and-by   10
Will be exhausted of its tears.
   All earthly pain must sometime cease,
   If not in life, death bringeth peace
To last through God's eternal years.

161. COFFINING THE PAUPER

(Suggested by an incident recently reported in the *Weekly Mail*.)

A worn and weary woman
  Lay on a poorhouse bed;
She knew that she was dying,
  She wished that she was dead.

For her years had all been dreary,   5
  And her cares a mighty throng,
And her heart had grown a-weary
  That she should have lived so long.

'Let me die,' she whispered softly,
  In a slow and silent prayer;   10
'Take me from earth's gloomy shadows,
  'Twill be brighter "over there."'

But she knew not that the angels
  Watched and waited at her side,
Till she saw their glorious faces   15
  When they took her, as she died.

And as Lazarus was carried
  From a beggar's grave away,
So the pauper woman's spirit
  Rose with angel hosts that day.   20

Never more to see a shadow,
  Never more to know a care;
Far away from all earth's sorrows,
  She is happy 'over there.'

As her wan and wasted body   25
  Lay unmourned upon its bier,
Careless strangers washed it roughly,
  Not a single friend came near.*

---

* Prov. xix, 4-7

For when care her strength had wasted,
  When in daily need of aid,   30
Every earthly friend had failed her—
  To their charge it will be laid.

As friends grudged what would have fed her,
  Grudging 'Guardians' had to feed;
Even now, with sore begrudging,   35
  They supply her latest need.

See the scanty poorhouse coffin,
  For her wasted frame too small;
She is crushed and smashed to fit it!
  Soon the grave will cover all.   40

Yet the Lord looked down from Heaven,
  Though they thought He would not see;
And He said, 'As thus they did to her,
  They did it unto Me!'

Not of kings, or queens, or princes,   45
  However great they be,
Hath Christ said, 'Your deeds towards them
  I count as done to Me.'

But He said this of the stranger,†
  Of the ragged, starving poor,   50
Of the sick and lonely pris'ner,
  Of the beggar at your door.

For Christ scorns the pride of riches,
  And the rank by worldlings prized;
And He holds the nearest to Him   55
  Those whom this world hath despised.

---

† Matt. xxv, 42-45

Tremble for your pride, ye scorners,
  Guilt lies darkly at your door;
And 'Rejoice in tribulation'
  Ye who suffer with the poor.   60

162. A SHOWER OF FALLING STARS

I wakened in the silent night,
   And through my window bars
I gazed upon a glorious sight—
   A shower of falling stars.

They fell as from the fig-tree boughs,   5
   When shaken by a mighty breeze,
The unripe figs snap off and fall
   Untimely from the trees.

So from one centre in the sky,
   As from a single tree,   ·   10
Did shooting stars in thousands fly—
   A wondrous sight to see.

'Is this,' I cried, 'the awful sign*
   That Jesus Christ hath given
To show when draweth near the time   15
   Of His return from heaven?'

'Tis said that in the ancient days
   Such scenes as this were all unknown;
But now their frequency displays
   A sign that all should own.   20

Soon may the Lord return again
   His Kingdom to restore—
That sin, and grief, and death, and pain
   May trouble earth no more.

---

* Matt. xxiv, 29,30; Rev. vi, 13

163. PATIENCE

(Suggested by the words that a child used to explain the meaning of
'Patience.')

'Bide a wee and dinna weary'—
   Sweetly sound those words to me.
Let your spirit aye be cheery,
   Thinking of the joys to be.
'Bide a wee and dinna weary,'   5
   Though the waiting time be long;
Heaven's days are never dreary,
   Never ends its joyous song.

Count earth's troubles 'light afflictions',
   Since they are but for a day;   10
They may gain you benedictions
   That will never pass away.*
Having hope so full of glory,
   Wherefore is your soul cast down?
For the joy that's set before ye   15
   Bear the cross and win the crown.

Never let your thoughts be dreary—
   Think of what's laid up for thee;†
Oh, be sure you 'dinna weary'
   Though you have to 'bide a wee'.   20
With each grief this hope is blended,
   Taking half its pain away—
Soon our sorrows will be ended
   And our joys endure for aye.

---

* 2 Cor. iv, 17
† 2 Tim. iv, 8

164. THE SCOTTISH MARSEILLAISE

Ye sons of Scotland, rise in union,
  To set your native mountains free;
For wealth and greed, in base communion,
  Enslave the land from sea to sea.
From lands that were their sires' possession,   5
  Behold, your neighbours are exiled;
Submission strengthens harsh oppression—
  Shall Scotland be a forest wild?
    Brave sons of Scotland, rise!
      Arise, and not in vain;   10
      Drive out the sportsmen and their deer,
      And claim your hills again!

Think how your brethren and their children
  Are driven to a foreign shore;
Now drive out those who dispossessed them,   15
  Recall them to their hills once more!
The price of land is fairly given
  By paying twenty years of rent,
Yet many now from Scotland driven
  Would pay thrice o'er and be content.   20
    Arise, ye Scots, arise!
      Insist on Nature's plan,
      Drive out the sportsmen and their deer,
      God gave the land to *man*.

'Give back the land,' cries Alexander,*   25
  Ah! no; *'tis given* by God's own hand;
Then let your battle cry be even grander—
  Not *'give.'* 'Tis yours; *'take'* back the land!
When sire and son have given rental
  For holdings lairds now choose to clear.   30
This wrong is more than sentimental,
  'Tis plunder without shame or fear.
    Arise, ye Scots, arise!
      Contend for Nature's plan,
      Drive out the sportsmen and their deer,   35
      God gave the land to man.

---

* Alexander Murdoch, in the *Weekly Mail*, Oct. 17, 1885.

165. WANTED

Wanted, quickly, a host of dry nurses,
To take entire charge and control
Of those men whom the drink traffic curses,
 And rescue them, body and soul.

To guard them from being run over,   5
 Or plundered upon the wayside,
Or getting mixed up in a murder,
 Or dropping themselves in the Clyde.

To protect them from evil companions,
 Past the public-house safely to steer;   10
To receive and to lay out their wages
 Upon all things save whisky and beer.

For, you know, when the wife has the money,
 The poor drunkard can take it by force;
But it would not appear quite so funny   15
 To attack the dry nurse, as of course

She would give him in charge to the 'pollis,'
And would make him repent of his strife;
For a man has to smart for such follies
 When the victim is not his own wife.   20

Wanted also, some wise legislation
 That will give the dry nurses control,
Thus to act for the drunkard's salvation,
 And the good of mankind on the whole.

It is mournful to see the position   25
 Of those mindless, incapable elves,
As they helplessly drift to perdition,
 No one caring, not even themselves.

Alas! the poor, overgrown babies!
 We must guard them as well as we can;   30
And, perhaps, after years of dry-nursing,
 Everyone may at last be a man.

166. ACROSTIC SONNET—ELIZABETH MOUAT

Enduring bravely, with unshaken mind,
Lonely, and lost upon the storm-tossed waves,
In their dark gulfs beholding yawning graves,
Zionward turn her thoughts, nor fail to find
'An anchor of the soul' that wave or wind   5
By no means can disturb. The tempest raves
Even more wildly still; but He who saves
Those who believe and pray, hath now inclined
His gracious ear to his lone servant's cry.
Many will say that angels took the helm;   10
Or how through such a sea reach such a shore?
Until the last the sea raged furiously;
And when it threatened most to overwhelm
Then she was saved—her fears and perils o'er.

167. ON THE DEATH OF A FAVOURITE PET
THAT HAD EVERY VIRTUE AND NO FAULT

Her voice when she was dying
   I never shall forget;
The echo of her crying
   In my heart lingers yet.

That voice was changed completely;   5
   The music of its tone,
That sounded once so sweetly,
   Was tuned to pain alone.

Death has a tragic history;
   That such as she should die   10
Is fraught with awful mystery—
   My spirit questions, 'Why?'

There cometh no suggestion
   From all the world around—
No answer to my question;   15
   What answer can be found?

A fonder heart hath never
   By Death's cold hand been stilled;
Nor was one purer ever
   With life's warm pulses filled.   20

So loyal and so loving,
   So patient, kind, and meek,
All truest virtues proving
   For which God's grace we seek.

Oh, can that guileless spirit   25
   Have perished with the dust;
Or can a beast inherit
   The heaven in which we trust?

God loveth all His creatures;
   Methinks He never can   30
Despise in beasts the virtues
   That would be blest in man.

He who reproved the prophet
   That did unjustly smite*
The patient beast, will never   35
   Cast goodness from His sight.

When first He set the rainbow
   In the dark cloud above
He gave 'all living creatures'
   The promise of His love.†   40

---

* Num. xxii, 32
† Gen. ix, 12, 15, 16, 17

168. NOTHING NEW

(Postscript to a letter.)

'For all things there is a place and a time—
To weep and to pray, and to laugh' and to rhyme;
But 'there is nothing new under the sun'
That has not been said or has not been done.
—M. R. S.

Answer to the above.

Though truly there's nothing new under the sun
That hasn't been said or that hasn't been done,
Scribble on, from domestic economy learning
That old things are made new by *carefully turning.*

169. ROBERT BURNS

Oft it moves my indignation
   That the envious eye discerns
Nought of holy exaltation
   In the life of Robert Burns.
On his faults will many dwell,   5
His repentance few will tell.

Few of Adam's sons inherit
   Robert Burns's simplicity,
And his meekly noble spirit,
   Sorrowing submissively,   10
Willing, 'mid his grief and loss,
Openly to bear the cross.*

How the Scottish minstrel raises
   Holy hymns to God above,
And, like Hebrew David, praises   15
   All His everlasting love!
Striving to be true and just,
In the Lord he puts his trust.

Scorn of pride, and base oppressions,
   Pity for th' oppressed ones' wrongs,   20
Deep regret for all transgressions
   Breathe throughout his noble songs.
Honour to his name belongs,
Fame immortal as his songs.

Those who love the Psalms of David   25
   Should not sneer at Robert Burns;
Each has sinned, and each is savéd,
   Each to God repentant turns;
And God never hides His face
From a soul that seeks His grace.   30

---

*He submitted to open censure in the church for his irregular marriage
with Jean Armour, which her ill-advised father and minister mistakenly
declared to be illegal. Though not permitted at that time to repair the
supposed wrong by a regular marriage, he afterwards took the earliest
opportunity of doing so.

By temptation's power assailed,
    Each betrayed the guilt within;
Each his sinfulness bewailed,
    And 'God put away' his 'sin.'
Both among the saints are set,   35
Wherefore call them sinners yet?

When will envy cease from sneering?
    Fain to cast a cloud of blame
On the Bard, whose name endearing
    Well deserves a Christian's fame.   40
Yet some dare to say that he
Had not Christianity.

Some there have been in all ages
    Fain to mar a good man's praise,
Slandering the saints and sages   45
    Who denounce their evil ways.
These all faults exaggerate,
Hiding virtues which they hate.

Thus detraction's envious finger
    Points out spots upon the sun,   50
Happy on some fault to linger,
    Grieving if it findeth none.
Glad are all God's foes to say
That His flock can go astray.

Thus it is the guilt of David   55
    Still can make God's foes blaspheme
(Though by deep repentance savéd,
    Owned of God, and blessed by Him):
Hear them whispering apart,
'Guilt is after God's own heart'?   60

Thus hath Scotland's sweetest poet
    Been defamed and slandered long;
Those who love him best should show it,
    Nor permit this cruel wrong.
Suffer not reproach to rest   65
On the mem'ry of our best.

Now let Scotland's justice waken
  For the Bard whose songs she sings;
Let detraction's dust be shaken
  Off, as from an angel's wings.   70
Even God would ne'er rebuke
Any sins his saints forsook.[†]

Burns was good as any mortal
  Who had sins to be forgiven
Ere he reached the pearly portal,   75
  He was purified for heaven;
For no guile[‡] dwelt in his breast,
And no errors unconfessed.

Blest are they at whose repentance
  God hath washed away their sin—   80
Who escape the rebel's sentence,
  And to glory enter in.
God hath blessed them. Who shall say
Aught accusing such as they?[§]

[†] Ezek. xxxiii, 16
[‡] Ps. xxxii, 2
[§] Rom. xii, 23

170. A SUMMER DAY

Sweet lilacs bloom and bright laburnum trees
   Appear like golden tasseled fairy bowers,
And hawthorn fragrance scents the summer breeze,
   And bees sip honey from the flowers.
Listen! what a merry song   5
Birds are singing all day long.
'The summer day is bright,' they say,
   'The summer flowers are sweet,
Here's leafy shadow overhead,
   And green grass at your feet.'   10

Outshining Solomon like living blooms
   Those cheerful preachers—bright-winged butterflies,
But lately risen from their dark still tombs,
   Now flit in freedom through the skies.
O, how sweet must freedom be   15
After long captivity!
How fair, how bright the glorious light
   After the long, long gloom!
An image of life's dearest hope—
   New life beyond the tomb.   20

The sunny hours have passed away:
   Now comes the pleasant evening shade,
A welcome sequel to the day,
   For rest and quiet made.
'Tis sweet to rest beneath the trees   25
After the day's activities.
The summer night is starry bright,
   The moonbeam seems to be
A silver bridge to fairyland
   Across the shining sea.   30

The op'ning morn, the closing eve,
　　Resound with choral songs of praise
From birds, while mutely we receive
　　New blessings all our days.
O that men would thus rejoice.　　　　　　　　35
Praise the Lord with heart and voice.
All earth-cares leave at morn and eve,
　　Begin and end each day
With thanks to God for mercies given
　　And troubles kept away!　　　　　　　　　40

171. THE NAME OF THE LORD

By many names is God made known
To many souls that are His own,
And in each diff'rent name we see
Some symbol of divinity.

The sapphire throne above the sky,   5
We think on, naming 'God Most High,'
Who sits thereon, while Heaven rings
With homage to the 'King of kings.'

Who shall not glorify Thee, 'Lord'?
Let all that live, with one accord   10
Confess Thy greatness, and recall
That Thou art 'Maker' of us all.

Who that hath prayed will not declare
Thy praise, 'O Thou that hearest prayer'?
While all Thy gracious powers proclaim   15
'Almighty Saviour' as Thy name.

Unto the pure, their 'Shepherd,' Guide,
Who leads them safe through paths untried;
Unto the meek, the 'Prince of Peace,'
Bidding remorseful terrors cease.   20

But yet, while contrite souls draw near,
Rebellious sinners quake with fear;
The 'Lawgiver,' who will condemn
Th' 'Avenging Judge' Thou art to them.

'Tis said Thou hast a name above   25
All other names, and that is 'Love';
But, O my God! Thou seem'st to be
Most perfectly revealed to me.

By that dear name Thou deign'st to share
With common mankind everywhere,   30
That doth Thy loving care proclaim—
'Our Father' is Thy dearest name.

172. FORWARD MARCH!

There was a time when years seemed long,
   But now how short they seem!
Scarcely begun ere they are gone
   Like changes in a dream.

Shall we regret the years passed o'er,   5
   And wish, with longings vain,
That friends who cheered our hearts of yore
   Might come to us again?

Nay, forward march, and murmur not,
   Though rough the path we tread;   10
There is no sadness in our lot
   With Heaven overhead.

The pathway to that Land of Bliss
   Is free to every soul;
Then let our hearts rejoice in this,   15
   And make that land our goal.

However dark the path, 'tis brief,
   And hope should make us strong;
Waste not the hours in idle grief,
   But sing a cheering song.   20

Yes! forward march, and murmur not,
   Though rough the path we tread;
There is no sadness in our lot
   With Heaven overhead.

173. VANITY FAIR

Hard as the nether millstone
  The worldly hearts around,
Hard are their worldly faces,
  Harshly their voices sound.
Were love divine among them   5
  'Twould soften heart and tone,
'Twould soften looks and language;
  But love is all unknown.

E'en in the house of worship
  Coldly their prayers arise,   10
(Lacking love's sacred incense
  They cannot reach the skies).
No generous emotion
  Within their hearts is known:
The god of their devotion   15
  Is Self, and Self alone.

Oh, cold and heartless worldlings,
  What shall your portion be?
Your wealth wrought no thanksgiving,
  Your griefs no sympathy.   20
Your hearts' most valued treasure
  Would not be found above:
How can you gain an entrance
  Where reigns Eternal Love?

174. THE BEAUTIFUL SPRING

All that's bright and beautiful
   Comes with the beautiful spring—
Leaves and buds are opening,
   Birds are beginning to sing;

And the radiance of the skies   5
   Daily brighter beams.
Vanished are the snow and ice—
   Freely flow the streams.

The merry sunshine seems to say,
   'Now that the winter's passed away,   10
Let the reviving earth be gay,
   Rejoice in the beautiful spring!'

Now the early butterflies
   Wake from the chrysalis tomb
Clad with beauty they arise   15
   Like living flowers in bloom.

Blossoms not more bright than they
   Deck the leafy trees,
Make the grassy meadows gay,
   And scent the pleasant breeze.   20

While all the birds of every wing
   Their songs of love and gladness sing,
The woods with sweetest music ring,
   Rejoice in the beautiful spring!

175. A WISH

Earth is not home
   Nor earth-life rest:
Changes must come,
   And death's sad quest
Finds out our dearest,   5
   Beloved, and nearest,
Till the heart's forlorn as an empty nest.

Yet would I live
   If I might choose,
While life can give   10
   One hour to use
In work that's given
   To me from heaven,
For that blessed labour I wou'd not lose.

Small is my strength,   15
   Yet to complete
My task at length
   Would seem so sweet.
I only ask
   To end that task,   20
And lay my work at the Master's feet.

Then let me die,
   If such His will;
I would not sigh
   To linger still: 25
Let earth forget me;
   My hopes await me
On the heavenly Sion's eternal hill.

176. APOTHEOSIS

The work day week was over,
   The day its course had run,
They welcomed in the Sabbath
   At setting of the sun.

In those times not at midnight   5
   Did each new day begin;
The day went out at sunset,
   The morrow then came in.

For so the word was given,
   In ages past away;   10
'From even until even
   Observe your Sabbath-day.'*

The early saints of Scotland
   This word remembered long,[†]
Though now it seems unheeded,   15
   Like some forgotten song.

'This day,' said Saint Columba,
   'This seventh day, most blest,
Is called in Holy Scripture
   The sacred day of rest;   20

And I shall truly find it
   A day of rest to me;
This night, as Christ hath showed me,
   I go with Him to be.'

It was the solemn midnight,   25
   When in the house of prayer
They found the good Columba,
   Who met his summons there.

---

* Lev. xxiii, 32
[†] For more than a thousand years, until the observance of the ancient
Sabbath was forcibly suppressed, under Margaret, 'saint and queen.'

A flash of heavenly radiance
  Revealed him to their eyes—   30
The glory of the angel
  That bore him to the skies.

Thus in the Sabbath midnight
  He entered into rest;
Then dawned upon his spirit   35
  The Sabbath of the blest.

177. TO A CAPTIVE BIRD

Bird that hast sung in the forest bowers,
Mingling thy strains with the breath of flowers,
As the prayers of saints with the incense rise
From the altar, borne to the far-off skies,
Never again wilt thou wander free,   5
Happy is innocent liberty;
Never again wilt thou spread thy wing,
And in thy careless wanderings sing
As thou hast sung in the days of yore,
In the happy times that come no more,   10
When thy days, like the summer sun were bright,
And thy sleep was watched by the stars at night.
Thou art torn from thy nest on the forest bough,
A cheerless prison confines thee now.
And if thou singest, thy songs must be   15
The songs of a sad captivity.
Oft wilt thou gaze to yon azure skies,
Grieving to feel that thou canst not rise;
In vain would thy light wings essay
To burst those bars and soar away.   20
Sweet bird, I cannot set thee free
Or solace thy captivity;
There must thou pine till death's release
Shall give to thee oblivion's peace.

178. TREASURES GRATIS

I have many fine treasures
That add to life's pleasures,
And my house is too small
To make room for them all.
So I'll give some away;   5
Now, let anyone say
Who will take them, and prize them,
And never despise them,
Or cast them away.
For, so precious are they,   10
They'd be prized by the Queen,
And would not be too mean
An off'ring for her;
But I should prefer
To let lesser folks be   15
The sharers with me
In treasures so dear
As those I have here.
And what are these treasures
That add to life's pleasures?   20
They are dear cats and kittens.
A genius like Lytton's
Is needed to tell
Their history well;
Or justly to praise   25
Their sweet, winsome ways.
I've a bonnie young pair
Of black kittens to spare;
They are sister and brother,
So fond of each other,   30
It would sadden my heart
To give them apart.
Therefore, I say, who
Takes one must take two.
'Two are better than one.'   35
If you care about fun,
Your care 'twill repay
To see them at play.
They will fence with your hand
And you should understand   40

That 'tis Pussy's delight
To have a sham fight—
Make-believe scratch and bite;
But you'll find it all right
When their teeth only press   45
In a gentle caress,
And their paws softly stroke
Your face for a joke.
With purring they'll come
To welcome you home: 50
On your shoulder they'll ride
If permitted to bide.
They know they are wise
Yet never advise
Or scold or contend   55
But worship their friend
All others above,
And pay love with love
More tender and true
Than is given to you   60
By man, woman, or child.
Human friends make you wild
With their preaching or quarrelling,
      scolding or blame;
But sweet Puss only loves, and loves   65
      ever the same.
My address must be said—
'Tis Great George Street, Hillhead,
At number sixteen.
Yours,   70
      Marion Bernstein

179. POOR PUSSY'S SONG

(Suggested by the Editor's advice to a correspondent to take Puss to
the coast with the family, as change of air would be good for her the
same as others.)

Meeow, meeow!
Don't leave me now,
   Not knowing how to find you;
Don't go away,
For months to stay,   5
   And leave poor Puss behind you.

If friends can go
And leave me so,
   Not planning how to feed me,
I wonder not   10
That hard's my lot,
   And neighbours never heed me.

Hungry and sad,
Sometimes half mad,
   Through cruel foes and dangers,   15
I've had to roam
Without a home,
   Repulsed by heedless strangers.

Oh, do not leave
Me here to grieve,   20
   No peace or comfort knowing;
But take me, too,
Along with you
   Wherever you are going.

When you're away   25
'Tis hard to stay,
   Not knowing how to find you;
Meeow, Meeow!
Oh, take me now,
   Don't leave poor Puss behind you!   30

180. A VISION OF THE CROSS

'I was kneeling to pray, and I immediately saw, or thought I saw, a golden cross reaching from earth to heaven. I do not know what it meant, but it gave me unspeakable comfort.'—Letter from a Friend

Our father Jacob dreamed he saw
   A ladder from the skies,
Whereon the angels came and went
   Before his wond'ring eyes.

Your vision, too, doth represent   5
   A path from earth to heaven;
The path of suffering is meant,
   Yet bright with blessings given

To earnest prayer, to patient trust,
   To faithful human love,   10
Aye rising farther from the dust
   And nearer heaven above.

What though that ladder be a cross?
   'Tis gloriously bright!
What though each step be pain and loss?   15
   It ends in yonder height.

Above the stormy clouds unrolled
   Around our pathway here,
Amid the shining streets of gold,
   Where there is nought to fear.   20

Where pain and sorrow enter not,
   Where life is joy and light,
Where earthly shadows are forgot,
   And there is no more night.

Oh! may we walk together there,   25
   When earth's dull days are o'er;
And find among those regions fair
   Our loved ones gone before.

Old as the world, yet ever new,
   That blessed hope will be,   30
For ever sweet, for ever true,
   Unto eternity.

181. HAVE PATIENCE

Have patience, O ye suff'ring saints!
 Let not your faith grow dim,
God's mighty patience never faints,
 Commit your ways to Him.

Forget not the unsleeping eye   5
 That seeth all you bear,
That watcheth o'er you from on high
 With kind, unfailing care.

The furnace of affliction tries
 Our souls as gold is tried,   10
It burns the dress, and purifies
 All things that should abide.

Was not our Lord made perfect thus
 By keenest suffering?
And shall we murmur if to us   15
 Come griefs, as to our King?

Rather rejoice in Christian trust
 That all is meant for good;
That God, most merciful and just,
 Thus giveth fortitude.   20

Souls equal with the angels made,
 In conq'ring strength must stand;
Can those who yield a vanquished field
 Join that heroic band?

Each earthly chief his army trains   25
 All hardships to despise;
And shall we shrink from any pains
 That train us for the skies?

Nay; but triumphantly endure
 All trials on the road   30
That leadeth to our home secure—
 Our Father's bright abode.

182. YE HAPPY BIRDS

'Thou makest the outgoings of the morning and the evening to sing.'—
Ps. lxv, 8

Ye happy birds, whose tuneful voices
    Sing songs first learned in Paradise,
At morn and eve the grove rejoices
    Whene'er your thankful anthems rise.

I doubt not that you hold communion   5
    With Him who notes the sparrow's fall;
All guileless spirits dwell in union
    With God the Father of them all.

Some call you soulless, but your singing
    Telleth of thought earth's cares above,   10
E'en to man's world-worn spirit bringing
    New trust in all-protecting Love.

Away, vain cares! my soul rejoices
    To hear these winged minstrels raise
The music of their happy voices,   15
    And mine shall join their song of praise.

Glory to God, who reigns above us,
    Yet deigns to heed the songs we sing!
His kind heart ceaseth not to love us,
    Weak as we are in everything—   20
    Prone as we are to wandering.

Will he who heeds a sparrow's falling
    Neglect one human grief or fear?
Though countless worlds on Him are calling,
    Each voice among them He doth hear.   25

183. PEACE AT THE LAST

Oh, it seemed hard to die! To leave
   His wife and children here
Unsheltered to the chilling blasts
   Of this world's atmosphere.

But ere the parting moment came,   5
   A happier thought was given,
That he might still watch over them
   And wait for them in heaven.

And there he hoped to meet again
   Friends who had gone before;   10
His first and best beloved child
   Had reached that golden shore.

His father there awaited him,
   His mother, too, was there,
With many, many a long-lost friend,   15
   Set free from earthly care.

Lamented once with loving tears
   When laid in kindred clay,
Though half-forgotten through the years
   That since have passed away.   20

Remembering them all again,
   He deemed not death a foe—
Through death he quickly would regain
   All he had lost below.

'Heaven is no stranger land,' he cried;   25
   'Of all I ever knew,
The best, the dearest, there abide,
   And there I'll wait for you.'

184. THE PASSING YEARS

The years, like shadows, come and go;
   Darkly they pass by me,
Though there are some who only know
   Years bright with gaiety.

My days would be accounted dull,   5
   My outward life seems drear,
Yet fancies, bright and beautiful,
   My inmost spirit cheer.

For mine hath been a happy heart,
   'Mid sternest frowns of fate,   10
And hopefully, 'neath every smart,
   For happier days I wait.

Those happier days are slow to come,
   Yet do I not despair;
Hope, smiling, points beyond the tomb,   15
   Joy reigns immortal there.

And even 'mid life's cares below,
   There's true felicity
To those God comforteth, who know
   His love and sympathy.   20

'Tis not by gifts of worldly wealth,
   Man is most truly blest;
Nor yet by sturdy strength and health,
   But by a heart at rest.

A 'mind that's stayed on Thee,' O Lord!   25
   No earthly ills can fear,
'Mid wintry storms will faith afford
   A calm and brave New Year.

185. LINES ON THE DEATH OF DR W. T. M'AUSLANE

(Respectfully inscribed to Mrs M'Auslane.)

One by one our loved ones leave us,
    Gath'ring on the brighter shore;
Why should their departure grieve us?
    Soon we too shall journey o'er,
    Meet them all, and part no more.   5

Oh, how many there will meet us!
    All who here were tried and true.
God, with all the saints, will greet us,
    And forebears we never knew,
    Who have known and loved us too.   10

They will tell how they watched o'er us.
    We 'shall know as we are known,'*
When, with those who died before us,
    We shall live (all sorrows flown)
    Life that's filled with joy alone.†   15

Mid this dark world's strife and madness,
    Blest are they whose sorrows cease,
Who in Jesus sleep.‡ Life's sadness
    Hurts them not. They rest in peace,
    Waking to eternal bless.   20

Angel hosts the saints will gather,§
    Jesu's voice will wake the dead;‖
To the welcome of our Father
    All His children will be led,
    And for ever comforted.**   25

---

* 1 Cor. xiii, 12
† Ps. xvi, 11
‡ Rev. xiv, 13
§ Matt. xxiv, 31
‖ John v, 25
** Rev. xxi, 4

'Wherefore comfort one another
   With these words'[††] of what shall be.
Blessed hope of sweet reunion
   With the friends you long to see,
   Yours to all eternity.   30

[††] Thess. iv, 18

186. 'IN THE OLD LIKENESS'

'Could you come back to me Douglas, Douglas, in the old likeness that
I knew?'

When I shall meet with my long-lost loved ones
    When the dull days of this life are through,
Will they appear, 'mid the light of Heaven,
    'In the old likeness that I knew?'

Well do I know they will rise in beauty,   5
    Fairer than mortal eyes may view;
Yet do I wish that I might behold them
    'In the old likeness that I knew.'

Thou who wilt raise us from death, immortal,
    Thou wilt worn age to bright youth renew—   10
O, wilt thou spare, in that wondrous changing,
    Aught of the likeness that we knew?

If I may meet with my long-lost loved ones,
    When the sweet dream of our faith comes true,
Let me behold them, if but for one moment,   15
    'In the old likeness that I knew.'

187. THE HORRORS OF WAR

(Suggested by the Armenian tragedies.)

You can talk of the horrors of war,
But the horrors of peace may be more,
It is dreadful to fight,
But sometimes it is right.
Now suppose that one night   5
Some tramps killed your neighbour next door,
And proceeded in spite,
Attempting to slaughter
His son and his daughter;
Would you get up and fight   10
With the whole of your might
To defend them? 'Not quite,'
You would say, 'It's not right
To do murder.' The sight
Is quite sickening. Their screams   15
Are ear-piercing. It seems
That they all must be slain.
I would help, but refrain,
Because it is dreadful to fight.
They might kill me; I fear that they might.   20
And their fathers, and brothers, and cousins
Might come round and attack us by dozens.
Many men they might slay
In a fearful affray.
It might lead to a riot,   25
So I'd better be quiet,
And allow three or four
To be murdered next door.
'Tis not everyone argues that way.
If a p'liceman should hear the affray   30
He would force his way in,
Take no care of his skin,
But he'd drag the assassins away;
And he'd not brag about it, but say
'It's my duty to fight   35
Against wrong for the right,
I know nothing of fright,
And as little of flight,

Or hiding away out of sight.'
Better die in a right manly way   40
Than see crime, and do nothing to stay
The murderer's arm,
But in selfish alarm
Refuse to take part in the fray.

188. BLUE

(Answer to Mrs C. Jobling's Poem, 'Green.')

Nay, 'tis the blue that's changeless,
    Though night and clouds may come,
Above the clouds remaineth
    Heaven's starry, azure dome.
There, of all hues most constant,   5
    The truest of the true,
Is the colour of the 'sapphire throne,'
    The holy, heavenly blue.

How can the green be steadfast
    When winter makes it fade?   10
How can the green be cheerful
    That o'er the dead is laid?
The green grows from earth's bosom
    Like earthly hopes that fail.
But the blue looks down from heaven,   15
    Where joy and peace prevail.

Only by looking upward
    We look toward the light,
Faith's eye can pierce the cloudland,
    And see beyond the night.   20
Above the moon and starlight
    The sapphire throne shines through,
Therefore, is Hope's true symbol
    The holy, heavenly blue.

189. THE DARK BEFORE THE DAWN

They say that it is darkest ere the dawning,
    I know not, it may be.
But oh; it seemeth long before the morning,
    In brightness beams on me.

I've seen one life by trouble overshaded,   5
    Through years of deep'ning gloom,
Fade, as the autumn's latest flowers have faded,
    Fall'n in a wintry tomb.

But is there not a 'land of light and beauty,'
    A home of joy and love,   10
Where those who here were mindful of their duty
    Find happiness above?

I'll hope that with those closing shades, so dreary,
    The night from her is gone.
I'll deem those final hours so sad and weary,   15
    The dark before the dawn.

190. A FABLE

(Respectfully Inscribed to the A. S. E.)

    There was war in the land
    'Twixt the head and the hand,
And each party resolved to be master.
    As they would not agree,
    All outsiders could see   5
It must end in a double disaster.

    Losing patience outright,
    The hands rose in their might,
And determinedly cut off the head.
    Then the hands quickly fell   10
    (As a child might foretell);
Parted thus, head and hands were all dead.

191. HALF-WAY DOWN THE SHADOWY VALLEY

Halfway down the shadowy valley
   I have wandered in the gloom;
Then, called back, returning upward,
   For awhile escaped the tomb.

Oh, the darkness of that valley!   5
   And my spirit loves the light.
Day shines fair beyond the valley,
   But within is dreadful night.

Oh, the chill blast from the river
   Flowing through that gloomy vale!   10
Still remembering I shiver,
   At the thought my cheek grows pale.

Fear not, oh, my soul, look yonder,
   Far beyond the vale of night,
See the eternal hills arising   15
   Crowned with everlasting light.

There await the friends and kindred
   Who have trod the vale before,
They shall meet thee, they shall greet thee,
   When thy awful charge is o'er.   20

Ah, my spirit would be willing,
   But my trembling heart is weak,
From the dark unknown it shrinketh
   With a dread no words can speak.

And I have a work to finish,   25
   One most dearly cherished task.
Call me not till I have done it,
   Father, this is all I ask.

Then I'll seek no more to linger
   In this wilderness below   30
At the beck'ning of Thy finger
   Through the vale I'll gladly go.

192. 'WILLIE BREWED A PECK O' MAUT'

(A New Version, for Teetotallers.)

Willie brewed a peck o' maut,
  An' ca'd the neebors ben tae pree,
Noo, Willie wisna' worth his saut,
  He lo'ed o'er weel the barley bree.
As canny Jock met Donald Clyde,   5
  'Are ye gaun ben tae Will's?' said he.
Said Donald, 'Na, we'd better bide
  Awa' frae ony drucken spree.
    We are na fools, we're no sic fools
      As waste guid siller on the spree;   10
    Let folly think there's joy in drink,
      But I'll no taste the barley bree.

Will winna work, an' canna play,
  A drucken ne'er-dae-weel is he.
His wife gangs oot tae work a' day,   15
  While Willie tastes the barley bree.
He has the makin's o' a man,
  But ne'er made up, it seems tae me.
An ass is wiser, if he can
  Hae sense tae leave the barley bree.   20
    We are na fools, we're no sic fools
      As waste guid siller on the spree;
    Let folly think there's joy in drink,
      But I'll no taste the barley bree.

Willie spent fu' half the nicht   25
  Drink, drinkin' wi' the folk aroun',
An' at the blink o' mornin' licht
  He lay in sleep sae still an' soun',
He'll wake nae mair till Judgment Day,
  An' O, what will the wakin' be?   30
Wae's me, tae live sae far astray,
  An' sic a waefu' death tae dee!
    We are na fools, we're no sic fools
      As waste guid siller on the spree;
    Let folly think there's joy in drink,   35
      But I'll no taste the barley bree.'

193. TO KING EDWARD ON HIS CORONATION

To-day thou dost receive the British crown,
    Ancient, yet new;
And the anointing oil on thee drops down
    Like heavenly dew.
Twice hath the Lord our God vouchsafed to hear   5
    Thy people's prayer,
And in the hour of sickness and of fear
    Thy life to spare.
Now, may He make that life 'one grand sweet song,'
    Joyous as grand;   10
And, like thy mother's days, thy days prolong
    To bless our land.
God bless thy Consort, too, our beauteous Queen
    On whose fair face
The only impress of Time's touch hath been   15
    The added grace
That comes of thought, and love, and suffering,
    And is, in truth,
More beautiful than the first blossoming
    Of early youth.   20
God bless thy children, and their children, whom
    Thine eyes have seen,
And may their children come to birth and bloom
    Within thy reign.
These brief notes of a songbird caged, ascend,   25
    'God speed,' to say;
And may thy list'ning ear one moment bend
    To hear the lowly lay.

194. ST VINCENT LOCH

Calmest of lochs! no tempests rise
Where thy bright waves reflect the skies,
No wreck beneath thy surface lies.
No merchant ships sail over thee
With cargoes of anxiety.
No emigrants e'er leave thy strand   5
As exiles from their native land.
No ships of war go forth from thee
To work destruction. Thou art free
From all the 'sorrow on the sea.'
Thy white-sailed yachts glide to and fro,   10
I love to see them as they go;
Because I know their human freight,
Not bowed by Care's oppressing weight,
Travel in peace, for pure delight
In all things beautiful and bright.   15
On and around thee they can find
A beauty of serenest kind,
Smooth lawns, green trees, among whose boughs
Many a song bird builds its house.
I hear their voices all day long   20
Charming the hours with happy song,
I see the children, free and gay,
Upon the green grass at their play,
Beside the smooth and shining waves
That roll not over hidden graves,   25
Like greater lochs, whose dark depths hold
Many a tragedy untold.
How well I love this peaceful scene,
Where all is evermore serene,
As changing seasons come and go,   30
'Neath summer sun, or winter snow,
For ever sweet, for ever bright,
This tranquil pleasance charms my sight,
And wakens thoughts of calm delight.

195. 'JE PENSE A TOI'

Dearest friend, I'm thinking to you,
    And I wish my thoughts might be
Whispered to you by the angels
    Who watch over you and me.

There are thoughts of every spirit   5
    That cannot be told in words,
Though they sound sometimes in music,
    Like the wordless songs of birds.

Swifter than the eagle's pinions
    They can fly o'er land and sea,   10
And be felt across the distance
    By two hearts in sympathy.

Will my thought thus fly, I wonder,
    As I'm thinking here alone,
Sending you a silent message   15
    By some spirit telephone?

Will it cross the space between us?
    Are our spirits so in tune
That my silent thought can reach you
    And bring back an answer soon?   20

196. SONG OF A 'SHUT IN'

Sweet summer comes, but not for me,
Not for me, oh, not for me;
For I in my captivity
Its loveliness can never see.
   These gloomy walls shut out the flowers,   5
   And darken summer's sunny hours.

Sweet summer comes, but not for me,
Not for me, oh, not for me!
Hear you the murmur of the sea?
Feel you the wild breeze blowing free,   10
   And bearing from far distant bowers
   The perfume of a thousand flowers?

Fairest scenes are now most fair,
Summer's richest robes they wear;
But to me the fairest scene   15
Is as though it had not been.
   I can ne'er its beauty see—
   Summer cometh not for me.

197. SONNET: THE RAINBOW

See, God's memorial arch is in the sky.
   It is His messenger, to say that yet
   He thinketh on us, and will not forget
His creatures, that from His bright home on high
He looketh down upon us constantly.   5
Our every deed and thought He doth behold,
And, with a love that never will grow cold,
He careth for us, hears each pleading cry,
Watcheth our ways with His all-seeing eye;
Noting the grief, the struggle, and the pain   10
That are the medicines by which we gain
Strength to our souls for immortality.
After the storm God sendeth calm again,
And waits for prayer, to prove it not in vain.

198. A MEDITATION

Year after year is passing by,
   And time should sweep all wrongs away,
   Yet error flourishes to-day,
Upheld by custom's tyranny.
And ever the all-seeing Eye   5
   That watches all things may behold
   Truth unregarded, falsehood bold,
And mankind in perversity.
If all the churches would agree
   To walk in all the light that's given   10
   By Him who giveth light from heaven,
How many changes we should see!
How many an ancient sophistry
   Discarded, as increasing light
   Revealed its error, and set right   15
Mistakes of false philosophy!
Then ev'ry kind of church would be
   The holy, happy meeting-place
   Of souls that seek increasing grace,
And upward climb unceasingly,   20
Until the perfect unity
   Of perfect truth at last is gained,
   And perfect sympathy attained
By all God's children, even as He
Himself desires, and so do we.   25

Notes on Individual Poems

(Citations for sources quoted in these Notes are provided in the Selected Bibliography.)

Poems Published 28 February 1874 to 8 April 1876 and Collected in *Mirren's Musings*

1. ON HEARING 'AULD LANG SYNE'
First published (with the third stanza omitted) in the *Glasgow Weekly Mail*, 28 February 1874, p. 7; collected in *Mirren's Musings*, p. 6. This early poem is the first of a thread of sentimental lyrics, woven throughout her collected verses, in which Bernstein laments the loss of times past. Readers must have responded sympathetically to her melancholy discourse and conveyed their concerns to the editor; for in the subsequent issue, 7 March 1874, he wrote: 'M. Bernstein, if unlucky at all, is unlucky in the possession of a facility for rhyming. But, after all, the amusement is a very innocent one, and in Marion's hands it is irreproachability itself' (p. 7).

2. WANTED IN GLASGOW
First published (with lines 13–14 omitted) in the *Glasgow Weekly Mail*, 4 April 1874, p. 3; collected in *Mirren's Musings*, p. 7. In this poem—together with 'A Song of Glasgow Town' (23)—Bernstein presents her first impressions of the city. Her attention to the squalor of urban life counters the romanticised picture of pre-industrial Glasgow suggested in John Mayne's 'Glasgow: A Poem' (1783) and advances the conflicted representation—'A sacredness of love and death / Dwells in thy noise and smoky breath'—created in Alexander Smith's 'Glasgow' (1857).

3. 'THE WETCHED SEX'
First published (with the first stanza omitted) in the *Glasgow Weekly Mail*, 11 April 1874, p. 3; collected in *Mirren's Musings*, p. 8. Declining a poem from another contributor, on 21 March 1874, the editor of the *Weekly Mail* had declared: '"Women's Rights" is a topic we are specially

desirous of avoiding. As *Punch*'s swell puts it, we decidedly "Pwefer the wetched sex with all its wongs"' (p. 7). The cartoon—'Extremes That Meet'—had appeared in *Punch* on 14 March 1874, p. 110. The extremes are a fair and fashionably dressed young lady and a plain woman severely coiffed and clothed. A swell observes a crowd of gentlemen admirers flocking to 'the famous champion of women's rights' and 'feasting on the sad and earnest utterances wrung from her indignant heart by the wrongs of the wretched sex!' A second swell replies: 'Wather pwefer *she*-women myself—wather pwefer the wetched sex with all its wongs.' Bernstein subsequently appropriated portions of the text from *Punch* as the title and the epigraph for her poem, and these elicited another response from the editor—printed below her text—in which he first addressed her as 'Mirren' and opined that 'if woman had many of the rights her self-elected advocates contend for, she would be very much wronged indeed'.

4. CREMATION
First published (with lines 25–35 and 52–54 omitted) in the *Glasgow Weekly Mail*, 23 May 1874, p. 3; collected in *Mirren's Musings*, pp. 10–11. This poem is composed in closed triplets, and the reference to Swift (lines 37–42) is an allusion to 'A Modest Proposal' (1729). Four months before the poem appeared, English surgeon and polymath Sir Henry Thompson, 1820–1904, had published a seminal article—'Cremation: Treatment of the Body after Death'—in the *Contemporary Review* (January 1874), pp. 477–84. His opposition to traditional burial, expressed in language laced with gruesome details of 'grave-yard pollution' and of the post-mortem state of the body, stirred considerable controversy. The principal issue was the uncertain legal status of cremation, and the debate was reported widely and variously in the press. Bernstein was inspired by a number of stories published in the pages of the *Weekly Mail*: 'Burning the Dead in Germany' (4 April 1874, p. 6); 'The Cremation Propaganda' (18 April 1874, p. 6); and 'Burning the Dead in England' (25 April 1874, p. 6). One of her concerns here and in 'Cremating a Mother-in-Law' (91) addresses whether cremation might be used to conceal the cause of death when a woman died by misadventure.

5. THE SULKY MAN
First published in the *Glasgow Weekly Mail*, 20 June 1874, p. 7; collected in *Mirren's Musings*, p. 12. The archaic word 'glumpy'—in line 2—appears in both texts and is listed as a synonym for 'glum', 'sullen', or 'sulky' in *Webster's Revised Unabridged Dictionary* (1913).

6. TO THE EDITOR OF THE 'WEEKLY MAIL'
First published as 'An Amatory Lay' in the *Glasgow Weekly Mail*, 20 June 1874, p. 7; collected in *Mirren's Musings*, pp. 28–29. The lyric addresses the editor's anonymity and his refusal to publish love poems.

7. FASHIONS AND FOLLIES
First published in the *Glasgow Weekly Mail*, 18 July 1874, p. 7; collected in *Mirren's Musings*, p. 15. The reference to 'manly sports' anticipates Bernstein's scornful poem (16) of the same title.

8. SQUARING THE CIRCLE
First published in the *Glasgow Weekly Mail*, 18 July 1874, p. 7; collected in *Mirren's Musings*, p. 29. In its correspondence column—on 11 July 1874—the *Weekly Mail* had published a mathematical formula, submitted by a reader, for calculating 'the square contents of a circle' (p. 4). The poetry editor included Bernstein's quatrain in his 'response' column and identified her as the contributor.

9. LOVE AND DEATH AND THE 'WEEKLY MAIL'
First published in the *Glasgow Weekly Mail*, 25 July 1874, p. 7; collected in *Mirren's Musings*, pp. 30–31. This comic lyric refers to a note in the *Weekly Mail* on 18 July 1874 in which the editor states: 'There are three kinds of poems that we object to—the amatory, the epistolary, and the obituary' (p. 7). To Bernstein's poem the editor responded: 'We'll be shot if we do.' For Bernstein's reply, see 'To the Editor' (89).

10. A ROMANCE OF THE MORGUE
First published in the *Glasgow Weekly Herald*, 25 July 1874, p. 2; collected in *Mirren's Musings*, pp. 26–27. On 4 July 1874, the *Glasgow Weekly Mail* had related the following

story: 'There are many romances of real life that find their *dénouement* in the Morgue; but the strangest that I have ever heard happened quite recently. The body of a girl exposed on one of the dreadful slabs was of such surpassing beauty that the Morgue was thronged all day with sight-seers, and one poor lunatic actually drowned himself in order, as he took care to explain in a letter found in his lodgings, that he might rest for a time next to the only creature he had ever admired, and whom he had seen too late' (p. 7).

11. TO AN ATHEIST
First published in the *Glasgow Weekly Mail*, 1 August 1874, p. 7; collected in *Mirren's Musings*, p. 46. The poetry editor of the *Weekly Mail* routinely rejected submissions that expressed 'strictly religious sentiment'. Bernstein was becoming a regular and popular contributor, however, and he tended to indulge her. He printed this poem above a caveat: 'Mirren has promised not to do this again, if we will let her pass this time. Let her see to it.' After this date Bernstein published most of her religious and philosophical verses in the more conservative *Glasgow Weekly Herald*.

12. THE DONKEYS' DUEL
First published in the *Glasgow Weekly Mail*, 8 August 1874, p. 7; collected in *Mirren's Musings*, p. 43.

13. REPLY TO J. B. M. ['Oh! "J. B. M.," you must be stupid']
First published under a heading of 'Bernsteiniana' in the *Glasgow Weekly Mail*, 15 August 1874, p. 7; collected in *Mirren's Musings*, p. 33. These lines were directed to a correspondent who had contributed verses defending Bernstein's 'Love and Death and the "Weekly Mail"' (9) against the editor's censorship of amatory lyrics: 'Oh, resolute, unbending man, / Say how can you refuse / The simple wish of Marion, / This daughter of the muse!'

14. TO D'ODEURS
First published in the *Glasgow Weekly Mail*, 22 August 1874, p. 7; collected in *Mirren's Musings*, p. 37. This poem is directed to a pseudonymous correspondent who had contributed verses professing his love for Bernstein: 'O,

Marion! With thy wise-like head, / As mirrored in thy
verse, / I hope thou'lt not lay down unread / This tribute,
though not terse.'

15. THE RIVER OF TIME
First published in the *Glasgow Weekly Herald*, 22 August
1874, p. 2; collected in *Mirren's Musings*, p. 51. Bernstein's
birthdays—she would turn twenty-eight on 16 September—
often inspired melancholy poems on the passage of time.

16. MANLY SPORTS
First published in the *Glasgow Weekly Mail*, 29 August
1874, p. 3; collected in *Mirren's Musings*, p. 48. The original
focus of the Society for the Prevention of Cruelty to
Animals, established in 1824 and granted royal patronage in
1837, was to protect cattle, working and domestic creatures,
and animals subjected to baiting as a form of entertainment.
The popularity of fox hunting peaked after the middle of
the nineteenth century, but opposition to this institution—
and its 'manlier pleasures'—was generally class based rather
than gender based.

17. A RULE TO WORK BOTH WAYS
First published in the *Glasgow Weekly Mail*, 5 September
1874, p. 7; collected in *Mirren's Musings*, p. 42. To judge by
the number of sensational cases narrated in the local newspapers, instances of wife beating reached epidemic propor-
tions in Britain in the last quarter of the nineteenth century.
In the first six months of 1874, for example, the *Weekly
Mail* reported more than sixty accounts in which wives
were pushed, punched, or pummelled by their spouses. In
one case a woman died after she was kicked repeatedly and
then thrown by her inebriated husband down a flight of
stairs. Almost as appalling as the details of these assaults
were the inconsequential penalties meted out to the per-
petrators. For other examples of Bernstein's treatment of
the theme of domestic abuse, see ' "The Wetched Sex" ' (3),
'Woman's Rights and Wrongs' (40), 'A Dream' (53), and
'A Woman's Logic' (86).

18. QUITE BEWILDERED
First published in the *Glasgow Weekly Mail*, 5 September

1874, p. 7; collected in *Mirren's Musings*, p. 47. On 20 August 1874, at the annual meeting of the British Association for the Advancement of Science, John Tyndall, 1820–93, had delivered his famous 'Belfast Address' in which he argued for the superior authority of scientific over religious explanations for the construction of the universe. The *Weekly Mail* and the *Weekly Herald* published accounts of Tyndall's address in their issues for 22 and 29 August, and both referred to the tensions he had traced between the scientific inquiry into the 'origin of things' and the 'advent of Christianity'.

19. CHANGES
First published in the *Glasgow Weekly Mail*, 12 September 1874, p. 7; collected in *Mirren's Musings*, p. 50. This poem about aging and the loss of 'youthful hopes' was published four days before Bernstein's twenty-eighth birthday. The first two lines are quoted from a poem by the Irish melodist Thomas Moore, 1779–1852.

20. REPLY TO J. B. M. ['Dear J. B. M., I was but joking']
First published as 'To J. B. M.' in the *Glasgow Weekly Mail*, 19 September 1874, p. 7; collected in *Mirren's Musings*, p. 35. On 12 September 1874 the editor of the *Weekly Mail* had printed—as an example of 'our epistolary poets' adulation'—a poem in three quatrains addressed to 'our clever correspondent, Marion Bernstein' (p. 7) and submitted by J. B. M. in defense of Bernstein's initial 'Reply' (13).

21. THE THUNDERSTORM
First published as 'Thunderstorm' in the *Glasgow Weekly Herald*, 19 September 1874, p. 2; collected in *Mirren's Musings*, pp. 64–65.

22. A SONG FOR THE WORKING MAN
First published in the *Glasgow Weekly Mail*, 3 October 1874, p. 7; collected in *Mirren's Musings*, p. 13. Like William Penman, Jessie Russell, and other local contributors to the *Weekly Herald* and the *Weekly Mail*, Bernstein populated her poems with an array of ordinary citizens.

23. A SONG OF GLASGOW TOWN

First published in the *Glasgow Weekly Mail*, 10 October 1874, p. 7; collected in *Mirren's Musings*, pp. 54–55. On 5 September 1874, the editor had complained that contributors to the *Weekly Mail* had a tendency 'to run in a rut' and to submit poems on 'conventional country life' (p. 7). More polished than 'Wanted in Glasgow' (2), this poem is one of several responses to his challenge: 'Has city life no phases worthy of poetic mention?' Other sources—including David Walker Brown's *Clydeside Litterateurs* (1897) and George Eyre-Todd's *The Glasgow Poets* (1903)—would present similar critiques. S. G. Checkland, in *The Upas Tree* (1976), argues that the litterateurs of the later nineteenth century 'showed little real interest in their city' and asserts that 'their urgent feeling for the idyllic and the heroic made them curiously impervious to the real circumstances which dominated their lives' (p. 83). In *Noise and Smoky Breath* (1983) and *Mungo's Tongues* (1993), however, Hamish Whyte has included many Victorian 'condition of Glasgow' poems, similar to Bernstein's, which celebrated the variety of the city and examined the tensions there between wealth and want, learning and ignorance, beauty and ugliness.

24. OH, SCENES OF BEAUTY!

First published in the *Glasgow Weekly Herald*, 17 October 1874, p. 2; collected in *Mirren's Musings*, p. 38.

25. THE DANGER OF DELAY

First published in the *Glasgow Weekly Mail*, 7 November 1874, p. 3; collected in *Mirren's Musings*, p. 24. The scriptural quotations in lines 3 and 15—on the theme of Christian charity—are taken from James 4:13 and Luke 12:20.

26. SIGH NOT FOR YESTERDAY

First published in the *Glasgow Weekly Herald*, 5 December 1874, p. 2; collected in *Mirren's Musings*, p. 39.

27. WANTED A HUSBAND

First published in the *Glasgow Weekly Mail*, 19 December 1874, p. 7; collected in *Mirren's Musings*, p. 53. This poem was composed in response to 'Wanted'—printed in the

Weekly Mail, 12 December 1874, p. 7—in which a poet identified as 'Eleve' enumerates the economies 'devolving on
housewives'. At a time when there were many 'redundant'
women in Britain, men were often perceived as dawdling in
their pursuits of wives. Here, Bernstein cleverly constructs
her search for a spouse as an advertisement; in the end,
however, she abandons her entry into the marriage market
and opts instead for independence.

28. ON THE CLOSING YEAR
First published in the *Glasgow Weekly Herald*, 26 December
1874, p. 2; collected in *Mirren's Musings*, p. 56.

29. ON NEW YEAR'S DAY
First published in the *Glasgow Weekly Mail*, 2 January
1875, p. 3; collected in *Mirren's Musings*, p. 57.

30. THE HERO OF THE CLYDE
First published in the *Glasgow Weekly Mail*, 9 January
1875, p. 7; collected in *Mirren's Musings*, pp. 58–59. On 28
November 1874, the *Glasgow Weekly Herald* had published
the story of 'A Hero and a Martyr' (p. 5), and on 5 December 1874 the *Weekly Mail* had published the same 'Story of
a Glasgow Hero' (p. 1). Born in 1808 James Lambert had
lived for many years on the banks of the Clyde and had
claimed 'to have saved the lives of more than a hundred
persons' swept away by the currents. The 'Story' was based
on a sketch of Lambert's life written by Charles Reade and
published in the *Pall Mall Gazette*. The episode celebrated
in Bernstein's poem recalls, in epic diction, the capsizing of
a ferry overloaded with workers employed at the Somerville
Street mills. Lambert had saved more than twenty lives that
night, but according to Reade's account he had lost his sight
on another occasion whilst trying to rescue a child. From
1869 Lambert had been an inmate of the Asylum for Indigent Old Men in Rotten Row. Subsequent articles—on
'The Lambert Fund'—appeared in the *Weekly Herald* and
the *Weekly Mail* in January 1875 and encouraged charitable
contributions to acknowledge 'his humane services'.

31. TO AMATORY POETS
First published in the *Glasgow Weekly Mail*, 16 January

1875, p. 7; collected in *Mirren's Musings*, p. 67. The several literary allusions—to poems and ballads by Burns, Douglas, Tannahill, and Lady Caroline Keppel—reveal Bernstein's familiarity with popular Scottish poetry. In issue after issue, the editor of the *Weekly Mail* had explained that 'we do not publish amatory or love poems except in rare instances of conspicuous merit'. In a note appended to this poem, he wrote: 'If Mirren will have her little joke and misrepresent our motives, we must submit to it.' The following week, 23 January 1875, the *Weekly Mail* published a comic poem—'A Word to the Amorous Poets Again'—in which A[lex] W[ardrop] defended the editor's policy: 'I'd rather be progged w' a big roosty nail / Than rhyme ower my courtship to folk through the *Mail*' (p. 7). Six years later Wardrop would reprint his poem, with the second stanza of Bernstein's 'To Amatory Poets' as his epigraph, in *'Johnnie Mathison's Courtship and Marriage' with Poems and Songs* (Coatbridge: Wardrop, 1881), p. 88.

32. THE BEST KIND OF WIFE

First published in the *Glasgow Weekly Mail*, 23 January 1875, p. 7; collected in *Mirren's Musings*, pp. 68–69. Here Bernstein appropriates a classical rhetorical device, the maxim, and concludes each stanza as if repeating a common truth. Like 'Wanted a Husband' (27) this lyric responds to a poem by 'Eleve'—'The Expostulation of the Ambitious Bachelor'—printed in the *Weekly Mail*, 2 January 1875, p. 7; the speaker seeks a woman of 'beauty', 'virtue', 'wisdom and worth'. 'Cœlebs'—in addition to being the Latin word for 'bachelor'—was the central character in a novel by Hannah More, *Cœlebs in Search of a Wife*, 1809. In the narrative, the young bachelor travels from the north of England to London, where he encounters a number of eager and fashionable mothers and daughters. He chooses, however, a young woman who possesses both domestic and intellectual qualities. The lesson Bernstein forwards from More's didactic novel is that a good marriage is one in which a couple are matched rather than merely joined. In reply, a poem titled 'The Lass We Lo'e Best' and addressed to Bernstein from a correspondent named 'Cynic' was published in the *Glasgow Weekly Mail*, 30 January 1875, p. 7: 'Marion, you're richt, an' I beg to confess't, / We would get a guid wife in the lass we lo'e best; / But there's *ae* little obstacle stands in the way. / We canna aye buckle the lass we would ha'e; / It's ower aften the case—tae its truth I'll attest— / The things we aft *lose* are the things we *lo'e best*.'

33. AN ABLE ADVOCATE
First published as the first of two 'Scraps' in the *Glasgow Weekly Mail*, 30 January 1875, p. 7; collected in *Mirren's Musings*, p. 70.

34. THE WELL OF TRUTH
First published as the second of two 'Scraps' in the *Glasgow Weekly Mail*, 30 January 1875, p. 7; collected in *Mirren's Musings*, p. 70.

35. 'ENDING IN SMOKE!'
First published in the *Glasgow Weekly Mail*, 6 February 1875, p. 7; collected in *Mirren's Musings*, p. 78. Like 'Cremation' (4) and 'Cremating a Mother-in-Law' (91), this poem reveals Bernstein's continuing fascination with the cremation controversy reported both seriously and humourously in the press. The generous attention given to this topic in the *Weekly Mail* is explained by the interest of Charles Cameron, the proprietor of the paper, who was a leading advocate of cremation as an alternative to the interment of human remains. Indeed, as MP for Glasgow, he would rise in the House of Commons on 30 April 1884 to read and support the Disposal of the Dead (Regulations) Bill.

36. THOUGHTS
First published in the *Glasgow Weekly Herald*, 6 February 1875, p. 2; collected in *Mirren's Musings*, pp. 128–29; reprinted in D. H. Edwards's *One Hundred Modern Scottish Poets*, 1880, pp. 54–55. An obscure but likely source for this poem is the second stanza—'Yes, time has dimmed the picture / And thrown its veil across / And now and then a golden link / From memory's chain was lost'—of a lyric by Mary T. Lathrap, 'To the Friend of My Childhood' (1860). Lathrap, 1838–95, was an American poet, orator, minister, and advocate for temperance.

37. COURTSHIP ON VALENTINE'S MORNING
First published in the *Glasgow Weekly Mail*, 13 February 1875, p. 7; collected in *Mirren's Musings*, pp. 76–77.

38. COME AGAIN, COME AGAIN, BEAUTIFUL SPRING
First published in the *Glasgow Weekly Mail*, 20 February 1875, p. 7; collected in Mirren's Musings, p. 90.

39. A QUESTION
First published in the *Glasgow Weekly Herald*, 20 February 1875, p. 2; collected in *Mirren's Musings*, p. 71. Bernstein's source for the epigraph is Psalms 14:1; her source for the question quoted in line 16 is 1 Corinthians 15:55.

40. WOMAN'S RIGHTS AND WRONGS
First published in the *Glasgow Weekly Mail*, 27 February 1875, p. 7; collected in *Mirren's Musings*, p. 81. This poem was composed in response to 'Woman's Rights *versus* Woman's Wrongs'—published in the *Weekly Mail* on 20 February 1875—in which Jessie Russell had embraced equality but not suffrage for women. Russell subsequently composed 'A Recantation' which she dedicated to Bernstein and published in *'The Blinkin' o' the Fire' and Other Poems* (Glasgow: Cossar, Fotheringham & Co., 1877), p. 31.

41. RULES FOR HOUSE-HUNTING
Published in the *Glasgow Weekly Mail*, 13 March 1875, p. 7; collected in *Mirren's Musings*, pp. 82–83. In the second half of the nineteenth century, the rising cost of living forced many Glaswegians to rent flats within converted townhouses. The preferred locations in these three- or four- or five-storey tenements were above the ground floor, where the noise and dust from the street intruded, and below the upper floors, to which there were steep flights of stairs. Leases conformed to the traditional legal calendar, and searches for new accommodations would begin some months in advance of a removal. See 'A Rainy Day Flitting' (128).

42. 'MOVE ON!'
First published in the *Glasgow Weekly Mail*, 20 March 1875, p. 7; collected in *Mirren's Musings*, pp. 86–87. Whilst

loitering was perceived as a problem in Victorian Glasgow, overcrowding in the city's housing made lagging on street corners an unenforceable offence. In suburban neighbourhoods, however, the local constabulary was expected to discourage such 'scenes of idleness'.

43. REFLECTIONS
First published in the *Glasgow Weekly Mail*, 10 April 1875, p. 7; collected in *Mirren's Musings*, p. 79.

44. LOOK FORWARD AND LOOK UPWARD
First published in the *Glasgow Weekly Mail*, 17 April 1875, p. 7; collected in *Mirren's Musings*, p. 80. The theme of trust and faith in God suggests Proverbs 3:25–27 as the principal source for this poem. The source of Bernstein's allusion to gloom—'a dark and stormy night'—is the infamous opening of Edward Bulwer-Lytton's novel *Paul Clifford* (1830).

45. A DOUBTFUL STORY
First published in the *Glasgow Weekly Mail*, 24 April 1875, p. 7; collected in *Mirren's Musings*, pp. 84–85.

46. COME BACK TO ME, YE HAPPY DREAMS
First published in the *Glasgow Weekly Herald*, 24 April 1875, p. 2; collected in *Mirren's Musings*, p. 75.

47. MARRIED AND 'SETTLED'
First published in the *Glasgow Weekly Mail*, 1 May 1875, p. 3; collected in *Mirren's Musings*, pp. 88–89. In this poem Bernstein's sharp-edged humour is sustained by a sprightly rhythm strangely at odds with the theme of domestic violence.

48. THE HEATHER AND THE BROOM
First published in the *Glasgow Weekly Mail*, 8 May 1875, p. 7; collected in *Mirren's Musings*, p. 91. After this poem appeared, a reader from Kilbarchan wrote to Bernstein and explained that the heather and the broom did not bloom simultaneously; Bernstein would later acknowledge her botanical error in 'An Awful Mistake' (81).

49. ON RECEIVING THE FIRST FLOWERS OF THE GARDEN FROM A FRIEND IN LONDON

First published in the *Glasgow Weekly Mail*, 15 May 1875, p. 7; collected in *Mirren's Musings*, p. 92. The true topic of this lyric is friendship, but the identity of the caring person who sent this 'welcome gift' of spring flowers remains unknown.

50. I REALLY DON'T KNOW WHAT TO SAY

First published in the *Glasgow Weekly Mail*, 5 June 1875, p. 7; collected in *Mirren's Musings*, pp. 98–99. In this poem Bernstein transforms a case of writer's block into a catalogue of the editor's literary proscriptions.

51. A SLIGHT INCONSISTENCY

First published as ' "Vanity of Vanities" ' in the *Glasgow Weekly Mail*, 19 June 1875, p. 7; collected in *Mirren's Musings*, p. 99. Bernstein refers in this poem to the editor's rejection on 12 June 1875 of R. H. L.'s 'Water Lily': 'Love needs encouragement, and the more of general goodwill there is the better for us all' (p. 7). In response, in a note on Bernstein's poem, the editor wrote: 'Alas! it was only "love and goodwill" to mankind in general that we referred to, and our fair correspondent is only making game of the kindhearted poets.'

52. IN THESE STEAM-ENGINE DAYS

First published in the *Glasgow Weekly Mail*, 26 June 1875, p. 7; collected in *Mirren's Musings*, pp. 100–01. Several aspects of this poem—the quotation in line 3, the references to steam power, and the theme of separation by time and space—reveal the influence of Wordsworth.

53. A DREAM

First published in the *Glasgow Weekly Mail*, 10 July 1875, p. 7; collected in *Mirren's Musings*, pp. 101–02. This poem— one of Bernstein's most famous works—may be an expansion of 'Oh I wish that all women had power to vote' (76).

54. THE MUSIC OF THE STREETS

First published in the *Glasgow Weekly Mail*, 17 July 1875, p. 7; collected in *Mirren's Musings*, pp. 109–10.

55. SONG ['Oh, bring me a bunch of flowers to-day']
First published in the *Glasgow Weekly Mail*, 24 July 1875,
p. 7; collected in *Mirren's Musings*, p. 121.

56. GAS ON THE STAIR
First published in the *Glasgow Weekly Mail*, 31 July 1875,
p. 7; collected in *Mirren's Musings*, p. 103. This poem, which
suggests the difficulties Bernstein encountered in ascending
and descending stairs, is principally a commentary on local
politics. In 1869 the city of Glasgow had purchased a gas
works from a private corporation and, by a series of
improvements and enlargements of the plant, quickly
repaid the debts it had incurred for all services out of the
receipts from gas alone. Tensions arose, however, over the
disparity between services provided to the city proper and
to its contiguous suburbs, including the cost-cutting practice of curtailing the distribution of gas to the suburbs
during the summer months. Dunrobin Place, where Bernstein lived with her mother between 1874 and 1879, is identified in the 1871 census as located in Enumeration
District 14—'along the north side of Paisley Road to the
west side of Avondale Place'—and appears to have been
situated near the boundary between the municipal district
of Tradeston and the police burgh of Kinning Park, but
probably (according to the poem) within the latter.

57. THE GIANT-KILLER
First published in the *Glasgow Weekly Mail*, 7 August 1875,
p. 7; collected in *Mirren's Musings*, pp. 110–11. On 1 July
1875, the *Weekly Mail* had quoted a report on 'The Plimsoll
Scene'—from the London correspondent to the *Manchester
Guardian*—concerning a clamour created in the House of
Commons by Samuel Plimsoll, 1824–98. Elected MP from
Derby, Plimsoll had crusaded against the overloading of
ships, including those transporting emigrants from Ireland
during the Great Famine and from Scotland during the
Clearances. He achieved prominence by challenging the
indifference of his fellow statesmen, some of whom were
ship owners, and accusing them of profiting from the loss
of their heavily insured 'coffin ships'. The passage of the
Merchant Shipping Act, in 1876, would require that vessels
bear a load line—now known as the Plimsoll mark—which

saved the lives of countless seamen. The references in the poem to the 'imp' or 'dragon' of Wantley signal the influence of a popular mock-heroic ballad on 'The Renowned History and Rare Achievements of John Wilkes' first published in 1801 and composed by George Huddesford, 1749–1809.

58. ADVICE TO ANXIETY
First published as 'A Wet Blanket' in the *Glasgow Weekly Mail*, 14 August 1875, p. 7; collected in *Mirren's Musings*, p. 124. A poem titled 'Advice Wanted' and signed by 'Anxiety' had been published in the *Weekly Mail* on 7 August; in a note on that poem, the editor wrote: 'Here's a chance for Willie Penman, Jessie Russell, or some other of our "experienced" friends to "do the State some service"' (p. 7). In the next issue the *Weekly Mail* printed this response in verse from Bernstein, and in the succeeding issue 'Anxiety' expressed his gratitude: 'On Marion Bernstein's word I'll go— / "Yet till you try you cannot know." / I'll try, and if I fail; why then / I'll just be like the maist o' men.' (p. 7).

59. SONNET ['Fade not! oh, autumn flowers!']
First published in the *Glasgow Weekly Mail*, 21 August 1875, p. 7; collected in *Mirren's Musings*, p. 120. In her first of eight sonnets, Bernstein eschews the traditional elements associated with the form. She creates a rhyme scheme, ABBAACCAABBADD, with only four repeated sounds and constructs short lines chiefly in iambic and trochaic trimeters and tetrameters. The effect is to establish a parallel between economy of form and simplicity of theme.

60. MUSICAL REFLECTIONS
First published in the *Glasgow Weekly Mail*, 28 August 1875, p. 7; collected in *Mirren's Musings*, pp. 118–19. The couplet quoted in lines 21–22 is from Milton's *L'Allegro* (1645).

61. O, CALEDONIA! THOU ART FAIR
First published in the *Glasgow Weekly Mail*, 4 September 1875, p. 7; collected in *Mirren's Musings*, pp. 104–05. Bernstein's lines echo the tribute to Scotland's natural beauty

written by James Hogg, 1770–1835, in his 'Caledonia' of
the previous generation. Whereas he celebrated the martial
'valour' of Scottish forefathers who had repulsed invaders,
however, she urges readers to resist oppression that comes
not from without but within. Her reference to the 'power
of peaceful commerce' and her slightly mournful tone suggest that this poem was composed in response to the failure
of the Commercial Land Company, registered early in
1875, whose aim was to purchase landed estates, particularly in the Highlands, and to subdivide them into afford-
able smallholdings. Local Scottish newspapers reported,
with considerable disappointment, that the company's
public share subscription had failed to reach its investment
goal.

62. OH, I WISH I WERE A SWALLOW!
First published in the *Glasgow Weekly Mail*, 11 September
1875, p. 7; collected in *Mirren's Musings*, p. 125. This poem
provoked a response—'I Lo'e the Robin Best'—composed
by Mary Inglis and published, first, in the *Glasgow Weekly
Mail*, 16 October 1875, p. 7, and, second, as 'I Wadna
Be a Swallow', in her slim volume of *Croonings* (Glasgow:
Marr, 1876), pp. 26–28. Bernstein's subsequent reply—'The
Swallow' (110)—was collected in *Mirren's Musings*, pp.
126–27.

63. BLAME NOT THE BROKEN-HEARTED
First published in the *Glasgow Weekly Mail*, 18 September
1875, p. 7; collected in *Mirren's Musings*, pp. 94–95. This
poem was composed in response to the editor's callous
rejection of 'My Nellie's Grave'—submitted by an unidentified contributor—on 11 September 1875 (p. 7).

64. SERVANTS OF GOD, AWAKE!
First published as 'Hymn' in the *Advent Review and Herald
of the Sabbath*, 23 September 1875, p. 94; collected in
Mirren's Musings, p. 25. The references to the 'Servants of
God' and to the return of the 'Master' suggest James 5:8 as
the source for this poem.

65. AN APPEAL
First published in the *Glasgow Weekly Mail*, 25 September

1875, p. 7; collected in *Mirren's Musings*, pp. 112–13. Bernstein's explanatory note sets forth the substance of the unpopular Admiralty Order to naval officers, by which they were instructed not to receive fugitive slaves. If slaves were rescued in territorial waters, they were not to remain on board if it could be proved they were fugitives; if they were rescued on the high seas, they were to be surrendered when the ship came within the territorial waters of the countries from which they had escaped. This order—authored by Disraeli's First Lord of the Admiralty George Ward Hunt (1825–77)—provoked considerable agitation, and the Minister was subsequently accused of committing England to a furtive partnership with slave-owners. The Circular was suspended in October 1875, cancelled in November 1875, and revised in January 1876.

66. SONNET, ON RECEIVING A BOUQUET
First published in the *Glasgow Weekly Mail*, 9 October 1875, p. 7; collected in *Mirren's Musings*, p. 119. In this sonnet, with a traditional turn between octave and sestet, Bernstein employs an unconventional rhyme scheme and measures of chiefly trochaic and occasionally dactylic trimeter. She also creates a dramatic interaction between the poem's two speakers: the 'lonely invalid' who receives the flowers and the 'unknown friend' who sent them.

67. A REPLY TO 'TWENTY-EIGHT'
First published in the *Glasgow Weekly Mail*, 16 October 1875, p. 7; collected in *Mirren's Musings*, pp. 116–17. These lines—addressed to 'Miss Lavinia'—reply to verses titled 'Twenty-Eight' and published in the *Weekly Mail*, 9 October 1875, p. 7. Bernstein had turned twenty-nine just one month earlier, and the personal nature of her response is suggested in the shift to the first-person voice in the last two stanzas. She challenges the way marriage defined a middle-class woman's role in Victorian society and rejects the contemporary perception of unmarried women as unhappy and unfulfilled, eccentric and unnatural. Similar to 'Wanted a Husband' (27), in which the speaker values her independence even more than an ideal relationship with a spouse, she refuses to embrace the stereotypical view of

'old maidenhood' as a socially and economically vulnerable status.

68. HOPE
First published in the *Glasgow Weekly Mail*, 23 October 1875, p. 7; collected in *Mirren's Musings*, p. 74.

69. TOO SOON FORGOTTEN
First published in the *Glasgow Weekly Mail*, 30 October 1875, p. 3; collected in *Mirren's Musings*, p. 66.

70. FAR OUT AT SEA
Published in the *Glasgow Weekly Mail*, 4 December 1875, p. 3; collected in *Mirren's Musings*, p. 14.

71. SOARING UPWARDS TO THE LIGHT
First published in the *Glasgow Weekly Herald*, 11 December 1875, p. 2; collected in *Mirren's Musings*, pp. 16–17; reprinted in D. H. Edwards's *One Hundred Modern Scottish Poets*, 1880, pp. 53–54. A note to this poem, in the *Weekly Herald*, announced: 'The above will form part of a new volume of songs and poems, entitled "Mirren's Musings", which will be published as soon as a sufficient number of subscribers have sent in their names to the authoress. Price, 2s 6d. Cloth, gilt edges, with portrait.'

72. MUSINGS
First published in the *Glasgow Weekly Mail*, 18 December 1875, p. 3; collected in *Mirren's Musings*, pp. 1–2. The editors' notes on 'Soaring Upward to the Light' (71) and 'Fame' (73)—printed, respectively, in the poetry columns of the *Weekly Herald* and the *Weekly Mail*—convey Bernstein's intention to collect her poems and suggest that she had a sequence in mind when she composed this lyric. For although 'Musings' was first published at the end of 1875, she would place it at the beginning of *Mirren's Musings*, as if to assert that her 'songs of mirth' and 'hymns of praise' represented 'something more than idle musings'.

73. FAME
First published in the *Glasgow Weekly Mail*, 8 January 1876, p. 3; collected in *Mirren's Musings*, pp. 2–3. A note to

this poem advised: 'The above is taken from "Mirren's Musings" (now in the press), which contains over a hundred poems. With portrait, cloth, gilt edges, 2s 6d. Orders should be sent direct to the authoress.' Like 'Musings' (72), the lyric appears to have been inspired by Bernstein's decision to publish a volume in which her 'simple lays' would be preserved between hard covers.

74. THE FUGITIVE SLAVE
First published as 'A Dream' in the *Glasgow Weekly Mail*, 15 January 1876, p. 3; collected in *Mirren's Musings*, pp. 114–15. In 1875, the first Admiralty Order regarding fugitive slaves had been issued in September, suspended in October, and cancelled in November. The text of 'The New Admiralty Circular' was published in the *Weekly Mail* on 1 January 1876, p. 5, and a highly critical reading of this document—'The New Slave Circular'—appeared in the *Weekly Mail* on 8 January 1876, p. 4.

75. SONNET ['Life's sunny summer time']
First published in the *Glasgow Weekly Mail*, 8 April 1876, p. 3; collected in *Mirren's Musings*, p. 59. Bernstein employs the same rhyme scheme, ABBAACCAABBADD, as in 'Fade not! oh, autumn flowers' (59). In addressing once more the theme of time, she creates an opposition between the brief 'golden prime' and 'all the after time'.

Poems Published 25 April 1874 to 6 May 1876, but not Collected in *Mirren's Musings*

76. 'OH! I WISH THAT ALL WOMEN HAD POWER TO VOTE'
Published in the response column of the *Glasgow Weekly Mail*, 25 April 1874, p. 3; not collected in *Mirren's Musings*. Identifying the author of this 'declined' text, the poetry editor wrote: 'Marion Bernstein is becoming as ambitious as the man who wanted to get into the pulpit just to know how the minister felt when he preached.' Following the defeat of John Stuart Mill's women's suffrage amendment to the 1867 Reform Act for England and Wales, there began another long campaign to extend the franchise to women.

In Scotland the emerging women's movement was sustained by a culture of reform. 'The first women's suffrage society in Glasgow was formed in March 1870'—according to Sue Innes and Jane Rendall—and 'by 1874 there were twenty-four women's suffrage societies in Scotland' ('Women, Gender and Politics', p. 61). Bernstein may have withheld this piece from inclusion in *Mirren's Musings* because she published a revised and expanded version as 'A Dream' (53).

77. 'I AM VERY GLAD THAT I CAN SAY'
Published in the *Glasgow Weekly Mail*, 28 November 1874, p. 7; not collected in *Mirren's Musings*. In a headnote to this poem, the editor of the poetry column explained: 'Recently we had occasion to send to our lively correspondent, Marion Bernstein, a number of sympathetic addresses from admiring readers of the *Mail*. We have since received from her brief replies to each of these addresses; but as these would only interest a few, while their insertion would set an inconvenient fashion, we prefer to give an extract from the letter Marion sends with these replies. This concerns herself, and on that account is more likely to prove of general interest.' The 'friendly letters five'—the editor reported—were inquiries after Bernstein's health 'from D'Odeurs, Alex Strachan, J. B. M., H. E. Mosely, and D. C.'

78. WHAT THE POPE SAID
Published in the *Glasgow Weekly Mail*, 12 December 1874, p. 7; not collected in *Mirren's Musings*. Among the principal objections in Britain to the statement of papal infallibility, defined in the first Vatican Council in 1870, was the notion that one could no longer be both a good Catholic and a loyal subject of the Crown. Intolerance toward Catholicism peaked in October 1874 when William Gladstone published an article on 'Ritualism and Ritual'—in the *Contemporary Review*—in which he insisted that no one could become a convert to Rome 'without renouncing his moral and mental freedom' (p. 674). This essay, reprinted as a pamphlet and reviewed widely in the press, sold 150,000 copies by the end of 1874; many of the reviews were of an incendiary nature and provided tinder for numerous reports in the pages of the *Glasgow Weekly Herald* and the *Glasgow Weekly*

Mail. Bernstein's exclusion of 'What the Pope Said' from *Mirren's Musings* reflects good judgment on her part.

79. WHAT SOMEBODY SAID
Published in the *Glasgow Weekly Mail*, 6 March 1875, p. 7; not collected in *Mirren's Musings*.

80. MY BOOK
Published in the *Glasgow Weekly Mail*, 13 November 1875, p. 7; not collected in *Mirren's Musings*. This lyric is the first notice of Bernstein's intention to publish her 'Songs and Poems.'

81. AN AWFUL MISTAKE
Published in the *Glasgow Weekly Mail*, 20 November 1875, p. 7; not collected in *Mirren's Musings*. The previous week, when 'My Book' (80) was published in the *Weekly Mail*, Bernstein's address had been misprinted. Here she seizes an opportunity in verse to advertise her forthcoming collection and to identify the contributors with whom she had interacted during the past twenty months.

82. MY OWN DEAR NATIVE HOME
Published in the *Glasgow Weekly Mail*, 22 January 1876, p. 3; not collected in *Mirren's Musings*. Bernstein's 'native home' was England, but so little is known of her life there that it is difficult to suggest either what prompted her to compose this poem or why she decided to exclude it from *Mirren's Musings*. The well-worn phrase—'Absence makes the heart grow fonder' (line 7)—comes from a poem with a similar theme, 'Isle of Beauty', by Thomas Haynes Bayly 1797–1839.

83. 'HE PROMISED THAT EITHER BY HOOK OR BY CROOK'
Published in the 'response column' in the *Glasgow Weekly Mail*, 12 February 1876, p. 7; not collected in *Mirren's Musings*. In a note prefixed to the poem, the editor explained: 'Mirren writes that she has been greatly tried by the printers in getting out her book. One firm she gave up altogether; and now another.'

84. COME BACK, SWEET MUSE
Published in the *Glasgow Weekly Mail*, 6 May 1876, p. 6; not collected in *Mirren's Musings*. The decline in Bernstein's poetic productivity, in the first half of 1876, may be attributed to the difficulties she was encountering with the printing of her collection.

Poems Collected in *Mirren's Musings*, June 1876, but not Previously Published

85. ROBIN DONN'S LAMENT
Collected in *Mirren's Musings*, pp. 3–5. Rob Donn, 1714–78, laboured as a herdsman and served for a year or more in the Sutherland Highlanders. A Scottish Gaelic poet, he was virtually illiterate. Here Bernstein paraphrases not one of the several 'laments' attributed to him but a translation of his 'Shieling Song'.

86. A WOMAN'S LOGIC
Collected in *Mirren's Musings*, p. 9. On 11 April 1874—in a note on 'The Wetched Sex' (3)—the editor of the *Glasgow Weekly Mail* responded: 'Kicking is cruel—brutally, murderously cruel, and we would repay it with the lash. But kicking never degrades a woman, however much it may injure her physically. Now, if she had what some call her rights, she would be very seriously degraded indeed' (p. 3). Bernstein's epigraph to 'A Woman's Logic' suggests that she composed this poem—probably in April 1874—in response to the editor's note.

87. THE GREAT PASSOVER
Collected in *Mirren's Musings*, pp. 18–23. The source for the epigraph is 1 Corinthians 5:7.

88. EPIGRAM ['Love's a first-rate theme for rhyming']
Collected in *Mirren's Musings*, p. 29.

89. TO THE EDITOR
Collected in *Mirren's Musings*, p. 31. This poem was composed, probably in July 1874, in response to the snippy note appended to 'Love and Death and the "Weekly Mail"'

(9). The French word *mitrailleuse* refers to mounted rapid-firing weapons of rifle caliber, and 'Krupp's greatest gun' refers to a steel canon manufactured in Germany. Bernstein's allusions to these two pieces of artillery—often ranged against each other during the Franco–Prussian War—exaggerate the effects of the 'arrows and bows' at the centre of her poem.

90. A MEDITATION ['Again I see the radiant skies']
Collected in *Mirren's Musings*, pp. 40–41. In this lyric—as in others in which she confronts her 'captivity'—Bernstein finds 'solace and delight' in nature and in prayer.

91. CREMATING A MOTHER-IN-LAW
Collected in *Mirren's Musings*, pp. 44–45. On 13 June 1874 the *Glasgow Weekly Mail* published an article on 'A Case of Actual Cremation in London' which quoted a letter—apparently a hoax—signed 'H. T. Pelling, M.D., Ph.D., F.R.A.S.' and reprinted from the *Figaro*. In his lengthy treatise Pelling confesses: 'I give full details of the crowning experiment of my life, the cremation of my wife's deceased mother' (p. 1). Bernstein subsequently submitted this poem to the *Weekly Mail* and insisted—in response to the editor having truncated her verses on 'Cremation' (4)—that the new piece be printed in its entirety. On 4 July 1874 the editor responded: 'M. Bernstein—You say that unless we can find "space to print every stanza entire" you would desire that your communication should be "declined". The alternative is a cruel one, but we must "cremate" your "mother-in-law"' (p. 7).

92. EPIGRAM ['If a man has more malice than wit']
Collected in *Mirren's Musings*, p. 47.

93. OH STAY, SWEET SUMMER, STAY
Collected in *Mirren's Musings*, p. 52.

94. FIRST PARAPHRASE
Collected in *Mirren's Musings*, pp. 60–63. The 'original composition' to which Bernstein refers is a hymn—'Genesis I'—by Isaac Watts, 1674–1748.

95. TEACH ME HOW TO KEEP THY WAY
Collected in *Mirren's Musings*, p. 65. This poem in two stanzas is structured as a dialogue between a speaker who wanders through 'life's perplexing maze' and God who promises to light 'the path' (95). The biblical source is Psalms 119:105.

96. FRIDAY EVENING HYMN
Collected in *Mirren's Musings*, p. 72. In 1874 Good Friday fell on 3 April. In this poem and in several others—including 'At Sabbath Sunset' (97), 'Sabbath Eve' (102), 'The Seventh Day' (105), and 'The Sabbath of the Lord' (106)—Bernstein expresses her devotion to the Saturday Sabbath.

97. AT SABBATH SUNSET
Collected in *Mirren's Musings*, p. 73.

98. TO ANNIE ON HER BIRTHDAY
Collected in *Mirren's Musings*, p. 83, and dated 'Nov. 2, 1873'. Bernstein's sister, Lydia Annie, was born on 2 November 1844.

99. THE THREE GUIDES
Collected in *Mirren's Musings*, p. 87. The traditional guides for Christians are faith and wisdom and love. Whilst this poem contains echoes of Proverbs 29:23, its more likely source is a lyric with the same title composed by Anne Brontë and first published in *Fraser's Magazine* for August 1848. In that work, the three spiritual guides are the Spirit of Pride, the Spirit of Earth, and the Spirit of Faith.

100. ON TOOTHACHE
Collected in *Mirren's Musings*, p. 89.

101. MOTHER, WEEP NOT FOR THY CHILD
Collected in *Mirren's Musings*, p. 93.

102. SABBATH EVE
Collected in *Mirren's Musings*, pp. 96–97.

103. SONNET, TO THE STARS
Collected in *Mirren's Musings*, p. 97. These lines are cast

as yet another variant of the sonnet rhyme scheme—
ABBAACCAADDAEE—but the repeated sounds are predictable whilst the diction is gaudy.

104. A SLEEPLESS NIGHT
Collected in *Mirren's Musings*, p. 105.

105. THE SEVENTH DAY
Collected in *Mirren's Musings*, p. 106. The lesson of the
poem is given in Exodus 20:8–11.

106. THE SABBATH OF THE LORD
Collected in *Mirren's Musings*, p. 107; reprinted in the
Advent Review and Herald of the Sabbath, 21 February 1878,
p. 59. The diction in this poem paraphrases that of Exodus
20:10.

107. A SONG OF SUMMER
Collected in *Mirren's Musings*, p. 108.

108. HUMAN RIGHTS
Collected in *Mirren's Musings*, p. 113. In this enlightened
poem, Bernstein advocates not only gender equality but
racial equality as well.

109. REPLY TO THE FOREGOING
Collected in *Mirren's Musings*, p. 123. The poem is a response to 'Lines Sent to Miss Bernstein Anonymously with
a Bouquet and a Cluster of Grapes'—printed in *Mirren's
Musings*, p. 122.

110. THE SWALLOW
Collected in *Mirren's Musings*, pp. 126–27. The epigraph is
a stanza from a poem by Mary Inglis published first as 'I
Lo'e the Robin Best' in the *Glasgow Weekly Mail*, 16 October 1875, p. 7, and second as 'I Wadna Be a Swallow' in
Croonings (Glasgow: Marr, 1876), pp. 26–28. Inglis, who
appears not to have understood the swallow's migratory
nature, accuses the bird of seasonal infidelity. Bernstein, on
the other hand, draws upon the long-held notion that the
swallow is monogamous and commends its 'constancy' and
'affection true'.

Poems Published 8 July 1876 to 6 January 1906, Subsequent to the Printing of *Mirren's Musings*

111. JUST HEAVEN, DEFEND US
Published in the *Glasgow Weekly Mail*, 8 July 1876, p. 7.

112. A LEAP-YEAR ROMANCE
Published in the *Glasgow Weekly Mail*, 26 August 1876, p. 7. Unlike the speaker in 'Wanted a Husband' (27), who adheres defiantly to her single status, Rosalie effects an equally dramatic conclusion when her 'leap-year' initiative wins over the incredulous William.

113. THE SUN SHINES ON FOR EVER
Published in the *Glasgow Weekly Mail*, 2 September 1876, p. 7.

114. ONWARD YET! UPWARD YET!
Published in the *Glasgow Weekly Mail*, 16 September 1876, p. 7. In this poem Bernstein advances beyond her goals for 'womankind' and proceeds to her higher aspirations for 'all humankind'.

115. NATURE'S ARISTOCRACY
Published in the *Glasgow Weekly Mail*, 18 November 1876, p. 3. The title of this poem and the issues that Bernstein addresses suggest the influence of a book by Jennie Collins, *Nature's Aristocracy*, published in Boston in 1871. That book, radical in its time, combined both social criticism and feminist polemics; the tone of these pieces ranged from sarcasm to sentimentality. Like Jessie Russell and others of Bernstein's fellow Glasgow poets, Collins, 1828–87, had worked both as a mill girl and as a domestic servant; against tradition, she argued that labouring in a textile mill, even with its strict rules and regimented workday, offered greater independence to a woman than serving in another's household.

116. OUR CAT CAN SAY 'IM-PH-M'
Published in the *Glasgow Weekly Mail*, 20 January 1877, p. 7. James Nicholson, 1822–97, was a celebrated composer of hymns and temperance verses. His popular comic poem—

'Im-ph-m'—was first published in *'Kilwuddie' and Other Poems* (Glasgow: Scottish Temperance Union, 1863), pp. 146–48.

117. ON THE DEATH OF 'RHYMING WILLIE'
Published in the *Glasgow Weekly Mail*, 27 January 1877, p. 3. William Penman, 1848–77, worked as a blacksmith in the Star Foundry and was a regular contributor of comic and occasionally acidic verses to the *Weekly Mail*. He died suddenly and prematurely on 21 January 1877; his death notice appeared in the paper on the same day as Bernstein's poetic tribute to him; and his obituary was printed there on 3 February 1877, p. 4. Within a week of his death, the *Weekly Mail* had received 'no fewer than fifty-four' verse tributes to Penman.

118. CAPRICIOUS MAY
Published in the *Glasgow Weekly Mail*, 12 May 1877, p. 3.

119. JUSTICE, MERCY, AND TRUTH
Published in the *Glasgow Weekly Mail*, 25 August 1877, p. 3.

120. WELCOME TO MAY
Published in the *Glasgow Weekly Mail*, 11 May 1878, p. 7.

121. BIRTHDAY MUSINGS
Published in the *Glasgow Weekly Mail*, 21 September 1878, p. 7. Bernstein turned thirty-two on 16 September 1878. Her sad 'musings' evoked concern from William Reid, 1830–88, whose 'Birthday Verses to a Poetess / (Marion Bernstein) / Depressed By Long Illness' was published in *Romance of Song or The Muse in Many Moods* (London: Bogue, 1884), p. 59. His poem begins: 'Daughter of song! so long immured / Within thy solitary room, / Where thou in meekness hast endured / The silent shadow of thy doom, / Art thou so weary of this life— / E'en on thy birthday's glad return— / That thou shouldst plead to quit its strife, / And pass beyond its darkened bourne?'

122. THE GOVAN RIVETERS' STRIKE
Published in the *Glasgow Weekly Mail*, 14 December 1878, p. 7. This poem caused some discomfort for the *Weekly*

Mail, whose poetry editor wrote: 'While we permit the opinions of our correspondent, we do not of course endorse them; it is an easy thing to say but exceedingly difficult to prove that either strikes or trades-unions have influenced the Clyde trade in any degree.' Although the shipbuilding industry on the Clyde expanded spectacularly in the last three decades of the nineteenth century, there were also years of economic stagnation and decline. Between 1877 and 1879 the *Weekly Herald* and the *Weekly Mail* regularly reported news of financial collapse: threats of strikes, rising unemployment, and the disastrous failure of the City of Glasgow Bank. Week after week both papers published grim accounts of the 'State of Trade'. In October 1878 the Clyde Shipbuilders' and Engineers' Association averted a general strike by agreeing to reductions in the workers' wages and hours. But on 9 November the *Weekly Mail* reported that 'a few squads of boilermakers and riveters came out on strike' rather than accept these conditions: 'At the present time there are scores of starving families in Govan and Partick, and the prospects for the winter are anything but encouraging' (p. 5). Bernstein's political position on the strike is similar to the one advanced on 2 November in the *Weekly Herald*: 'The largest and most beneficial industry on which our city depends is once again to be banished elsewhere. Surely at such a time all this might have been avoided' (p. 5).

123. MARION'S REPLY TO M. M'M
Published in the *Glasgow Weekly Mail*, 11 January 1879, p. 7. In response to Bernstein's poem on 'The Govan Riveters' Strike', the *Weekly Mail* on 4 January 1879 had published lines 'To Marion Bernstein' in which the poet-correspondent wrote: 'I am sorry indeed / You are so much in need / Of a subject to render poetic; / For in days that are gone / You usually shone / In strains that were more sympathetic.' The poem—signed 'M. M'M'—admonishes her to 'abstain' from expressing 'unstable opinions' about trades unions and from writing of 'men's work'. Bernstein's liberal positions on many issues might have led readers to expect support from her for the striking riveters. In this instance, however, her sympathies lay with other workers adversely affected when the riveters were on the dole. In

addressing one of Bernstein's favourite topics—gender divi-
sions—M. M'M has unwittingly baited her into a defence
of women.

124. LIGHT THE FURNACE AGAIN!

Published in the *Glasgow Weekly Mail*, 8 February 1879,
p. 3. In this poem, which reads like a gloss on 'The Govan
Riveters' Strike' (122), Bernstein cites biblical passages to
support her plea for an end to the discord between 'masters
and men' in the local trades. An account of the deepening
economic crisis—submitted by a 'special commissioner'
and titled 'In the Homes of the Unemployed'—had
appeared in the *Weekly Mail* on 1 February 1879, p. 1. This
report quoted applications for help from ministers and mis-
sionaries in Govan, Partick, Springburn, Camlachie, and
elsewhere on behalf of many proud workers 'compelled to
apply for relief'.

125. HEARTSEASE

Published in the *Glasgow Weekly Mail*, 17 May 1879, p. 3.
The references here to the simplicity of this short-lived
perennial give way to suggestions of its 'power to please'
and of its medicinal properties.

126. REST

Published in the *Glasgow Weekly Mail*, 31 May 1879, p. 3.

127. SONNET: ON THE PREDICTION OF EXTRA-ORDINARY DARKNESS, &c

Published in the *Glasgow Weekly Mail*, 14 June 1879, p. 3.
This first-person sonnet is adventurous both in its rhyme
scheme—AAABBCCDDCCEEE—and its subject. The 'prediction' refers to a prophecy long attributed to Ursula
Sontheil, *c.* 1488–1561, an English woman also known as
Mother Shipton: 'The world to an end shall come, / In
eighteen hundred and eighty-one.' An article titled 'Mother
Shipton's Prophecy' had appeared in the *Weekly Mail* on 5
April 1879, p. 7, and reported that a contemporary arith-
metician had recalculated 'this estimable lady's prophecy'
and was convinced that the world would end in 1880.

128. A RAINY DAY FLITTING
Published in the *Glasgow Weekly Mail*, 6 September 1879, p. 3. Bernstein and her mother had lived at 5 Dunrobin Place, south of the Clyde, for more than six years. This 'flitting' to Glasgow's West End was the first of several removals she would experience as the years passed.

129. THE VICTIM OF INTEMPERANCE
Published in the *Glasgow Weekly Mail*, 27 September 1879, p. 3. The Glasgow papers regularly reported incidents of this sort, and Bernstein in her account rises above the sanctimoniousness that coloured many temperance poems.

130. HOME MUSIC
Published in the *Glasgow Weekly Mail*, 18 October 1879, p. 3. The 'sweet domestic choir' portrayed in this poem includes the principals of Bernstein's family—mother, father, sister, and brother—but the picture is strangely impersonal.

131. NEW YEAR'S MUSINGS
Published in the *Glasgow Weekly Mail*, 27 December 1879, p. 7.

132. MIRREN'S AUTOBIOGRAPHY
Published in *One Hundred Modern Scottish Poets*, ed. D. H. Edwards, 1880, pp. 52–53. Two other Bernstein poems— 'Thoughts' (36) and 'Soaring Upwards to the Light' (71)— appeared in this well-known collection; both were listed in the table of contents, whereas 'Mirren's Autobiography' was not. One may deduce that Bernstein composed this poem in response to the editor's invitation and submitted it late in the production process. In his headnote (pp. 51–52) on Bernstein, Edwards observes that 'she is vague on the subject of her birth' and assumes that she is vain with regard to her age; the truth is that she appears to be masking the *place* of her birth, lest her contribution be excluded.

133. LEAP YEAR VALENTINES
Published in the *Glasgow Weekly Mail*, 14 February 1880, p. 3. This poem elicited a response—'I Am a Merry

Bachelor'—signed by John S. Seaton and printed in the *Weekly Mail* for 21 February 1880; the speaker rejects a succession of leap-year overtures, including one from 'little Marion gentle' (p. 3).

134. THE RESURRECTION OF THE FLOWERS
Published in the *Glasgow Weekly Mail*, 6 March 1880, p. 3. The references here to 'Death's icy chain' and the 'icy hand of death' suggest the influence of 'Death the Leveler' by James Shirley, 1596–1666.

135. AN EVENING SONG
Published in the *Glasgow Weekly Mail*, 3 April 1880, p. 7.

136. TOILING UPWARDS
Published in the *Glasgow Weekly Mail*, 15 May 1880, p. 3.

137. HAPPY DREAMING
Published in the *Glasgow Weekly Mail*, 17 August 1880, p. 3.

138. TO THE GREAT INVENTOR
Published in the *Glasgow Weekly Mail*, 25 September 1880, p. 3. This poem was inspired by two accounts—'Telephones in Mines' and 'Money by Telephone'—that appeared in the *Weekly Mail* on 18 September 1880, p. 3. The first quoted a report in the London *Times* of an experiment that 'demonstrated the facility with which telephonic communication' could be established between miners at the bottom of the Carberry Coalpit and engineers on the surface. The second rehearsed a scam perpetrated by a 'hard-looking customer' who bilked 'the young lady in charge of the central telephone office' when he convinced her to advance him a sum of cash.

139. SONG ['In the morning sunlight']
Published first in the *Glasgow Weekly Mail*, 18 June 1881, p. 3; second, with minor differences in punctuation, in the *Glasgow Weekly Herald*, 2 July 1881, p. 2. The last line—'Light at evening time'—repeats the title of a sermon delivered on 25 October 1857 by the Reverend Charles Haddon Spurgeon, 1834–92; the scriptural source is Zechariah 14:7.

140. THE SCOTTISH EMIGRANT

Published in the *Glasgow Weekly Mail*, 15 October 1881, p. 3. In the 1870s and 1880s, in every issue of the weekly newspapers, readers were courted by advertisements for opportunities to emigrate; and during these years, according to Richards, more than 75,000 people left Scotland for New Zealand, Australia, North America, South Africa and other destinations (*Britannia's Children*, p. 181). Among those who emigrated were Highland cottars and crofters evicted or dispossessed by the Clearances. As Harvie asserts, however, 'the Scots who went abroad were mainly from the Lowlands, craftsmen with their certificates, clerks, weavers with their savings from the penny bank. They were concerned to get on, and they created an emigration ideology to justify their move' (p. 921). The emigrant described in Bernstein's poem is characterised chiefly by his poverty, so it is impossible to deduce whether she has in mind a man who flees a remote rural district experiencing economic decline or one who leaves an urban area with surplus labour. Notable here, too, are deeply ingrained views about the savagery that one might encounter in new and godless lands; such notions were just as much a part of the Scottish collective imagination as the overarching British imperialism.

141. THE EAST COAST FISHERMEN

Published in the *Glasgow Weekly Mail*, 5 November 1881, p. 3. This poem was inspired by a report Bernstein read in the *Weekly Mail*, 22 October 1881, p. 3, of a 'fearsome gale that swept over the entire kingdom'. More than 160 fishermen were drowned, and the few who survived described the 'awful suddenness', the 'howling north-east wind', and the 'terrible surf' as the worst they had ever encountered.

142. THE FLOWER SERMON

Published in the *Glasgow Weekly Mail*, 8 July 1882, p. 3. The second stanza of this poem contains several echoes of an untitled lyric—'When days of beauty deck the Earth'— by Emily Brontë, 1818–48.

143. BEATITUDES

First published in the *Glasgow Weekly Herald*, 30 December 1882, p. 2. The poem was reprinted in Silver City, Idaho—

as 'Blest'—in the *Owyhee Avalanche*, 17 March 1883, p. 3; and in East Canterbury, New Hampshire in the Shaker periodical *The Manifesto*, February 1894, p. 50. The first four stanzas were reprinted in London—also as 'Blest'—in *The Christian Life: A Unitarian Journal*, 8 November 1884, p. 533; and in *New-Year and Midwinter Exercises*, edited by Alice M. Kellogg (Philadelphia: Penn, 1907), p. 42. The first stanza was reprinted in *Behold a Sower! A Book of Religious Teaching for the Home*, selected and arranged by Louise C. Hastings (Boston: Beacon, 1919), p. 149.

144. THE POINTSMAN
Published in the *People's Journal for Glasgow and Edinburgh*, 6 January 1883, p. 3. On 16 December 1882 the *People's Journal* had reported on a meeting in Glasgow of the Amalgamated Society of Railway Servants for Scotland. Tensions had arisen between the men, who had 'frequently to work 70 and 90 hours in the week' but had demanded 'a day of ten hours', and the directors of the several railway companies, who had declined to confer with them; a representative for the petitioners insisted that 'the concessions asked are not only reasonable, but absolutely necessary to the interests and the safety of the travelling public' (p. 6). Just one week later, in a grim coincidence, the same newspaper reported three serious railway collisions—at junctions near Glasgow, at Kilbirnie, and at Essendene—in which three miners were killed and scores of passengers were injured (*People's Journal*, 23 December 1882, p. 6).

145. THE LIGHT-GLINT ON LOCH LOMOND
Published in the *Helensburgh and Gareloch Times*, 10 January 1883, p. 3. The source for this poem was a story first published in *Chambers's Journal* and then reported in the *Helensburgh and Gareloch Times*, 13 December 1882, p. 3. Bernstein's version of the tale is just as sentimental as the texts on which her poem was based.

146. A WOMAN'S PLEA
Published in the *Glasgow Weekly Herald*, 20 January 1883, p. 2.

147. ROBERT BURNS ['While others will tell of thy triumphs']
Published in the *People's Journal for Glasgow and Edinburgh*, 3 February 1883, p. 3. In this surprisingly self-reflexive lyric, Bernstein identifies the burdens and the sorrows that she shares with the Scottish Bard.

148. SHIPWRECKED
Published in the *Glasgow Weekly Herald*, 31 March 1883, p. 2. On 24 March 1883 the *Weekly Herald* reported four accounts of shipwrecks: 'Loss of a Barque'; 'Wreck of a Dundee Whaler'; 'Loss of a Fishing Boat and Seven Lives'; 'Wreck of a Norwegian Brig' (p. 3). Bernstein's poem, with its references to a 'fragile bark' and the loss of twenty-four lives, draws principally upon the first of these four accounts.

149. FAR AWAY IN THE WEST
Published in the *Glasgow Weekly Mail*, 31 March 1883, p. 3. Here Bernstein offers a more realistic treatment of the emigrant theme than in 'The Scottish Emigrant' (140).

150. THE STAR OF BETHLEHEM
Published in the *Christian Leader*, 21 June 1883, p. 327. The 'sweet white starlike' perennial, *Ornithogalum umbellatum*, blooms in the spring—when this poem was probably written—but is named after the star that rose over Bethlehem to reveal the birth of Christ.

151. THE HIGHLAND LAIRD'S SONG
Published first in the *Christian Leader*, 23 August 1883, p. 3; second, in the *People's Journal for Glasgow and Edinburgh*, 25 August 1883, p. 2; third, in the *Glasgow Weekly Mail*, 25 August 1883, p. 3. By the mid-1870s, after years of evictions and forced removals from the lands they had worked for generations, the Highlanders began to agitate in earnest for the restoration of their traditional farming and grazing rights. Thenceforward the cottars and crofters took the battle to the landlords and sought to wrest control of the land from their masters. A result of these protests was the appointment of a Royal Commission—chaired by Lord Napier—into the condition of the former tenants, and the

testimony taken in representative communities was reported variously in the press. The *Scotsman* and other allies of the landlord interests offered only general accounts of the proceedings and expressed few opinions, but in the spring of 1883 the liberal papers began to publish excerpts—many sarcastic in tone and incendiary in substance—that included recollections of violent dispossessions and dislocations. On 4 August 1883 the *Weekly Mail* quoted a clergyman who deposed that 'the management of most Highland estates was despotic in nature' and asserted that 'one man's will ruled whole parishes' (p. 3). Bernstein's refrain—'all for me, all for me'—portrays the laird as greedy, arrogant, and contemptuous of the 'common people'.

152. NEARER TO THEE
Published in the *Christian Leader*, 18 October 1883, p. 575. The foundation of this poem is the hymn 'Nearer, My God, to Thee' composed by Sarah Flower Adams, 1805–48, and based loosely on Genesis 28:11–19.

153. THE CHRISTMAS PARTY
Published in the *Glasgow Weekly Herald*, 29 December 1883, p. 2.

154. NEW-YEAR THOUGHTS
Published in the *Glasgow Weekly Herald*, 5 January 1884, p. 2. This poem contains echoes of 2 Samuel 22:3 and of a hymn composed by Vernon J. Charlesworth, 1839–1915, 'The Lord's Our Rock, in Him We Hide, a Shelter in the Time of Storm' (*c.* 1880).

155. THE DEATH OF DOUGLAS
Published in the *Glasgow Weekly Herald*, 24 May 1884, p. 2. The words of the popular song 'Annie Laurie' are traditionally attributed to William Douglas, *c.* 1672–1748. A member of the Royal Scots, Douglas fell in love with the young Annie, 1682–1764; but political differences between their families apparently doomed the romance. First published in *Sharpe's Ballad Book* (1823), the lyrics were emended and set to music in the mid-1830s by Lady John Scott, 1810–1900.

156. A DREAM OF REST
Published in the *Glasgow Weekly Herald*, 12 July 1884, p. 2.

157. ON THE FRANCHISE DEMONSTRATION OF THE 6TH INST
Published in the *Glasgow Weekly Herald*, 20 September 1884, p. 2. On 13 September 1884 the *Weekly Herald* devoted a full page to a report on the 'great franchise demonstration' in which 'the number of processionists was estimated at 35,000 and the apparently sympathetic on-lookers at half-a-million' (p. 5). The participants had included men 'who represented the principal trades unions and liberal associations' and some 'who were witnesses of the stirring events of the first Reform period' half a century before. This poem elicited a 'Reply' in verse from Mrs M. A. Smith which appeared in the *Weekly Herald* on 4 October 1884 and in turn inspired an 'Answer' (159) by Bernstein.

158. A BIRTHDAY MEDITATION
Published in the *Glasgow Weekly Herald*, 4 October 1884, p. 2. The occasion of this sad poem is Bernstein's thirty-eighth birthday.

159. ANSWER TO M. A. SMITH
Published in the *Glasgow Weekly Herald*, 18 October 1884, p. 2. On 4 October 1884, the *Weekly Herald* had published Mrs M. A. Smith's 'Reply to Marion Bernstein on the Franchise Demonstration of the 6th Ult' (p. 2). Smith was born in England in 1827, removed to Glasgow after her husband's death, and published a volume of *Poems and Songs* in 1877. A vein of gentle humour runs through most of her verses; but a few pieces, especially those on temperance concerns and gender matters, are scornful in tone. In her 'Reply' to Bernstein, she expresses anger at those who 'say a woman's right sphere is her home' and anticipates a subsequent stage of political discourse: 'But now these preliminaries so far arrang'd, / There's a question we can't do without— / Who's to head our procession, to glory lead on, / Who's our leader? Now, Marion, speak out.'

160. SONNET—TO MARY CROSS

Published in the *Glasgow Weekly Herald*, 31 October 1884, p. 2. Born in Liverpool, in 1860, Cross had migrated to Glasgow and was, like Bernstein, a frequent contributor of verses to the local newspapers. On 18 October 1884, the *Weekly Herald* had published 'His Wedding Eve' (p. 2), in which Cross constructs the memories of a husband who has lost his bride to 'the tide of time'. In Bernstein's sonnet the traditional turn, between the octave and the sestet, is situated instead between the two seven-line stanzas and shifts the sentiments expressed from grief to consolation. Her rhyme scheme replicates precisely the pattern of Dante Gabriel Rossetti's 'Lovesight' (1869).

161. COFFINING THE PAUPER

Published in the *Glasgow Weekly Mail*, 5 September 1885, p. 7. This poem was inspired by a brief account—tucked into the lower left corner of the *Weekly Mail*, 8 August 1885, p. 6—of a complaint filed in Dublin against a supplier of shoddily made coffins for the poor. Bernstein transforms the sensational story into a parable with Christian undertones suggested by Proverbs 19 and Matthew 25.

162. A SHOWER OF FALLING STARS

Published in the *Glasgow Weekly Herald*, 3 October 1885, p. 2.

163. PATIENCE

Published first in the *Christian Leader*, 24 December 1885, p. 798; second, in the *Glasgow Weekly Herald*, 26 December 1885, p. 2. The first line comes from a short poem—'Bide a Wee!'—written by William Arthur Dunkerley, 1852–1941, an English journalist who also published fiction and verse under the pseudonym of 'John Oxenham'.

164. THE SCOTTISH MARSEILLAISE

Published in the *Glasgow Weekly Mail*, 9 January 1886, p. 3. This poem was composed in response to the passage of the Crofters' Holdings (Scotland) Act, 1886. Fellow poet and poetry editor of the *Weekly Mail* from 1878, Alexander G. Murdoch, 1843–1901, had published a poem in the paper— 17 October 1885, p. 7—similar in sentiment but titled 'Give

Back the Land'. Where Murdoch addresses the lairds and pleads for the return of the crofters' lands, Bernstein addresses the crofters themselves and enjoins them to *take* action.

165. WANTED
Published in the *Glasgow Weekly Herald*, 23 January 1886, p. 2. This poem touches on a concern addressed repeatedly in Bernstein's poems: inadequate penalties imposed on men, either sober or inebriated, who battered their wives.

166. ACROSTIC SONNET—ELIZABETH MOUAT
Published in the *Glasgow Weekly Herald*, 10 April 1886, p. 2. Mouat, sixty years old, was rescued off the coast of Norway on 7 February 1886 after drifting helplessly from the Shetland Islands in a fishing smack for seven days and nights. She survived the stormy crossing by lashing herself to the hatchway. Bernstein's source for this poem—the 'Narrative of Elizabeth Mouat'—appeared in the *Weekly Herald*, 20 February 1886, p. 1. Another account of the adventure, together with Mouat's photograph, appeared in the *Illustrated London News*, 13 March 1886, p. 266. The sonnet illustrates Bernstein's poetic discipline both by responding to the demands of an acrostic and by conforming to the traditional Petrarchan rhyme scheme and its iambic pentameter cadence.

167. ON THE DEATH OF A FAVOURITE PET THAT HAD EVERY VIRTUE AND NO FAULT
Published in the *Glasgow Weekly Herald*, 13 November 1886, p. 2.

168. NOTHING NEW
Published in the *Glasgow Weekly Herald*, 20 November 1886, p. 2.

169. ROBERT BURNS ['Oft it moves my indignation']
Published in the *Glasgow Weekly Herald*, 29 January 1887, p. 2. In this second of her Burns Day poems—see also 'Robert Burns' (147)—Bernstein sneers at hypocrites intent on judging the Bard's transgressions. She celebrates instead his 'noble songs' and his 'noble spirit'.

170. A SUMMER DAY
Published in the *Christian Leader*, 7 July 1887, p. 428.

171. THE NAME OF THE LORD
Published in the *Christian Leader*, 10 November 1887, p. 714.
The quotation in line 14 is from Psalms 65:2.

172. FORWARD MARCH!
Published first in the *People's Journal for Glasgow and Edinburgh*, 31 December 1887, p. 3; second, with minor differences in punctuation, in the *Glasgow Weekly Mail*, 7 January 1888, p. 7. This poem inspired verses composed by David R. Williamson, addressed 'To a Glasgow Poetess', and first printed in the *Christian Leader*, 19 January 1888, p. 31. Williamson, 1855–1941, was Minister of Kirkmaiden, Wigtownshire. His lines—acknowledging Bernstein's 'thoughts of mortal cares and fears'—were reprinted in his *Poems of Nature and Life* (Edinburgh: William Blackwood and Sons, 1888), p. 75.

173. VANITY FAIR
Published in the *Christian Leader*, 2 February 1888, p. 72. The reference in line 1 to the 'nether millstone' is an allusion to Job 41:24.

174. THE BEAUTIFUL SPRING
Published in the *Glasgow Weekly Herald*, 19 May 1888, p. 2. The first line of this poem paraphrases the opening line of the popular Anglican hymn—'All Things Bright and Beautiful'—composed in 1848 by Cecil Frances Alexander, 1818–95.

175. A WISH
Published in the *Christian Leader*, 31 May 1888, p. 348. The reference to 'Sion's eternal hill' is from Milton's *Paradise Lost*, Book I, line 10.

176. APOTHEOSIS
Published in the *Glasgow Weekly Herald*, 27 October 1888, p. 2. According to Alban Butler's *Lives of the Fathers, Martyrs and Other Saints*, first published in London in the 1750s, Columba foretold his death on a Saturday and said to a

disciple: 'This day is called the Sabbath, that is, the day of rest, and such will it truly be to me, for it will put an end to my labours.'

177. TO A CAPTIVE BIRD
Published in the *Glasgow Weekly Herald*, 23 February 1889, p. 2.

178. TREASURES GRATIS
Published in the *Glasgow Weekly Herald*, 28 September 1889, p. 2. The references to 'Lytton' and 'history'—in lines 22–24—suggest Edward Bulwyer-Lytton (1803–73) and his historical fiction *The Last Days of Pompeii* (1834).

179. POOR PUSSY'S SONG
Published first, as 'Pussy's Petition', in the *Glasgow Weekly Herald*, 5 July 1890, p. 2; second, with minor differences in punctuation, as 'Poor Pussy's Song' in the *Glasgow Weekly Mail*, 23 August 1890, p. 7. The poem was inspired by a response published in the 'Correspondents' Column' in the *Weekly Herald*: 'Puss.—No "home" for pussies left behind when families go to coast has yet, to our knowledge at least, been established in Glasgow' (7 June 1890, p. 2).

180. A VISION OF THE CROSS
Published in the *Glasgow Weekly Herald*, 9 May 1891, p. 2.

181. HAVE PATIENCE
Published in the *Glasgow Weekly Herald*, 2 January 1892, p. 2.

182. YE HAPPY BIRDS
Published in the *Glasgow Weekly Herald*, 6 August 1892, p. 2.

183. PEACE AT THE LAST
Published in the *Glasgow Weekly Herald*, 8 October 1892, p. 2.

184. THE PASSING YEARS
Published in the *Glasgow Weekly Herald*, 21 January 1893, p. 2. In line 25, the phrase 'a mind that's stayed on Thee' echoes Isaiah 26:3.

185. LINES ON THE DEATH OF DR W. T. M'AUSLANE
Published in the *Glasgow Weekly Herald*, 15 July 1893, p. 2.
William Thomson M'Auslane, 1832–93, was a Scottish
poet, journalist, and Secretary to the Association for
the Relief of Incurables for Glasgow and the West of
Scotland.

186. 'IN THE OLD LIKENESS'
Published in the *Glasgow Weekly Herald*, 15 September
1894, p. 2. The epigraph is from a poem—'Douglas,
Douglas, Tender and True'—by Dinah Mulock Craik,
1826–87.

187. THE HORRORS OF WAR
Published in the *Glasgow Weekly Herald*, 17 October 1896,
p. 2. On 3 October 1896 the *Weekly Herald* had printed a
despatch from a missionary on the Anatolian frontier who
had assisted in smuggling an Armenian girl out of harm's
way and thereby had 'cheated the unspeakable Turk of one
of his victims' (p. 1).

188. BLUE
Published in the *Glasgow Weekly Herald*, 9 January 1897, p. 2.
Charlotte Jobling was born in Belfast, settled with her
husband in Glasgow, and removed to Dublin after his
death; she published more than 800 poems in the *Weekly
Herald*, the *Weekly Irish Times*, and other local newspapers in
Scotland and Ireland. Her poem 'Green' had appeared in
the *Weekly Herald* on 26 December 1896, p. 2.

189. THE DARK BEFORE THE DAWN
Published in the *Glasgow Weekly Herald*, 30 October 1897,
p. 2.

190. A FABLE
Published in the *Glasgow Weekly Herald*, 25 December
1897, p. 2. This poem chastises both management and
labour of the Amalgamated Society of Engineers. Workers
in Britain's major cities had walked out in early July 1897—
when the leading firms refused to grant them the 'eight
hours day'—and accounts of the protracted national strike

continued to dominate the newspapers through the end of the year.

191. HALF-WAY DOWN THE SHADOWY VALLEY
Published in the *Glasgow Weekly Herald*, 2 July 1898, p. 2.

192. WILLIE BREWED A PECK O' MAUT
Published in the *Glasgow Weekly Herald*, 8 February 1902, p. 5. This poem, with its temperance leanings, parodies a song composed in 1789 by Robert Burns and Allan Masterson. The piece reveals Bernstein's ear for language and demonstrates her facility for incorporating Scots into her verse.

193. TO KING EDWARD ON HIS CORONATION
Published first in the *Weekly Leader*—formerly the *Christian Leader*—21 August 1902, p. 319; second, in the *Glasgow Weekly Herald*, 23 August 1902, p. 5. Both texts are dated '9th August 1902'. In her application for a grant from the Royal Literary Fund, Bernstein wrote that this poem 'was forwarded to the king in manuscript and graciously acknowledged through his majesty's secretary' (Royal Literary Fund, File No. 2686, 4 October 1904).

194. ST VINCENT LOCH
Published in the *Glasgow Weekly Herald*, 19 September 1903, p. 5. The site Bernstein describes was originally named 'Stobcross Estate' and was developed in 1849 by the architect Alexander Kirkland, 1824–92, as a middle-class residential property. The elegant serpentine of 'Stobcross Crescent' was the first and only part of this ambitious project to be built. Fronting the houses were gardens, bowling greens, and a large pond where children sailed toy boats in the summer and skated in the winter. Eventually, the neighbourhood came to be called 'St Vincent Crescent' and Bernstein was living at No. 30 in the summer of 1903.

195. 'JE PENSE A TOI'
Published in the *Glasgow Weekly Herald*, 15 July 1905, p. 5. The wish to communicate by 'some spirit telephone' recalls the reference to a 'spirit telegraph' in 'To the Great Inventor' (138). By this poem, composed less than a year before

she died, Bernstein hopes to bridge the divide between 'two hearts in sympathy'—hers in this world and an unknown friend's in the next.

196. SONG OF A 'SHUT IN'
Published in the *Glasgow Weekly Herald*, 29 July 1905, p. 5. Into her last year, this poem reveals, Bernstein could not escape the sense of confinement that her disability imposed.

197. SONNET: THE RAINBOW
Published in the *Glasgow Weekly Herald*, 23 September 1905, p. 5. This sonnet on God's 'memorial arch' fulfils the traditional parameters of fourteen lines in iambic pentameter. But the rhyme scheme confounds both the Petrarchan and Shakespearean patterns.

198. A MEDITATION ['Year after year is passing by']
Published in the *Glasgow Weekly Herald*, 6 January 1906, p. 5. Bernstein's final poem, published one month before she died, echoes the 'vision' she had experienced more than thirty years earlier—in 'A Dream' (53)—in which all the churches had agreed to discard their 'ancient sophistry' and to set aside their differences.

Selected Bibliography

Primary Sources

Bernstein, Marion, *Mirren's Musings: A Collection of Songs and Poems* (Glasgow: McGeachy [and] Bernstein, 1876).

Boos, Florence S., ed., *Working-Class Women Poets: An Anthology* (Peterborough, ON: Broadview, 2008), Bernstein, pp. 337–47.

Cohen, Edward H., and Linda Fleming, 'A Scottish Dozen: Uncollected Poems by Marion Bernstein', *Victorians Institute Journal* 37 (2009), Bernstein, pp. 93–119.

Crawford, Robert, and Mick Imlah, eds. *The New Penguin Book of Scottish Verse* (London: Penguin, 2000), Bernstein, p. 367.

Edwards, D. H., ed., *One Hundred Modern Scottish Poets* (Brechin: Edwards, 1880), Bernstein, pp. 51–55.

Leonard, Tom, ed., *Radical Renfrew: Poetry from the French Revolution to the First World War by Poets Born, or Sometime Resident in, the County of Renfrewshire* (Edinburgh: Polygon, 1990), Bernstein, pp. 296–303.

Morgan, Edwin, *Glasgow Poets Past and Present: The Story of a City* (Hamilton, NZ: University of Waikato, 1993), Bernstein, p. 8.

Whyte, Hamish, ed., *Mungo's Tongues: Glasgow Poems 1630–1990* (Edinburgh: Mainstream, 1993), Bernstein, pp. 141–43.

Critical and Contextual Sources

Andrews, J. N., 'On Arriving at Glasgow', *Advent Review and Herald of the Sabbath*, 17 July 1879, p. 28; *Signs of the Times*, 24 July 1879, p. 220.

Anonymous review of *Mirren's Musings* by Marion Bernstein, *Glasgow Weekly Mail*, 24 June 1876, p. 7.

Anonymous review of *Mirren's Musings* by Marion Bernstein, *The Graphic*, 27 January 1877, p. 91.

Bold, Valentina, 'Beyond "The Empire of the Gentle Heart": Scottish Women Poets of the Nineteenth Century', in *A History of Scottish Women's Writing*, eds. Douglas Gifford and Dorothy McMillan (Edinburgh: Edinburgh University Press, 1997), pp. 246–61.

Bold, Valentina, *James Hogg: A Bard of Nature's Making* (Oxford: Peter Lang, 2007), Bernstein, pp. 261–64.

Boos, Florence S. 'Cauld Engle-Cheek: Working-Class Women Poets in Victorian Scotland', *Victorian Poetry* 33.1 (1995), pp. 53–73.

Cohen, Edward H., and Linda Fleming, 'Constructing the Collected Poems of Marion Bernstein', *Journal of the Edinburgh Bibliographical Society* 5 (2010), pp. 98–104.

Cohen, Edward H., and Linda Fleming, 'Mirren's Autobiography: The Life and Art of Marion Bernstein (1846–1906)', *Scottish Literary Review* 2.1 (2010), pp. 59–76.

F[leming], L[inda], 'Marion Bernstein', in *The Biographical Dictionary of Scottish Women: From the Earliest Times to 2004*, eds. Elizabeth Ewan, Sue Innes, and Sian Reynolds (Edinburgh: Edinburgh University Press, 2004), p. 34.

King, Elspeth, *The Hidden History of Glasgow's Women: The Thenew Factor* (Edinburgh: Mainstream, 1993), pp. 83–87.

Leonard, Tom, 'The Buried Voices: Forgotten Scottish Poets on Class and Gender', in *Hidden Voices*, ed. Frances Campbell (Glasgow: Lapidus, 2007), pp. 15–17.

'Sabbath-Keepers in Scotland', *Advent Review and Herald of the Sabbath*, 1 January 1875, p. 6.

S[mith], U[riah], Review of *Mirren's Musings* by Marion Bernstein, *Advent Review and Herald of the Sabbath*, 30 November 1876, p. 176.

General Literary Sources

Bailin, Miriam. *The Sickroom in Victorian Fiction: The Art of Being Ill* (Cambridge: Cambridge University Press, 1994).

Bell, Eleanor, and Gavin Miller, eds. *Scotland in Theory: Reflections on Culture and Literature* (Amsterdam: Rodopi, 2004).

Brake, Laurel, *Print in Transition, 1850–1910: Studies in Media and Book History* (Basingstoke: Palgrave, 2001).

Brown, D[avid] Walker, *Clydeside Litterateurs: Biographical Sketches, Portraits, Etc.* (Glasgow: Carter and Pratt, 1897).

Dunn, Douglas, 'The Representation of Women in Scottish Literature', *Scotlands* 2 (1994), pp. 1–23.

Easley, Alexis, *First-Person Anonymous: Women Writers and Victorian Print Media, 1830–1870* (Aldershot: Ashgate, 2004).

Eyre-Todd, George, ed., *The Glasgow Poets: Their Lives and Poems* (Glasgow and Edinburgh: Hodge, 1903).

Frawley, Maria H., *Invalidism and Identity in Nineteenth-Century Britain* (Chicago: University of Chicago Press, 2004.

Goodridge, John, 'Some Rhetorical Strategies in Later Nineteenth-Century Labouring Class Poetry', *Criticism* 47.4 (2005), pp. 531–47.

Holmes, Martha Stoddard, *Fictions of Affliction: Physical Disability in Victorian Culture* (Ann Arbor: University of Michigan Press, 2004).

Houston, Natalie M., 'Newspaper Poems: Material Texts in the Public Sphere', *Victorian Studies* 50.2 (2008), pp. 233–42.

Hughes, Linda K. 'What the Wellesley Index Left Out: Why Poetry Matters to Periodical Studies', *Victorian Periodicals Review* 40.2 (2007), pp. 91–125.

Riach, Alan, 'The Literature of Industrialisation', in *The Edinburgh History of Scottish Literature: Enlightenment, Britain, and Empire (1707–1918)*, ed. Susan Manning (Edinburgh: Edinburgh University Press, 2007), pp. 236–43.

Ricoeur, Paul, *Time and Narrative*, I, trans. Kathleen McLaughlin and David Pellauer (Chicago: University of Chicago Press, 1984).

Whyte, Christopher, ed., *Gendering the Nation: Studies in Modern Scottish Literature* (Edinburgh: Edinburgh University Press, 1995).

Whyte, Hamish, ed., *Noise and Smoky Breath: An Illustrated Anthology of Glasgow Poems 1900–1983* (Glasgow: Third Eye Centre and Glasgow District Libraries, 1983).

General Critical and Contextual Sources

Abrams, Lynn, *The Making of Modern Woman: Europe, 1789–1918* (Harlow: Longman, 2002).

Alexander, Wendy, 'Women and the Scottish Parliament', in *New Gender Agenda: Why Women Still Want More*, ed. Anna Coote (London: Institute for Public Policy Research, 2000), pp. 81–88.

Anderson, Benedict, *Imagined Communities: Reflections on the Origin and Spread of Nationalism* (London: Verso, 1983).

Brown, Callum G., 'Religion', in *Gender in Scottish History since 1700*, ed. Lynn Abrams, Eleanor Gordon, Deborah Simonton, and Eileen Janes Yeo (Edinburgh: Edinburgh University Press, 2006), pp. 84–110.

Cameron, Ewen A., *Land for the People?: The British Government and the Scottish Highlands c. 1880–1925* (East Linton: Tuckwell, 1996).

Carswell, Donald, *Brother Scots* (New York: Harcourt, 1920).

Checkland, S. G., *The Upas Tree: Glasgow 1875–1975* (Glasgow: University of Glasgow Press, 1976).

Devine, T. M., *Clanship to Crofters' War: The Social Transformation of the Scottish Highlands* (Manchester: Manchester University Press, 1994).

Gordon, Eleanor, 'Women's Spheres', in *People and Society in Scotland*, II, *1830–1914*, ed. W. Hamish Fraser and R. J. Morris (Edinburgh: John Donald, 1990), pp. 206–35.

Gordon, Eleanor, and Gwyneth Nair, *Public Lives: Women, Family and Society in Victorian Britain* (New Haven: Yale University Press, 2003).

Harvie, Christopher. *Scotland and Nationalism: Scottish Society and Politics, 1707–1977* (London: Allen and Unwin, 1977).

Hatvany, Doris, *The Royal Society for the Relief of Indigent Gentlewomen of Scotland: A History, 1847–1997* (Edinburgh: Royal Society for the Relief of Indigent Gentlewomen of Scotland, 1997).

Herron, Andrew, comp., *Historical Directory to Glasgow Presbytery* (Glasgow: Presbytery of Glasgow, 1984).

Innes, Sue, and Jane Rendall, 'Women, Gender and Politics', in *Gender in Scottish History since 1700*, ed. Lynn Abrams, Eleanor Gordon, Deborah Simonton, and Eileen Janes Yeo (Edinburgh: Edinburgh University Press, 2006), pp. 43–83.

Leneman, Leah, *A Guid Cause: The Women's Suffrage Movement in Scotland* (Aberdeen: Aberdeen University Press, 1991).

Lightwood, Joan, *The Park School 1880–1980* (Glasgow: Park School and MacLehose, 1980).

Nenadic, Stana, 'The Victorian Middle Classes', in *Glasgow*, II, *1830–1912*, ed. W. Hamish Fraser and Irene Maver (Manchester: Manchester University Press, 1996), pp. 265–99.

Richards, Eric, *Britannia's Children: Emigration from England, Scotland, Wales and Ireland since 1600* (London: Hambledon, 2004).

Richards, Eric, *The Highland Clearances: People, Landlords and Rural Turmoil* (Edinburgh: Birlinn, 2008).